Poor Policy

POOR POLICY

How Government Harms the Poor

D. Eric Schansberg

WestviewPress

A Division of HarperCollins*Publishers*

Copyright © 1996 by Westview Press, Inc., A Division of HarperCollins Publishers, Inc.

Published in 1996 in the United States of America by Westview Press, Inc., 5500 Central Avenue, Boulder, Colorado 80301-2877, and in the United Kingdom by Westview Press, 12 Hid's Copse Road, Cumnor HIll, Oxford OX2 9JJ

A CIP catalog record for this book is available from the Library of Congress
ISBN 0-8133-2824-1—0-8133-2825-X (pbk.)

The paper used in this publication meets the requirements of the American National Standard for Permanence of Paper for Printed Library Materials Z39.48-1984.

10   9   8   7   6   5   4   3   2   1

Contents

Preface

Why should you read this book? Let me appeal to your self-interests first. This book can be read as an explanation of how political markets function—how special interest groups use the political process to redistribute income from you, the general public, to themselves. With concerns over the growth of government and the burden of taxation, the recommendations that follow would benefit the country overall and individuals who do not derive most of their income from belonging to an interest group. As Dave Barry says, "If the entire $1.3 trillion budget were divided up among the 260 million men, women and children in the United States, you wouldn't get any of it. That's why they call you an 'ordinary taxpayer.'" If you are an "ordinary taxpayer," this book documents how government policy affects you and explains how it happens.

Or this may be read as an analysis of current policy and prospective reforms. This book contains a potpourri of economic topics. Are you interested in welfare reform? Education reform? What about taxation and the growth of government, discrimination, protectionism versus free trade, the minimum wage and other labor market restrictions, drug prohibition, health care, housing policy, foreign aid, or environmental issues? In the next 21 chapters, you will find substantive and intuitive explanations of contemporary policies and how they affect people, especially the poor.

Especially the poor. This brings me to the main reason I wrote this book—to explain the origin and impact of policies that affect the poor. In Part 3 I analyze the most popular topic concerning the poor—welfare programs. However, Part 2 covers a set of issues whose impact on the poor is usually ignored but is at least as important—how government consistently (and inadvertently) harms the poor. As such, Part 2 provides a fresh approach to the typically stale ("welfare only") analysis of policies that affect the poor. If you want something to discuss besides welfare when it comes to the poor, "you've come to the right place."

The Book in a Nutshell

The book opens in Part 1 with background material on poverty in the United States—the measurement of poverty, trends in poverty and government's redistribution to the poor, and the non-government reasons people are poor. The goal is to put today's poor in perspective, setting the stage for a look at the impact of various policies.

Government's efforts to help the poor are well documented. However, the bulk of government policies redistribute money to the non-poor and inadvertently hammer the poor. This is the subject of Part 2. For example, because of farm price supports, the poor face higher prices for food; because of tariffs and quotas on textile imports, the poor pay more for clothing. In propping up the incomes of two special interest groups, government has decided to increase the prices of two categories of items for which the poor spend a disproportionate amount of their income. Similarly, the poor are often harmed by government intervention in a variety of other markets. My analysis includes two of the most important issues for the poor: education reform and drug prohibition.

In Part 3, I turn to the topic that receives the lion's share of attention in discussions of the poor—government's attempts to help through welfare programs. The solutions in this area are not as clear cut, but there are a number of practical ideas that would clearly improve the situation. The book closes in Part 4 with the primary causes of international poverty and the general solution to this problem.

The Role of Economics in Explaining and Fighting Poverty

Poverty is a complex topic. Vast energies have been spent in studying its causes and pursuing strategies for its elimination. The attack on poverty has come from many sides. In the trenches, private charities were the predominant benefactors into the 20th century. Beginning with the New Deal and especially the programs of the Great Society, the role of government in trying to help the poor increased dramatically.

Academics from many disciplines in the social sciences have been engaged in the battle as well. As an economist, my primary goal is to focus on how various government policies have harmed or helped the poor. I will only sparingly discuss the contributions of fields other than economics. This does not imply irrelevance, just that for me to present them would largely be an example of how a little knowledge can be a dangerous thing. Besides, the economic aspects of poverty are numerous and complex enough to fill at least this book.

The discipline of economics does not fit neatly into any category. It is a combination of business, social science (as a study of individual behavior), and philosophy (as an approach to thinking about problems). This last function is perhaps the most important. G. L. Bach says that "economics is a way of thinking about problems, not a set of answers to be taken off the shelf." Given the subject of this book, then, the task involves identifying the causes of poverty and analyzing the costs and benefits of policies that affect the poor. The subsequent step, which involves some degree of subjectivity, is for readers to weigh the costs and benefits and reach their own conclusions about the policies in question.

Although this element of subjectivity allows some flexibility, many results of economic policy are beyond debate. For instance, if we hold all else constant, the minimum wage causes an increase in unemployment for unskilled labor. Period. If the price of something rises, people will want less of it. In this case, since the price of unskilled labor rises, firms will demand less of it. We can disagree about how much additional unemployment is caused or whether we should pursue the policy, but its contribution to unemployment remains. Because economics has a normative (subjective) flavor, people too often assume one cannot reach any solid conclusions or alternatively, that all opinions, even those that ignore economic theory, are equally valid. This leads to the unfortunate circumstance that "everyone thinks they're an economist."

Identifying all the relevant costs and benefits of a given policy would seem to be a relatively simple task. However, for reasons I enumerate throughout the book, this task is not done as well as one might expect or hope. A failure to see the "whole picture" is especially troublesome in the context of poverty. In sum, it is the reason I wrote this book.

Before We Begin . . .

Although I am an economist and an academic, my passion and abilities are centered in teaching. I hope this will allow me to effectively communicate some basic principles that laypeople typically find frustrating. I have taken great care to make this book completely within the reach of laypeople. As a means to this end, a number of editors with little or no background in economics assisted me with proofreading. I will be disappointed if my book is unable to reach a broad audience.

A note on style: Because this book attempts to reach laypeople while continuing to be appropriate for the classroom, the endnotes range from technical details to anecdotes, from reference citations to bits of information. Although even the more interesting endnotes are not paramount to understanding the text, they often provide useful insights. I encourage you to peruse them.

Some people have dedicated their lives to trying to eradicate poverty—on an individual level or for whole nations. I hope this book allows
them to find constructive answers to the problem of poverty. There are
countless others who are concerned with this issue but do not know
what to do. This book can provide them with a place to begin.

D. Eric Schansberg

Acknowledgments

This project originated with the Poverty and Redistribution course I con structed and then taught at Texas A&M University in spring 1992. I have tremendous gratitude for those who had confidence in my teaching at an early date. Without the opportunities they provided, this book may not have been possible.

Many professors contributed to my intellectual development as an economist. Mark Crain at George Mason University introduced me to public choice economics and put Texas A&M University on my list of potential graduate schools. From there, Bob Reed and Morgan Reynolds greatly influenced the way I think about economics and public policy. My fellow students in graduate school were also instrumental; our countless hours of discussion and debate provided a forum for the proverbial "iron sharpening iron."

Of people I hardly know, Professor Walter Williams of George Mason University has had the most significant influence on my "substance and style." I have usually been impressed by his analysis of public policy. But more important, I respect that he will go *anywhere* to spread his message. This is particularly noteworthy, since he chooses to emerge from the stuffy confines of academia. I hope to channel my passions for these issues as effectively as he has.

As for the preparation of this book, I owe a great debt to a diverse band of friends (ranging from homemakers to graduate students in economics) who willingly played the role of editor for me. Matt Dickerson, Dr. Ann Gillette, Michelle Cohen, Jessica Phipps, Rusty Russell, Chris and Lee Schansberg, and Greg Vest read various chapters and provided valuable comments. Jon Bingham, Pat Boucher, Laura Jenkins, Dr. Joseph and Mary Ann Nagyvary, and Tracy Wood read about half of the manuscript; their efforts greatly improved the quality of my work. Most of all, I would like to thank those who ran the entire marathon with me—Dave Borden, Dr. Edgar (Butch) Browning, Steve Cuellar, Edward J. Lopez, and Jill Sewell.

It is often said that "hard writing makes easy reading and vice versa." I hope that readers will find my writing "hard enough" so that the reading is pleasant. Although I still have much to learn about writing more effectively, this project has been a supreme learning tool. In particular, Jill Sewell's comments on my writing style are responsible for vast improvements in the way my ideas have been translated onto paper. Despite the efforts of my friends, errors probably remain. Of course, I retain sole responsibility.

I also want to thank the people at Westview Press who have been helpful in walking me through my first book: Alison Auch for acquiring the project, Rebecca Ritke for guiding me through the process, Scott Horst for coordinating production, and Diane Hess for her fabulous editing.

Foremost, I owe everything to Jesus Christ—"the author and perfecter of my salvation." To the extent possible, I give the glory to God who gave me the providence to enter this project and the passion to finish it.

D.E.S.

Part 1

An Introduction to Poverty and Redistribution

1

Measuring Poverty: Who's Poor?

"The poverty rate was 15.1% for 1993, up .6% from 1992 and at its second-highest level since 1965." Reading such a statement in the newspaper, one might think it an accurate report on poverty in the United States. The poverty rate is the most frequently cited number concerning the poor, but it provides an inadequate picture. Determining the extent of poverty is considerably more complex than merely looking at the poverty rate, but fortunately, the reasons for this complexity are easy to grasp.

The Poverty Rate

The poverty rate is defined as the percentage of people who live in households with cash incomes below the "poverty line." The poverty line is not a fixed dollar amount; there are 48 different poverty lines, varying by family size and type. For example, the poverty line for a single person was $7,357 in 1993; the level for a typical family of four was $14,764. These income thresholds are adjusted each year for inflation.

How does the government know where to "draw the line"? The original measure debuted in the mid-1960s when economist Mollie Orshansky first estimated the cost of a nutritionally adequate diet.[1] Given that poor families spend approximately one-third of their incomes on food, the U.S. Census Bureau computed the poverty line as three times the dollar amount needed to purchase the Department of Agriculture's "economy diet."[2]

Table 1.1 provides a look at how the poverty rate and the actual number of people below the poverty line have changed over time. There are a few things to note. First, since 1973, the number of people designated as poor has risen along with the population. Second, the poverty rate fell very quickly throughout the 1960s. Third, since the 1960s, changes in the poverty rate have been less consistent. In fact, the poverty rate was higher in 1993 than it was in 1969. Paradoxically, consistent improvement in the poverty rate ended when the War on Poverty began in earnest in the

TABLE 1.1   The Poverty Population

Year	U.S. Population (in millions)	Number of Poor (in millions)	Poverty Rate (% of poor)
1959	176.3	39.5	22.4
1965	191.9	33.2	17.3
1969	199.2	24.1	12.1
1973	207.2	23.0	11.1
1977	212.9	24.7	11.6
1981	227.1	31.8	14.0
1985	236.4	33.1	14.0
1989	246.1	31.5	12.8
1993	260.3	39.3	15.1

SOURCE: U.S. Bureau of the Census, *Statistical Abstract of the United States* (Washington, DC: U.S. Department of the Treasury), 1994, Table 727; 1975, Table 654.

late 1960s. Just when the elimination of poverty was made an explicit goal, progress against it apparently ended. Clearly, we want to reach some conclusions about why the poverty rate behaved in this way.

Note also that government transfers decrease the amount of measured poverty at a point in time. If behavior remained constant (an assumption I analyze in Part 3), the poverty rate would be much higher if we eliminated government's cash transfers from consideration. For instance, in 1984, approximately 48 million people *earned* incomes below the poverty line.

The poverty rate is an important number in the arena of public policy. Conservatives read the statistics as an indictment of failed policy. Because the poverty rate numbers have not improved, they argue that the welfare state extended under the Great Society has failed. Liberals argue that poverty would have been worse in the absence of government activism. To them, the statistics are a strong rationale for a reinvigorated War on Poverty with more money. In 1992, the fact that the poverty rate was 1.2 percentage points higher than in 1980 was used to help defeat George Bush and to discredit "trickle-down economics." So who is right? The impact of welfare policies and the War on Poverty are discussed in Part 3.

The Distribution of Income

The distribution of income is another oft-cited statistic. Table 1.2 shows how real incomes for families have changed over time. The numbers are calculated before taxes and include all money income (earned and unearned, adjusted for inflation). Note that incomes improved dramatically until 1970 and have remained relatively unchanged since then.[3]

TABLE 1.2   Percentage Distribution of Families by Money Income Levels

Income Class	1950–1975, various years, in constant 1977 dollars				
	1950	1960	1965	1970	1975
Under $5,000	24.6%	17.1%	13.2%	10.0%	9.9%
$5,000–$6,999	14.4	8.8	7.9	6.7	7.2
$7,000–$11,999	43.5	29.8	22.5	18.9	19.2
$12,000–$24,999	16.6	36.8	44.6	46.3	44.3
Over $25,000	.8	7.4	11.8	18.2	19.4
Median income	$8,356	11,500	13,362	15,399	15,477

	1970–1990, various years, in constant 1991 dollars				
	1970	1975	1980	1985	1990
Under $10,000	9.2%	8.7%	8.9%	9.7%	8.9%
$10,000–$14,999	7.6	8.6	7.7	7.5	7.2
$15,000–$24,999	18.0	18.0	17.3	16.5	15.5
$25,000–$49,999	43.9	41.3	39.0	36.4	35.7
Over $50,000	21.4	23.6	27.3	29.9	32.7
Median income	$32,540	33,248	34,791	35,107	36,841

SOURCE: U.S. Bureau of the Census, *Statistical Abstract of the United States* (Washington, DC: U.S. Department of the Treasury), 1979, Table 734; 1993, Table 711.

Remember that the poverty rate stopped falling about the same time. Clearly the two measures are related, since they both deal with income. As incomes have stagnated, it should come as little surprise that advances against poverty—measured in terms of rising incomes—have been frustrated. Economic growth is evidently an important weapon in the fight against poverty.

Another way to look at income is to see what percentage of national income is earned by the wealthiest or poorest people. Table 1.3 shows the percentage of national income earned by each quintile (20% of the population) over time. The inequality between the quintiles is striking: In 1991, the people in the richest quintile had incomes that exceeded those in the poorest quintile by nearly tenfold. However, the most compelling feature of this table is the remarkable stability of the relationships over time; there is little deviation from the end of World War II to 1991. By this measure, inequality has increased somewhat since 1980. However, the changes have been relatively small, and the importance and causes of this change are the subject of some debate.[4] Again, the relative numbers are puzzling, especially in light of the War on Poverty. One would think incomes would have become more nearly equal after 1965—when the programs of the Great Society were instituted.

TABLE 1.3   Distribution of Money Income Among Families

Year	Percentage Share				
	Lowest Quintile	Second Quintile	Third Quintile	Fourth Quintile	Highest Quintile
1929	3.5	9.0	13.8	19.3	54.4
1950	4.5	12.0	17.4	23.4	42.7
1965	5.2	12.2	17.8	23.9	40.9
1980	5.2	11.5	17.5	24.3	41.5
1991	4.5	10.7	16.6	24.1	44.2

SOURCE: U.S. Bureau of the Census, *Statistical Abstract of the United States* (Washington, DC: U.S. Department of the Treasury, various years).

The Use of Statistical Proxies

Charles Murray's *In Pursuit of Happiness and Good Government* includes a discussion of the statistics used to measure success and failure in public policy arenas. He points out that all statistics are merely proxies for the state of the world we are trying to measure.[5] For instance, if the inflation rate for a given year was 4%, this does not mean each individual's inflation rate was 4%. The 4% increase in prices refers to what happened to the price of a "representative basket of goods" over the previous year. If my basket deviates substantially from the representative basket, my inflation rate may be quite different. Although the inflation rate is merely a proxy, it is generally effective at approximating the impact of rising prices on individuals.

The unemployment rate is a more significant example. It is calculated as the percentage of the labor force that is "unemployed"—a status conferred on those over the age of 16 who do not have a job and are looking for a job. One major flaw in the calculation is the omission of "discouraged workers"—those who do not have a job and are no longer looking. If the number of discouraged workers doubled over a five-year period, this would be a cause for concern, but it would not be registered by an increase in the unemployment rate. A statistic that measures the state of the world of employment would ideally include discouraged workers as well. Further, the unemployment rate says nothing about income or wages. If unemployment decreases because of the creation of many low-paying jobs, are we better off? In the past, the Eastern bloc countries reported unemployment rates near zero. Should we have embraced their economic system?

The point is that we should be cautious in relying on statistics that by definition are only proxies for the state of the world we are trying to measure. The same is true of the poverty rate.[6]

Problems with the Poverty Rate as a Proxy

What comes to mind when you think of people living in poverty? Many would picture relative squalor—people living in a run-down house, wearing ill-fitting clothes, eating low-budget meals, driving a rusted-out car, and so on. For a variety of reasons, this is an inaccurate stereotype for many people whose incomes are below the poverty line.

Probably the most important point of confusion is the distinction between being "poor" as measured by the Census Bureau and truly "living in poverty." Remember that being poor as measured by the government is determined by *cash* income. Thus, sources of noncash income—in particular, government in-kind transfers—are not included. These include food stamps, Medicare/Medicaid, and housing subsidies.[7] The existence of these transfers makes the poverty statistics less relevant to a discussion of those "living in poverty." And as the extent of in-kind transfers has grown over time, the poverty statistics have become even less meaningful.

Further, the Census Bureau's measure is a function of *reported* income. Often, the poor decide not to report money given to them or earnings from odd jobs and black market activity in order to remain eligible for government assistance and to decrease their tax liability. Thus, a poverty rate of 15.1%, is an exaggeration of the number of those living in poverty.

The poverty rate is also deficient as a proxy because it focuses solely on income while ignoring assets. Thus, many wealthy people are included in the poverty statistics, particularly the elderly. Many retirees are measured as poor because their cash incomes are below the poverty line—regardless of whether they are "living in poverty." Also remember that in-kind transfers (including Medicare) are not included. Some of the elderly do live in squalor, but their numbers are exaggerated by the poverty rate.

The poverty rate also ignores "life-cycle earning" considerations. Over the course of one's life, income generally rises with age as one gains experience and greater skills. Thus, there are many people who are counted as poor only in their early careers; over the course of time, they will come to lead rather comfortable lives. For instance, many students are poor for a few years while they attend graduate school. Do they deserve much pity? No. A "snapshot" of incomes in any given year will include people who would not elicit any great sympathy. Further, because the poverty rate is only a snapshot, it includes middle-class families who have "bad income" years. In 1991, 4.2% of those under the poverty line were in households headed by someone with at least a college degree; the corresponding number for those with some college was 12.2%. Again, a view of their income over time would not evoke much sympathy.[8]

Distribution Versus Dynamics of Income

A factor closely related to the distribution of income is the "dynamics" of income—how one's income changes over time. (Whereas the distribution of income is a snapshot, the dynamics of income are a motion picture.) Suppose that you could choose between world A, where half the population earns $20,000 per year and the other half earns $40,000 a year, and world B, where each half earns an additional $1,000 each year. World B seems the more desirable. Now let me add a wrinkle: In world B, people are stuck in their categories for life; in world A, they have a 40% chance of changing income classes later in life. Which world seems more desirable? Most would say world A, since some people in world A would have opportunities to become rich.

Two studies released in 1992 help to illustrate the dynamics versus the distribution of income in the United States. The Treasury Department's Office of Tax Analysis surveyed 14,351 representative taxpayers over the period 1979–1988. It found that every quintile had at least a 33% turnover rate. And of those in the bottom quintile in 1979, 65% had moved up at least two quintiles by 1988.[9] Isabel Sawhill and Mark Condon of the Urban Institute used data on 25 to 54-year-old adults to report that "when one follows individuals instead of statistical groups defined by income, one finds that on average, the rich got a little richer and the poor got much richer."[10] Moreover, they find that income dynamics are very similar when comparing 1967–1976 and 1977–1986. Their results for the latter period are reproduced in Tables 1.4 and 1.5. Finally, the Census Bureau reported that 25.7% of those measured as poor in 1987 left poverty in 1988; the number for 1991–1992 was 21.2%.[11]

TABLE 1.4   Changes in 1977 Family Income Distribution Levels by 1986

	Family Income Quintile in 1986 (%)				
	Bottom	Second	Third	Fourth	Top
Family income quintile in 1977					
Bottom	10.6%	5.0%	2.2%	1.3%	0.8%
Second	4.3	6.0	5.1	2.9	1.7
Third	2.9	3.8	5.9	4.8	2.6
Fourth	1.0	2.9	4.3	6.8	5.0
Top	1.2	2.2	2.5	4.1	10.0
All	20.0	20.0	20.0	20.0	20.0

Note: Sample limited to adults aged 25 to 54 in starting year.
SOURCE: I. Sawhill and M. Condon, "Policy Bites," no. 13, Urban Institute, Washington, D.C., June 1992.

Understanding income dynamics is crucial for many reasons: (1) Dynamics provide a much better picture of those who truly "live in poverty" as opposed to those who live "under the poverty line" in a given year. (2) Dynamics are a close proxy for economic opportunity. If dynamics are limited, people are less able (for whatever reason) to improve their economic standing. (3) Dynamics are a fundamental determinant of whether class warfare exists in a country. If there is a widespread perception that one has little or no chance to move up, resentment is likely. This is a chief difference between the United States and many other countries. Compared to the United States, the distribution of incomes abroad is often not significantly different, but the dynamics are much more limited.

So if the poverty rate and the distribution of income are such poor proxies for the state of the world we are trying to measure, why do we use them? It is primarily a matter of cost. To calculate the standard measures is simply a matter of accumulating and sorting some census data each year. To measure dynamics, one must follow a set of individuals for an extended period of time. This is a costly proposition.

Demographics, Some Anomalies, and a Taste for Leisure

Independent of opportunity and dynamics, there are also some demographic reasons for a poverty rate that has not declined. The number of female heads of household has risen dramatically since the mid-1960s. There has been greater immigration in recent years, particularly for rea-

TABLE 1.5   Changes in 1977 Average Family Incomes by 1986 (1991 dollars)

| | Average Family Income | | |
	1977 Quintile in 1977	1977 Quintile in 1986	Percent Change
Quintile			
Bottom	15,853	27,998	77
Second	31,340	43,041	37
Third	43,297	51,796	20
Fourth	57,486	63,314	10
Top	92,531	97,140	5
All	48,101	56,658	18

Note: Sample limited to adults aged 25 to 54 in starting year.
SOURCE: I. Sawhill and M.Condon, "Policy Bites," no. 13, Urban Institute, Washington, D.C., June 1992.

sons unrelated to productivity. In addition, the existence of welfare programs has been an enticement for some less skilled or less motivated natives and immigrants. All of these may contribute to a higher poverty rate.

The problems with the poverty rate also explain some seeming anomalies. According to the Census Bureau, in 1990, 22,000 poor households owned heated swimming pools or jacuzzis,[12] 38% owned their own homes,[13] 62% owned a car[14] (14% owned two or more cars[15]), and almost half had air conditioning.[16] In addition, the poorest 20% of the population consumed $1.94 for every $1.00 of "income."[17] Why? Again, with the omission of in-kind transfers, assets, and life-cycle earnings, the statistic fails to distinguish between those who are under the poverty line and those who are "living in poverty."

Furthermore, the average income per hour of work is almost identical for the bottom three quintiles of income and only a little higher for the fourth quintile.[18] This points to vast differences in preferences for work versus non-market activities (household work, school, and leisure). For the most part, this is a function of the demographics of the poverty rate: Because a disproportionate number of retirees and independent students are included in the poorest quintiles, the amount of work is biased downward. In fact, income per hour is perhaps a better proxy for opportunity than the poverty rate. If two people have identical rates of income per hour but one decides to work twice as many hours, there would be a large difference in income but no difference in opportunity.

There is also direct evidence that the number of hours worked by members of each quintile differ dramatically. Ray Battalio, John Kagel, and Morgan Reynolds found that within quintiles, tastes and preferences for leisure produce an income differential as large as that in the national economy.[19] Edgar Browning and William Johnson estimated that for three-person households headed by a 35- to 44-year-old, average annual hours of work for the highest quintile were 3,104 and for the lowest quintile, 1,328.[20] The economist Brooks Pierce found that in 1989, a random sample of workers in the highest quintile averaged 2,341 hours of work while those in the lowest quintile averaged 977.[21]

Finally, there are some relevant comparisons to help put today's poor in perspective. The poorest 20% in the United States eat more meat,[22] own more cars[23] and dishwashers,[24] and have more living space[25] and indoor toilets[26] (per person) than the average Western European or Japanese. And if one were to transplant today's poorest 20% back to 1955, they would be in the top half of the U.S. population in terms of consumption.[27]

Policy Ramifications

The fact that poverty statistics exaggerate the number of people "living in poverty" does not imply that poverty is not a problem. One needs only to look at the inner cities to know it is an important issue. For reasons that are complex but not difficult to understand, the Census Bureau's way of measuring poverty is inadequate for ascertaining the number of people who live in poverty. Because the bureau relies solely on cash income in a given year to determine the poverty rate, it overestimates the number of people living in poverty by ignoring in-kind transfers, wealth, and income dynamics. In sum, the poverty rate includes many people who few of us would consider poor.

Agreeing that poverty is not well measured is not equivalent to saying nothing should be done concerning poverty. First and most obvious, policymakers need better measures of true poverty. As we have seen, studies of income dynamics are useful, but the data are costly to obtain and require a relatively long time to interpret. The best method may be to use a consumption-based measure. It is relatively inexpensive and is a closer proxy for what we're trying to measure—standards of living.

Further, continued reliance on faulty measures may have policy ramifications. The "fairness debate," which focused on higher poverty rates and more inequality in income distribution through the 1980s, is a recent example. Susan Mayer and Christopher Jencks found that the ratio of consumption for the top 20% to the bottom 20% barely moved between 1973 and 1989 (4.78 versus 4.81) but that while the comparable ratios for income increased substantially over the same period (7.95 versus 9.79). Further, the poorest 10% of all households with children in 1988–1989 reported mean incomes of $5,588 while acknowledging spending $8,000 *more* on average.[28] Using the inferior proxy yields inappropriate conclusions about what happened to the poor during the 1980s.[29] Similarly, Daniel Slesnick found that the poverty rate significantly underestimates the progress against poverty as measured by consumption.[30] Unfortunately, although less costly than measures of income dynamics, consumption measures are more difficult to obtain than the poverty rate.

Another solution would be to examine statistics in specific categories rather than relying on a general proxy. For example, among blacks, Jencks points to specific areas—higher reading levels, fewer high school dropouts, a smaller percentage of single welfare mothers (83% to 56% from 1972–1987), lower birth rates among black teens (112 to 98 per 1,000 girls from 1975 to 1986) and lower crime rates (70 to 55 per 100,000 people from 1975 to 1986)—to express optimism about how living standards have improved.[31] The frequent use of the term "underclass" is also a move in this direction.[32] This concept correlates with poverty but points to more specific factors such as income, morals, crime, and culture. Statistics in specific categories are closer to what we are trying to measure and also allow for more effective solutions.

Nonetheless, Charles Murray argues that we have to be careful when interpreting any measure of poverty.[33] For instance, focusing on income or consumption ignores the non-monetary aspects of poverty—such as self-esteem and long-term financial independence. Dollar-denominated statistics measure only part of a complex picture.

Finally, because of the connection between increasing incomes and a decreasing poverty rate, emphasis needs to be placed on policies that promote economic growth, such as high-quality education and limited taxation. Increasing general living standards is probably the quickest and least painful way to help the poor. We have also seen that income dynamics are crucial. Thus, we need to focus policy efforts on allowing all people adequate opportunity to improve their lives. For instance, providing a high-quality education and opening access to labor markets are crucial. In sum, we should focus our attentions on programs that harm the poor and discover what can be done to improve those policies.

Notes

1. M. Orshansky, "Counting the Poor," *Social Security Bulletin,* January 1965, pp. 3–29.

2. I. Sawhill notes that the threefold multiplier stems from a 1955 survey showing that families with children spent (on average) 35% of their after-tax income on food. ("Poverty in the U.S.," *Journal of Economic Literature,* September 1988, pp. 1073–1119.)

3. One mitigating factor is that (non-taxable) fringe benefits have risen as a proportion of compensation as tax rates have increased. This also explains why productivity increases exceeded real wage gains between 1973 and 1993. *Economic Report of the President* (Washington, DC: U.S. Government Printing Office, 1995), Table B-45, B-47.

4. There are those who argue that growing inequality in income distribution is a new long-term trend. Hypotheses include a growing disparity in IQs (R. Herrnstein and C. Murray, *The Bell Curve: Intelligence and Class Structure in American Life* [New York: Free Press, 1994]), the choice of marriage partners by income (L. Thurow, *The Zero-Sum Society: Distribution and the Possibilities for Economic Change* [New York: Basic Books, 1980]), structural economic changes requiring a more highly skilled labor force (W. Wilson, *The Truly Disadvantaged: The Inner City, the Underclass, and Public Policy* [Chicago: University of Chicago Press, 1987]), work disincentives from welfare programs (C. Murray, *Losing*

Ground: American Social Policy 1950–1980 [New York: Basic Books, 1984]), and lower marginal tax rates since 1981 (B. Harrison and B. Bluestone, *The Great U-Turn: Corporate Restructuring and the Polarizing of America* [New York: Basic Books, 1988]).

5. The same also applies to test scores and grade point average versus learning and ability and is true when one tries to estimate the value of an individual in a team sport. In baseball, home runs, batting average, fielding percentage, and so on are used as proxies for performance. But these fail to hold team quality constant, and they cannot measure intangibles such as attitude and leadership qualities.

6. Ironically, the method used to calculate the consumer price index (the primary proxy for inflation) biases the poverty rate upward. The CPI's "representative basket of goods" is not representative of the goods consumed by the poor.

7. The poverty line is determined by the cost of an adequate diet—yet ironically, food stamps are not included in the Census Bureau's measurement of the poverty rate.

8. Note also that the bias can go the other way. For instance, people with moderate incomes who incur exorbitant medical expenses struggle financially but are not labeled as poor by the Census Bureau.

9. "Income Dynamics," *Wall Street Journal,* June 16, 1992.

10. I. Sawhill and M. Condon, "Policy Bites" no. 13, Urban Institute, Washington, D.C., June 1992. J. Davies, F. Saint-Hillaire, and J. Whalley provide estimates of lifetime income distributions in Canada ("Some Calculations of Lifetime Tax Incidence," *American Economic Review,* September 1984, pp. 633–649). They find that an annual pre-tax measure of income distribution yields 4.1% for the lowest quintile and 45.5% for the highest quintile. Estimating lifetime effects, they find 10.4% and 32.4%, respectively.

11. U.S. Bureau of the Census, *Poverty in the United States; 1992: Current Population Reports P60-185,* pp. xx, xxi.

12. U.S. Department of Energy, *Housing Characteristics 1987* (Washington, D.C.: U.S. Government Printing Office, 1989), p. 87.

13. U.S. Department of Housing and Urban Development, *American Housing Survey for the United States in 1987,* Current Housing Reports H-150-87 (Washington, D.C.: U.S. Government Printing Office, 1989), pp. 34, 84, 114, 304.

14. Ibid., p. 87.

15. Ibid.

16. Ibid., p. 40.

17. Bureau of Labor Statistics, *Consumer Expenditure Survey: Integrated Survey Data, 1984–86,* Bulletin #2333 (Washington, D.C.: U.S. Government Printing Office, August 1989), p. 6. Statistics in notes 12–17 are all cited in R. Rector, "How 'Poor' Are America's Poor?", *The Heritage Foundation Backgrounder,* The Heritage Foundation, Washington, D.C., September 21, 1990.

18. E. Browning and J. Browning, *Public Finance and the Price System,* 3rd ed. (New York: HarperCollins, 1987), p. 247. They report that income per hour—after taxes and transfers—was $5.78, $5.77, $5.68, $6.66, and $9.82 for the respective income quintiles in 1976.

19. R. Battalio, J. Kagel, and M. Reynolds, "Income Distributions in Two Experimental Economies," *Journal of Political Economy,* December 1977, pp. 1259–1271.

20. Browning and Browning, *Public Finance and the Price System,* p. 246, citing E. Browning and W. Johnson, *The Distribution of the Tax Burden* (Washington, D.C.: American Enterprise Institute, 1979).

21. By communication with the author. The numbers for men only are 2,416 and 1,391, respectively.

22. Foreign Agricultural Service, *World Livestock Situation* (Washington D.C.: U.S. Department of Agriculture, March 1990).

23. U.S. Department of Housing and Urban Development, *American Housing Survey for the United States in 1987,* Current Housing Reports H-150-87 (Washington, D.C.: U.S. Government Printing Office, 1989), pp. 46, 50; U.S. Department of Commerce, *Statistical Abstract of the United States: 1989* (Washington, D.C.: U.S. Bureau of the Census, 1989), Table 1418.

24. Organization for Economic Cooperation and Development, *Living Conditions in OECD Countries* (Paris: OECD, 1986), pp. 126–127.

25. Ibid., p. 133; United Nations, *Compendium of Housing Statistics* (New York: United Nations, 1983), pp. 251–261.

26. *Living Conditions in OECD Countries,* p. 133; *American Housing Survey,* p. 38, 44.

27. Bureau of Labor Statistics, *Consumer Expenditures in 1988* (Washington, D.C.: U.S. Department of Labor, February 26, 1990), Table 1; U.S. Department of Commerce, *Historical Statistics of the United States, Part I* (Washington, D.C., U.S. Bureau of the Census, 1975), pp. 297, 301. Statistics in notes 22–27 are all cited in R. Rector, "How 'Poor' Are America's Poor?", *The Heritage Foundation Backgrounder,* The Heritage Foundation, Washington, D.C., September 21, 1990.

28. J. Marshall, "Inconspicuous Consumption," *Reason,* July 1993, pp. 42–43.

29. This also contributes to the confusion over the extent of success for the programs of the Great Society. The two primary goals were to increase standards of living and to promote independence. At least with respect to the first goal, the poverty rate is not particularly instructive.

30. D. Slesnick, "Gaining Ground: Poverty in the Postwar United States," *Journal of Political Economy,* February 1993, pp. 1–38.

31. D. Whitman and D. Friedman, "The Surprising News About the Poor," *U.S. News and World Report,* January 1, 1990, pp. 73–76.

32. This term was popularized by K. Auletta (*The Underclass* [New York: Random House, 1982]); and Wilson (*The Truly Disadvantaged*).

33. C. Murray, *In Pursuit of Happiness and Good Government* (New York: Simon and Schuster, 1988). M. Kaus (*The End of Equality,* New York: Basic Books, 1992) also argues that "more than money matters."

2

Government as Robin Hood: Taxing the Rich and Redistributing to the Poor

One of government's primary activities is redistributing income. It turns out that many of these policies enhance the incomes of the middle class and the wealthy at the expense of the poor. Redistribution to the non-poor is covered in Part 2. This chapter provides an introduction to redistribution by the government and then focuses explicitly on its efforts to transfer income to the poor. The effectiveness of redistribution to the poor is covered in Part 3.

An Introduction to Government Redistribution

By definition, government spending and taxation redistribute income. Sometimes redistribution is the primary goal. For example, the explicit intent of welfare programs is to tax relatively wealthy people in order to supplement standards of living for poor people. Other times, redistribution is merely a by-product of another policy objective. One of the stated goals for "acreage-restriction programs" (paying farmers not to plant crops) is to help the environment by reducing soil exhaustion and erosion. A by-product of this policy is that farmers' incomes are enhanced at the expense of taxpayers.

Some government policies are meant to redistribute money indirectly. Quotas (limits) on foreign textile imports restrict competition for domestic textile producers and enable them to charge higher prices for their products. This amounts to a transfer of money from people who buy clothing to people who produce clothing. No money passes through the government's hands, but the quotas are effective in transferring money from one group to another.

Sometimes, redistribution is "progressive"—the percentage of taxes paid increases (or benefits decrease) as income rises. For example, income taxes are structured such that individuals pay higher percentages of their incomes to the government as their incomes increase (if we ignore tax loopholes). Other policies are "regressive." A tax on gasoline is regressive because poorer people spend a larger proportion of their budgets on gasoline.

Thus, government's redistributive efforts can be explicit or implicit; they can be achieved directly or indirectly; and they can target the poor, the middle class, or the wealthy.

Taxing the Rich

I identified the poor in Chapter 1, but who are the wealthy? According to the Census Bureau, in 1992 half of all households in the United States made at least $30,786. The top 20% was composed of those that earned at least $58,201.[1]

It is politically popular to have a progressive income tax schedule, that is, to tax the wealthy at a higher rate than other people. At times, the call to tax them at a considerably higher rate is particularly loud. Promoting class warfare can be good politics, especially during bad economic times. However, for a variety of reasons, soaking the wealthy has not been supported on a regular basis in the United States.

Many greatly admire the rich and feel that most wealth is earned. More important, many people perceive that the opportunity to earn a good living is generally available to those who are willing to work hard. The perception of considerable economic mobility—the income dynamics discussed in Chapter 1—is responsible for the attitude that a relatively comfortable standard of living is attainable. In addition, most Americans *are* relatively affluent by any worldwide standard.

Benjamin Page provides another explanation for why soaking the rich is not largely popular with voters: People are confused about the level of income redistributed by government.[2] It turns out that the amount of money transferred to the poor is relatively small compared to all the discussion that accompanies such transfers. Moreover, tax deductions extend the illusion that transfers from the wealthy are especially large. Confusion over marginal and average tax rates further clouds public perception of the amount of taxes collected from the rich. The average tax rate is the percentage of one's total income actually paid to the government; the marginal tax rate is that rate applied to a particular income bracket. In other words, if a taxpayer is in the 33% income tax bracket, that does not mean that the taxes actually collected are 33% of the person's income.

Table 2.1 illustrates the marginal and average tax rates for various incomes resulting from the 1980 tax code (the source of Page's complaint). Note that as income rises, marginal tax rates can increase dramatically at the same time that average tax rates are increasing relatively slowly. Conversely, marginal tax rates can fall dramatically without a corresponding decrease in the average tax rate. With marginal tax rates falling dramatically for the wealthy in the 1980s, some people may have mistakenly thought that redistribution through the tax code had become much more limited than in past years.

The Rich in the 1980s

Part of the recent impulse to tax the rich stems from the labeling of the 1980s as a "decade of greed" when the wealthy "prospered at everyone else's expense." How did the rich do during the 1980s? The wealthiest 20% gained substantially during the decade, but all other income classes gained as well. The wealthy also paid a higher proportion of the total taxes collected in 1990 than in 1980, while all other quintiles paid less.[3] Further, substantial income dynamics necessitate that the richest 20% in 1990 were a very different set of people than the richest 20% in 1980. The Urban

TABLE 2.1   The Difference in Marginal and Average Tax Rates with Progressive Taxation (in constant 1981 dollars)

Income Bracket Range (%)	Marginal Tax Rate (%)	Taxes Paid at Low End of Bracket	Average Tax Rate
0–3,440	0	0	0
3,440–5,500	14	0	0
5,500–7,600	16	294	5.3
7,600–11,900	18	630	8.3
11,900–16,000	21	1,404	11.8
16,000–20,200	24	2,265	14.2
20,200–24,600	28	3,273	16.2
24,600–29,900	32	4,505	18.3
29,900–35,200	37	6,201	20.8
35,200–45,800	43	8,162	23.2
45,800–60,000	49	12,270	26.8
60,000–85,600	54	19,678	32.8
85,600–109,400	59	33,502	39.1
109,400–162,400	64	47,544	43.4
162,400–215,400	68	81,464	50.2
> 215,400	70	117,504	54.6

Note: This table ignores the role of income deductions.
SOURCE: 1981 IRS tax form.

Institute's numbers (Table 1.5) for 1977 and 1986 point to massive gains by those in the lowest quintile compared to those in the highest quintile.

Each side in the debate over the policies of the 1980s cites only some of the statistics. Proponents note that the wealthy paid a greater percentage of taxes collected by the government.[4] Opponents point to the lower marginal tax rates and the increased incomes of the wealthy. Of course, one should consider all of the relevant statistics. The debate also raises questions about what the goals of our tax policy should be: If we have to choose, do we want the rich to pay higher tax rates or pay more taxes? Do we want to keep their incomes closer to the average or do we want them to put more money in the public till?

How could tax revenues from the wealthy rise while marginal tax rates decreased? When the top federal marginal tax rates fell from 70% to 28% in the early 1980s, the incentives confronting wealthy taxpayers changed in four ways. First, they had an incentive to work harder, since they were able to keep more of the fruits of their labor. At the higher marginal tax rates (70% not including state and local taxes), one kept only $30 of every additional $100 earned beyond the lowest boundary of the tax bracket. Second, such taxpayers had a greater incentive to report income. Not reporting $1,000 in income (or "finding" $1,000 in deductions) saved $700 in federal taxes before the tax rates decreased. Third, after the decrease, they were less likely to receive compensation in the form of fringe benefits, which are not subject to taxation. Fourth, they were less likely to use tax shelters to (legitimately) hide income from the government. One can easily imagine people behaving differently after marginal tax rates fell so dramatically.

Practically Speaking . . .

Even if one thinks it is desirable to tax the wealthy more than other people, higher tax rates on the wealthy may not achieve the goal. Incentives matter; behavior is determined to some extent by marginal tax rates. The tax increases in 1990 also illustrate this premise (marginal tax rates on the wealthiest rose from 28% to 33%). Although tax rates rose, tax revenues from the wealthy declined. Meanwhile, all other income classes paid more in taxes.[5] Ironically, if one wants to get money from the rich, the best way is probably to keep marginal tax rates low. The tax increases of 1993 will almost certainly provide additional evidence for this point.

Finally, even if one confiscated the incomes or even the wealth of the richest people in the country, it would not amount to much when one considers what our government spends every year. If you want to raise revenues, you have to go where the bulk of the money is— the middle class.

Government Spending on Social Programs

Table 2.2 provides some details of changes in federal government expenditures during 1965–1991. The first thing to note is that government spending as a percentage of national income has grown over time. Paradoxically, one might think that as a country became wealthier, there would be less for government to do. Then, total spending might rise, but not as a percentage of income. Apparently, government has found many additional things that require its attention.

Notice that defense spending declined as a percentage of government spending (from 42.8% to 20.6%) and as a percentage of national output (from 7.5% to 4.8%). Social spending increased dramatically after the Great Society programs of the 1960s (from 4.4% to 10.5% of national output).

However, Table 2.3 illustrates that only a small portion of social spending is expressly "pro-poor." Pro-middle-class spending on education and social insurance programs such as Social Security and unemployment

TABLE 2.2 Expenditures by Major Program Type (in billions of constant 1991 dollars) and as a Percentage of GDP and Total Government Spending

		As a % of GDP	As a % of Federal Spending
National defense			
1965	$218.8	7.5	42.8
1973	235.3	6.0	31.2
1980	221.5	5.0	22.7
1991	273.3	4.8	20.6
Major income-transfer programs			
1965	$127.2	4.4	24.9
1973	310.1	7.9	41.1
1980	425.3	9.6	43.5
1991	593.4	10.5	44.8
Total federal spending			
1965	$511.1	17.6	
1973	753.7	19.2	
1980	976.7	22.1	
1991	1323.8	23.5	

Note: GDP = gross domestic product. In 1991, expenditures on minor programs totaled $55 billion—for a total of 11.5% of GDP. (Browning and Browning, *Public Finance and the Price System*, 4th ed., p. 252.)

SOURCES: U.S. Bureau of the Census, *Statistical Abstract of the United States* (Washington, DC: U.S. Department of the Treasury various years); E. Browning and J. Browning, *Public Finance and the Price System*, 3rd and 4th eds. (New York: HarperCollins, 1987, 1994).

insurance is much higher than the amount of money allocated to the poor for welfare programs such as Medicaid, Aid to Families with Dependent Children (AFDC), food stamps, and housing vouchers. Although both the amount and proportion spent directly on the poor have increased dramatically since 1965 (the beginning of the War on Poverty), the numbers are still small compared to other types of spending. And much of this increase has been in the Medicaid program.[6]

Note also that contrary to popular belief, spending on social programs and spending on the poor (controlling for inflation) increased in the 1980s. The rate of growth fell, but the amount of money spent still increased. The "spending cuts" on social programs in the 1980s usually amounted to cutting the increases Congress proposed; for example, a decrease in the rate of growth from 10% to 6% would still amount to a spending increase.

At first glance, it might seem that Social Security, Medicare and unemployment insurance would also redistribute money to the relatively

TABLE 2.3   Expenditures on Major Income-Transfer Programs (in billions of constant 1991 dollars)

	1965	1973	1980	1991
Social insurance (targets general population)				
Social Security (OASDI)	71.3	148.2	193.6	265.6
Miscellaneous[a] (cash)	33.3	60.7	72.6	71.2
Medicare (in-kind)	–	29.1	57.9	116.7
Subtotal	104.6	238.0	324.0	453.5
Percentage of GDP	3.6	6.1	7.3	7.9
Major welfare programs (target the poor)				
Cash benefits				
Aid to Families with Dependent Children (AFDC)	7.4	21.5	23.1	20.9
Supplemental Security Income (SSI)[b]	11.7	10.1	10.6	15.9
Earned income tax credit (EITC)	–	–	2.1	9.5
In-kind benefits				
Medicaid[c]	2.2	27.9	41.7	53.4
Food stamps	–	7.7	15.0	18.7
Housing assistance	1.3	4.9	8.8	17.2
Subtotal	22.6	72.1	101.3	135.6
Percentage of GDP	0.8	1.8	2.3	2.4

[a]Miscellaneous programs include unemployment insurance, veterans' benefits, and railroad retirement.

[b]SSI was implemented in 1974. Before that, it had been referred to as Aid to the Blind, Aid to the Permanently and Totally Disabled, and Old Age Assistance.

[c]Called Medical Aid to the Aged in 1965.

SOURCES: E. Browning and J. Browning, *Public Finance and the Price System*, 4th ed. (New York: HarperCollins, 1994), p. 252; U.S. Bureau of the Census, *Statistical Abstract of the United States* (Washington, DC: U.S. Department of the Treasury, 1994), Tables 509, 573, 598, 600; Committee of Ways and Means, U.S. House of Representatives, *1993 Green Book* (Washington, DC: Government Printing Office, 1993), p. 1058.

poor. But for a variety of reasons, those programs are only somewhat progressive. Social Security is mildly progressive with respect to weekly benefits, but there is a cap on the amount of income subject to the Social Security tax. Medicare is a program designed for the elderly, who have a below-average poverty rate. Another relatively subtle factor is that the poor die at a younger age; thus they reap fewer benefits from Social Security and Medicare. Receiving payments from unemployment insurance is conditional on holding a job in the recent past. Thus, its benefits are regressive to the extent that the program does not pay those who have been jobless for a long time. In sum, these "social insurance" programs are largely a shell game within the middle class and between the young and old. The redistributive effects between income classes are only slight.

One other trend merits attention. Over time, spending on the poor has moved toward in-kind (non-cash) benefits. In 1965, welfare transfers were mostly in cash (85%); in 1991, much assistance subsidized the consumption of particular goods and services (cash transfers then were only 26% of total outlay). Remember that the "poverty rate" fails to include in-kind benefits, thus overestimating the number of people "living in poverty." As the proportion of assistance in the form of in-kind transfers has increased over time, the poverty rate has become less relevant.

In sum, for all of the concern about the level of social spending, programs that specifically target the poor are only a trivial part of the government's budget. However, the money transferred from taxpayers for programs that target the poor amounts to a large sum per poor person—approximately $5,800 each, or $23,200 for a poor family of four.[7] What happens to all of that money? Given the amount of money transferred, why aren't we making better progress in our war against poverty? Independent of concerns about the poverty rate as a proxy, I will analyze income transfers to the poor in Part 3.

Other Considerations

First, redistributive policies that are supposed to help the poor are often driven to some extent by special interest groups. The American Medical Association had a loud voice in the development of Medicaid (and Medicare). Government subsidies of health care for the poor (and the elderly) have driven up the demand for such services. The U.S. Department of Agriculture insisted on running the food stamp program out of its bureaucracy. In the face of declining numbers of farms and farmers, the bureaucrats needed additional tasks to justify their jobs. Labor unions have been vocal in extending unemployment insurance; their primary concern is to protect their workers, not help the poor.

Second, there is a popular, although somewhat misleading, distinction between Democrats—defined as fans of big government (especially social programs), and "small government" Republicans. Certainly there is some correlation, but most of our elected representatives encourage government spending, especially in their own districts. For example, Republican senators from farm states generally pursue smaller government except when it's time to vote for farm programs. Thus although Republicans tend to advocate smaller government, this approach is tempered by their desire to use government programs to redistribute income to their own constituents. Further, the distinction between the parties is not even clear when it comes to spending on the poor. Southern Democrats are not usually big proponents of welfare programs. And as we will see later, Richard Nixon was president during the vast growth of the Great Society programs in the late 1960s and early 1970s.

Government redistributes income in many ways. But only a small portion of the money goes to the poor. And in terms of financing current or additional government spending, soaking the rich is not a likely avenue because of the process of income dynamics and because opportunities to increase one's standard of living are still considered to be widely available. Further, rich people have numerous ways to protect themselves from high tax rates—taking advantage of loopholes, hiding income, "finding" deductions, moving to fringe benefits in lieu of cash, or just consuming more leisure.

In short, we are back to emphasizing policies that would increase the incomes of all people by improving education and infrastructure, lowering taxes, and promoting any other policy that leads to economic growth. It is often said that socialism makes everybody equal, but equally poor. Unseating the rich is an undesirable and impractical goal. Instead, we should move in directions that would allow more people to join them.

Notes

1. U.S. Bureau of the Census, *Income Supplement of the Current Population Survey* (Washington, DC: U.S. Department of the Treasury, March 1993).

2. B. Page, *Who Gets What from Government?* (Berkeley: University of California Press, 1983), pp. 21–23.

3. P. Gigot, "Oops! Weren't We Supposed to Soak the Rich?" *Wall Street Journal,* July 9, 1993. According to Gigot, tax receipts from the wealthiest fell 6.1% in 1991; tax receipts from everyone else rose by 1%.

4. L. Lindsay, "Estimating the Behavioral Response of Taxpayers to Changes in Tax Rates: 1982–1984," *Journal of Public Economics,* July 1987, pp. 173–206.

5. Gigot, "Oops!"

6. There are many other minor welfare programs designed to help the poor—including Head Start, Pell grants, and training programs. In 1990, 15 of them had expenditures of over $1 billion each. These add at least $55 billion to the $153 billion mentioned in Table 2.2, bringing the total to $208 billion. (E. Browning and J. Browning, *Public Finance and the Price System,* 4th ed. [New York: HarperCollins, 1994], p. 253.)

7. This calculation includes the $55 billion from miscellaneous programs that target the poor (for a total of $208 billion).

3

Discrimination: A Primary or Secondary Cause of Poverty?

This chapter concludes the introduction to the issues concerning poverty and redistribution. But before we discuss how government policies adversely affect the poor, we need to devote some time to the "non-government" factors that contribute to poverty—or more generally, why incomes differ between individuals and groups. Wages and incomes vary for many reasons, including everything from job skills to union participation and various forms of discrimination.

What Causes Income Differentials?

One crucial factor affecting income differentials is the level of human capital (job skills) that people bring to the labor market. Human capital can be endowed through natural ability or earned through investments in education, training, or job experience. In each individual's endowment, genetics and environment are significant—although their relative weights are the subject of an age-old debate. The pursuit of education and the accumulation of experience are perhaps the primary determinants of one's earnings potential. Further, the quality of education available, especially to the poor, is an extremely important issue.

One's geographical location is another important factor. For instance, poverty rates in 1989 ranged from New Hampshire's 6.4% to Mississippi's 25.2%.[1] In addition to being concentrated in the inner cities, (measured) poverty is greater in certain geographic areas—the lower Mississippi River and Rio Grande valleys, Indian reservations, and Appalachia. Further, in the context of income differentials that would cause little concern, it could be that of two equally talented and experienced engineers, one works in Mississippi and the other in Massachusetts. Because the cost of living is so much higher in New England, incomes overall are higher there. Although such differences would be measured as an "income differential," they refer to "nominal" income and are irrelevant in comparing "real" income or purchasing power.

Membership in a union also has a bearing on income. Because union workers are paid above what an equally qualified non-union worker would earn, differences in income are also a function of whether one belongs to a union.

Since wages are only part of the compensation one receives for working, there may be differences in wages without differences in compensation and vice versa. Some jobs have substantial fringe benefits; others have sizable pensions. Two people may begin the same job with one choosing to receive some compensation in the form of fringe benefits or a larger pension and the other choosing more cash. In such cases, where no difference in opportunity exists, statisticians would still report an income differential.

Individual tastes and preferences are another important factor. For certain job characteristics, there are "compensating wage differentials"—additional payments required to persuade workers to accept some undesirable aspect of a job. This explains the relatively high rates of pay for people who haul garbage or work in construction. The resulting income differential is not indicative of a difference in opportunity.

In addition, people have different tastes and preferences for "non-market activity"—schooling, household work, and leisure. These help determine whether people choose to work overtime, fulltime, parttime, or not at all. Two individuals (or families) may have equal abilities and opportunities but may make different decisions concerning the number of hours they work. Unfortunately, the resulting outcomes would be measured as an income differential.

The choice of statistical measures can also make a difference. For instance, even if per capita income is constant, family income and household income differ over time with changes in demographics—such as the age distribution, the propensities to get married and remain married, and the make-up of the household in terms of wage-earners and dependents (for example, college students or the elderly). It is possible that increases and decreases in household or family income are not an accurate reflection of the extent of economic change.

Sometimes the aforementioned differences that lead to income differentials are important only when comparing individuals. However, if a group is disproportionately represented in any particular category, that group would have a lower- or higher-than-average income.[2] For instance, a large proportion of blacks live in the deep South, where incomes and the cost of living are relatively low. To a limited extent, lower incomes for blacks as a group are a function of where many of them live. In fact, for non-southern families with both parents, black family income was 96%

of white family income as early as 1970.[3] Likewise, a large proportion of union labor is male; to some extent, lower incomes for women as a group are a function of their more limited involvement in unions.

Like the poverty rate, income is only a proxy for measuring standards of living and economic opportunity. Many of the previously mentioned variables cause differences in income that are unrelated to opportunity. Therefore, in order to be useful, statistics that measure income differentials between groups or individuals must take differences in these variables into account. Otherwise, one is comparing apples to oranges.

For example, newspapers report that on average, women earn about 75% of what men are paid. (Until the 1980s, this statistic remained around 60% for decades.)[4] However, this raw number does not account for differences in the groups' average job experience, training and education, and representation in various job fields, among others. This results in a comparison of one group of people who have more training and experience to another group that is disproportionately inexperienced and has less training. It should come as no surprise that the former group has a higher average income. Because important variables are not held constant, the raw number (75%) tells us nothing about income differentials between equally qualified men and women.

In a more useful comparison, June O'Neill found that a 27- to 33-year-old woman who has never had a child earns 98% of her male counterpart's income.[5] Likewise, fathers with working wives earn 20%–25% less than those who are sole breadwinners.[6] Some claim that this is a "daddy penalty," again arguing discrimination. A more compelling explanation is a difference in tastes and preferences between the two types of fathers.

The Role of Discrimination

Despite the importance of the previous factors, the most popular topic concerning income differentials between groups is discrimination. With a controversial subject, it is important to clearly define the terms to be used: Prejudice involves pre-judging something or someone—it is a belief or opinion; discrimination is prejudice in action. Note that in order to discriminate, one must (1) have a prejudice, (2) be in a position to turn the belief into action, and (3) be willing to bear the costs (if any) of those actions. In the context of economics, I will discuss how discrimination occurs in product and labor markets.

Discrimination can also be said to occur when an individual's wages or income is unrelated to his or her productivity and job characteristics. When labor economists measure discrimination, they control for the variables previously discussed. Whatever remains is considered "unexplained" differences in wages and is designated as (the upper boundary of the extent of) discrimination. There are two types of discrimination: personal and statistical.

Personal Discrimination

This type of discrimination is the most frequently discussed. Personal discrimination is a matter of indulging one's tastes and preferences concerning the buying or selling of products or the choice of whom to employ. For instance, I might get a kick out of not hiring or promoting women. Or I might decide against buying something from a certain store simply because it is operated by an Asian or a redneck. Or I might decide not to sell a product to people who are black or Jewish. Both parties are cheated out of a mutually beneficial trade because of one party's personal prejudices.

This type of behavior is costly to the one who is discriminated against. However, on average, the degree of competition in a given market and the number of discriminatory firms determines the extent of the cost. For example, in Houston a few years ago, one gas station owner decided to charge those with foreign automobiles a few cents more than the market rate. Since there were many gas stations in the city and only one station was participating, the cost was minimal to those discriminated against.

As long as the discrimination is limited to a few firms in a large market, the one significant result will be some segregation. If a large number of firms discriminate, non-discriminating entrepreneurs have an incentive to enter the market and sell to (or hire) those who have been discriminated against.

In addition, personal discrimination is usually costly to the one who discriminates. To indulge one's tastes and preferences, one may have to turn away good workers in favor of more expensive or less productive workers. The cost of such behavior may temper the desire to engage in it. Remember that discrimination is the willingness to put prejudicial opinions into action. The question may then become: "Do I really want to lower my income in order to discriminate against someone?"

Sometimes government policy encourages discrimination by reducing its cost to zero. When governments regulate a monopoly's prices and profits, they inadvertently provide an incentive for the firm to inflate its costs. If government is going to reduce my profits to "an acceptable level," why not lower profits myself by artificially raising costs? One way to do this is to indulge tastes and preferences concerning others—to discriminate. The cost is zero, since government would confiscate the "extra" profits anyway.

A more common case occurs when government prevents a market from functioning normally, creating a "market distortion." For instance, a price floor on wages (a minimum wage) creates a surplus of workers (unemployment). With a surplus of unskilled workers wanting to work at the minimum wage, employers can costlessly turn down any particular applicant because there are countless others looking for a job at that wage. The employer can costlessly discriminate because of the surplus created by government. Another example is rent control, which creates a housing shortage. With people waiting in line to get apartments at an artificially low price, landlords can costlessly choose those who fit their tastes and preferences.[7]

Government agencies are generally more interested in maximizing budgets than profits; they have an incentive to pursue (budget) size over efficiency. This inefficiency may include discriminatory hiring practices. If the goal is to expand budgets, bureaucrats may be unconcerned with hiring the best people for the job and may tend to hire less efficient workers who fit their tastes and preferences. (This tendency can lead to discrimination for or against individuals and groups.) Further, their monopoly power can allow discriminatory selling practices. If everyone must purchase a product or service through a government monopoly, there is little incentive to please customers of any type.

Finally, one should note that the greatest problems with discrimination against racial minorities have been caused or perpetuated by government, for example, slavery, police brutality, the Dred Scott decision, school segregation, Jim Crow laws, Davis-Bacon laws, apartheid in South Africa, and religious persecution around the world.[8]

The point is not that government agencies or landlords in cities with rent control always discriminate—or that personal discrimination never occurs in competitive markets. Rather, the point is simply that discrimination is less costly and therefore more likely in markets that are either not competitive or distorted by the government. In competitive markets, unless there are widespread discriminatory attitudes and a willingness to bear costs, personal discrimination is unlikely to substantially affect individuals and will not be a significant factor for a group.

If personal discrimination is widespread, enforcement of civil rights laws may be effective. But from economic analysis, we can see that promoting competition and eliminating government's market distortions would be a useful way to curb discriminatory behavior. Finally, because personal discrimination is difficult to prove by its very nature, our energies are probably better focused in areas where we know minorities are hurt on a routine basis. That is the subject of Part 2 and beyond.

Statistical Discrimination

Statistical discrimination is talked about only infrequently, although it is the more common of the two types—we all do it. That's right—all of us discriminate in this way. When you choose a can of beans at a store, do you select one with a dent in it (if it is the same price as an undented can)? Why not? Do you *know* there is something wrong with the can? If you are walking alone at night with three boisterous young men coming your way, do you get nervous? If possible, do you choose another path? Why? Do you *know* that the men intend to harm you? When you vote for offices at the bottom of a ballot, how do you decide? Name recognition? Party affiliation? Incumbent or not? Why? Do you *know* that the candidates you have chosen are more qualified than their opponents?

These decisions and many others have the following in common: We have incomplete information about the decision, information is costly to obtain, and the choice is of some importance. In other words, people make the best decisions they can with limited and costly information.

Part of this decision-making process involves using group information to form "best guesses" about what individuals in a group will do. When I joined our department's intramural softball team at Texas A&M, I asked the captain what position he wanted me to play. He looked at me for a moment and said, "We'll put you in right field." (Right field is where you put people who can't play very well, since balls aren't hit there very often.) Why did this happen? The captain had no idea how well or how poorly I played. But he knew that most individuals in the group I represent—tall, skinny guys with glasses—were not known for their athletic prowess. Until he observed my "productivity," I had to play right field.

In a November 1993 speech, Jesse Jackson expressed the concept this way: "There is nothing more painful for me at this stage in my life than to walk down the street and hear footsteps and start to think about robbery and then look around and see it's somebody white and feel relieved. How humiliating."[9] Jackson was using statistical discrimination to decide whether he could relax.

The same thing occurs in labor markets. Firms use signals of all types (group information) to do their best in selecting productive employees. Information is far from perfect, gathering information on prospective employees is costly, and hiring ineffective employees is a costly proposition. Thus, firms resort to using grades, college attended, standardized tests, and so on. It is not that all students who graduate with a 3.0 grade point average are better workers than those with a 2.5. But on average, a firm may have found this to be the case. It is not that all graduates of Princeton are more productive than those who graduate from "North-Northwest Idaho State University." But on average, firms may have found Princeton graduates to be more competent. A business may use a typing test for prospective secretaries. If someone is able to type 100 words per minute but suffers from "test anxiety" and can type only 40 words per minute during a test, he or she is unlikely to get the job.

Note that neither the employer nor the employee is happy about the failure of these signals to correctly predict productivity. The firm pays the cost of searching for the best people, but sometimes mistakes are made.[10] Likewise, even though particular applicants, say, a student from a less highly regarded university, might be a great asset to a firm, it is unlikely they will be able to signal their ability. Such workers "deserve better" in some sense but will have to start at a lower position to demonstrate their true productivity. Whereas statistical discrimination is "unjust" in an idealistic sense, it is comforting in that it is "nothing personal." People are simply doing their best to earn a living.

Additional Considerations About Discrimination

First, racial conflict is not simply a characteristic of the United States in the late 20th century. It is as old as time, it happens all over the world, and it occurs among many combinations of races. We often forget other countries and their histories, but discrimination is nothing new. In fact, one could argue that our troubles in this arena are relatively mild by any historical perspective.[11]

Second, neither political power nor the absence of personal discrimination are necessary or sufficient conditions for economic well-being. Blacks have struggled economically despite substantial political power, including nearly proportional representation in Congress and control of government in many large cities. In the past, the Irish held vast political power, but as a group, their incomes were well below average. Meanwhile, Asians have little political power but have done exceptionally well in economic arenas.[12] Further, Asians have been discriminated against by individuals and even government but have continued to thrive. Sowell points out that discrimination against the Chinese is legal in Malaysia but that they still dominate the country's economic activity.[13] Although discrimination and political power can influence outcomes, they are not primary explanations for income differentials between groups or economic outcomes for most individuals.

Third, degrees of integration and segregation occur naturally. For example, in dating and religion, people of different ethnic groups pair off and gather together voluntarily in a way that resembles racial discrimination. With respect to housing, people have tastes and preferences that are largely a function of income and independent of race. Thus, because incomes are disproportionately low for minorities, what is in fact a class issue is misconstrued as a racial issue. Walter Williams points to polls where concern over low-income families moving in, public housing, and "flight" to the suburbs are independent of race and completely an issue of income class; middle-class blacks have concerns remarkably similar to those of middle-class whites.[14]

Fourth, just as under-representation in a field does not necessarily imply discrimination, over-representation does not imply the absence of discrimination. For instance, blacks make up the majority of players in the National Basketball Association and Asians in the United States have higher incomes than the national average. But it is still possible that individuals in both groups suffer from discrimination.[15]

Higher Prices in the Inner City

One could accuse grocery stores of discrimination against minorities, since prices in the inner city are often somewhat higher than those elsewhere. Instead of some sort of conspiracy, such accusations usually reflect an ignorance about how markets work in general and specifically, how these particular markets work.

The higher cost of groceries in the inner city is the result of greater operating costs (especially for security and for crime and insurance premiums). In addition, higher rates of return are necessary to make such a relatively risky investment attractive. Certainly, events in many cities have proven these risks to be far from imaginary. Ironically, riots and unrest only exacerbate such problems—further driving up the cost of insurance and the rate of return necessary to attract entrepreneurs.

In regard to the concept of personal discrimination, charges of racism implicitly assume the market structure is not competitive. Otherwise, if store owners were charging "outrageous prices," entrepreneurs would have an incentive to enter the market and undercut their prices.

The same is true of bank-lending practices. Critics frequently complain about loan-rejection rates for minorities. But they fail to hold "productivity" concerns—for example, default and delinquency rates—constant. For instance, if blacks never default and whites have a 10% default rate, we can conclude that bankers are stupid (avoiding good loans), that they discriminate against blacks, or that they are constrained from lending to blacks by law.

Regardless, one could argue that to the extent there is discrimination, working diligently within an imperfect system is probably the best option.[16] Many Korean immigrants, for example, open inner-city grocery stores. They face some degree of discrimination and a language barrier but have chosen the route of hard work as opposed to incessant moaning about injustices. Many have had economic success. Presumably that option is open to all.

I have spent nearly an entire chapter on discrimination. However, I do not mean to imply that it is a significant explanation for poverty among groups or most individuals. This goes against conventional wisdom. A 1993 Gallup poll reported that 44% of blacks and 21% of whites believed discrimination is the *main* reason blacks (on average) have worse jobs, income, and housing.[17] Because discrimination is perceived to be so important and because it is a prominent part of discussions concerning the poor, it required a thorough treatment.

In fact, an overriding focus on discrimination is wrongheaded for two reasons. First, although it certainly exists, it is not a primary explanation for the plight of today's poor. Second and more important, from a practical standpoint, even if it were significant, it would be very difficult to stop. As we will see throughout the remainder of the book, there are plenty of poor government policies we can fix more easily than personal prejudices.

Notes

1. U.S. Bureau of the Census, *Statistical Abstract of the United States* (Washington, DC: U.S. Department of the Treasury, 1993), Table 741.

2. See T. Sowell, *Race and Culture: A Worldview* (New York: Basic Books, 1994).

3. J. Conti and B. Stetson, "The New Black Vanguard," *Intercollegiate Review*, Spring 1993, pp. 33–41. The 1991 poverty rate for all blacks was 32.7%; for whites it was 11.3%. (*U.S. Bureau of the Census Statistical Abstract of the United States*, Table 735.)

4. J. O'Neill, "The Shrinking Pay Gap," *Wall Street Journal*, October 7, 1994.

5. Ibid.

6. T. Lewin, "Fathers Get Ahead If Their Wives Stay at Home," *Louisville Courier-Journal*, October 13, 1994, citing studies by Linda Stroh (Loyola University of Chicago), Freida Reitmann (Pace University), and Jeffrey Pfeffer (Stanford University).

7. Remember that discriminatory behavior is independent of "productivity" issues—in this context, how good a tenant the prospective renter would be.

8. Note also that the fairly popular hypotheses of gender bias against females in (government) schools and the use of excessive force at Waco and Ruby Ridge are consistent with the government's ability to discriminate. The Davis-Bacon laws are covered in Chapter 7.

9. "A New Civil Rights Frontier," *U.S. News and World Report*, January 17, 1994, p. 38.

10. In a competitive market, firms who use "bad signals" will tend to be driven out of the market by those who use better signals.

11. T. Sowell's *The Economics and Politics of Race: An International Perspective* (New York: Morrow, 1983) provides substantial evidence about racial discrimination as a universal problem.

12. In 1992, blacks had a median household income of $18,660 versus the national average of $30,786; for Asians, the number was $38,153. (U.S. Bureau of the Census, *Statistical Abstract of the United States* [Washington, DC: U.S. Department of the Treasury, 1994] Table 712.) Blacks constitute about 10% of the representation in the House; Asians constitute less than 1%. For past Irish political power, see Sowell, *The Economics and Politics of Race*, pp. 69–71.

13. Ibid., pp. 26–27, 36–37.

14. W. Williams, *The State Against Blacks* (New York: McGraw-Hill, 1982), pp. 12–13.

15. Our over-reliance on numbers (proxies) is caused by the difficulty inherent in trying to measure discrimination.

16. At first glance, this would seem to contradict my thesis that we should try to change government institutions ("poor policy"). However, discrimination is different because it is difficult to measure and prevent if it is occurring. However, we know what effect poor policies have on the impoverished. Those policies can be more easily changed than attitudes.

17. *U.S. News and World Report,* June 13, 1994, p. 124.

Part 2

How the Government Hurts the Poor

4

Reversing Robin Hood: How to Transfer Income to the Non-Poor

As noted earlier, a vast array of government policies redistribute income to the non-poor in a variety of product and labor markets. Presumably, these efforts are not designed to hurt the poor; their harm is merely a by-product or an indirect effect of policies with other goals. Regardless of the intentions, the results hammer the poor all too often.

Political Versus Economic Markets

"Public choice" economics (a term I will use often) deals with the marriage of political science and economics—the idea that people behave in self-interested ways in political markets as well as economic markets. In other words, agents in political markets (elected officials, bureaucrats, and their constituents) make their decisions by implicitly weighing the benefits and costs of the available alternatives. Instead of merely viewing government officials as benevolent public servants, we understand they are also interested in enhancing their careers and increasing their incomes.

To some, this may seem like old news. But our current perspective comes after 30 years of growing cynicism with the people who represent us, the promises that are constantly broken, and the failed policies that emanate from all levels of government. When James Buchanan and Gordon Tullock developed public choice theory in the early 1960s, it was a novel approach.[1] Subsequently, Buchanan was awarded the Nobel Prize in economics in 1986.

Political markets are fundamentally different from economic markets in a number of ways. To generalize each: Political market transactions involve C taking money from A to give to B; economic market transactions involve A giving money to B in exchange for goods or services. What are the differences?

First, political markets are coercive—money is forcibly taken from A. Economic markets are voluntary—A willingly gives his money to B. Second, political markets make two parties better off (C and B) at the expense of somebody else (A). Economic markets feature "mutually beneficial trade"—both parties (A and B) perceive they will be better off. In the absence of coercion and fraud, both parties enter an economic arrangement expecting to benefit. Third, political markets merely move wealth around, transferring money from one party to another; economic markets create wealth, since both parties benefit from the trade. The former is a "zero-sum game": A loses $5, B gains $5; the sum is $0. In contrast, economic activity is "positive-sum." Fourth, political markets involve a third party—the "middleman" (C)—who must be paid a salary. (Thus, political market transactions are actually "negative sum.") Further, it is highly unlikely that C will spend A's money as well as A would have spent it. These are two reasons governments and their bureaucracies are more inefficient than economic markets. Fifth, in economic markets, self-interest gives producers an incentive to please their customers. In the "selfish" pursuit of greater income, producers inadvertently benefit others. In political markets, self-interested "producers" have an incentive to develop more sophisticated ways to take money from A to give to B.

Finally, governments and bureaucracies tend to be inefficient because they are typically motivated to maximize their budgets rather than maximizing profits and minimizing costs. The primary incentive for a government agency is to exhaust its yearly budget so it can return to the legislature and request additional funds the next year. If bureaucrats fail to spend their funds, it is likely they will have a smaller budget in the subsequent year. Anyone who has been involved with government enterprises knows stories about "trying to spend all the money."

In sum, although individuals exhibit self-interested behavior in both economic and political markets, the results are vastly different.

Interest Group Theory: The Politics of Redistribution

In *Welfare for the Well-to-do* (1983), Tullock argues that the bulk of government's redistributive efforts go to "the organized"—commonly known as "special interest groups."[2] These groups are primarily, although not exclusively, members of the middle class. They encourage government to intervene and redistribute income away from the general public through higher taxation or higher prices. How does this work and why do people tolerate it?

Let's establish a hypothetical government program where $260 million is taken from 260 million citizens through taxes to give to 10,000 people. The cost to each person would be a dollar; the benefit to each recipient would be $26,000.

First, think about those paying for the program—the general public. A dollar each for a family of four amounts to $4.00 per year, or $0.33 per month. Who would notice such a minor expense? Now imagine that instead, the $4.00 is extracted through slightly higher prices for some good bought throughout the year. Who would attribute the higher prices to the government program? These costs would be extremely subtle. Further, even if one did notice the additional cost, who would get excited about losing $4.00? Who would devote time and energy to defeat the government program? Only the most indignant would bother. In these matters, people are usually "rationally ignorant"—ignorant because they typically fail to see the small and subtle costs imposed upon them, and rationally so because individually these small costs are simply not worth the time and effort to pursue their removal.

Now, consider those receiving the transfer—the "interest group." As opposed to the apathetic general public, this group will be very excited. There is probably no other public policy issue they will care about more. They have an incentive to pursue this program with great time and energy. They have an incentive to be selective with or to twist information in any public debate. They have an incentive to create compelling stories for why the redistribution should occur—why it is good for the country or the general public, and so on. They have an incentive to support those in government who make the transfer possible—through a block of votes, campaign contributions of time and money, or even bribes. This amounts to mutually beneficial trade between government officials and the special interest group—at the expense of the general public.[3]

In sum, there is a small group receiving benefits that are large and easy to see (at least for it). There is another small group that facilitates the transfers—politicians and bureaucrats administering the program—that benefits as well. And there is a large group whose members absorb relatively small and difficult-to-see costs. The latter group hardly notices the loss; the first two groups pursue such intervention with great vigor and passion. A similar explanation is that people have a greater interest in the relatively few things they sell (which produce their income) as opposed to the innumerable things they buy.

Politics Continued: "How Do We Sell This?"

Imagine you are the public relations representative for one of these special interest groups. Here's what you *cannot* say to the public: "We want the government to increase your product prices (or taxes) because we want higher incomes." People would find this rationale outrageous. So how do you sell the policy to the general public and get it to accept and even enjoy your reaching into its wallet?

Many rationales will be discussed in the next few chapters. Probably the two most popular are spoken concerns about the best interests of consumers and appeals to nationalism or other emotions. The former consists, for example, of supposed concerns about the safety or quality of a good or service or the desire for stable prices. Often, incumbent firms seeking protection from outside competition speak on behalf of such proposals. For example, occupational licensing restrictions may be sought by the existing firms and practitioners in a given market. Further, any new requirements are usually subject to a "grandfather clause"— incumbents are immune to the new restrictions. If the well-being of consumers were the primary motivation, presumably all suppliers would have to measure up to the new standards.

Appeals to emotion are also popular. Through the years, we have heard about saving the family farm, the need to provide a living wage (a higher minimum wage), and the "giant sucking sound" that will supposedly result when NAFTA (North American Free Trade Agreement) "causes all of our jobs to go south of the border." Independent of any merit in their arguments, such ploys are primarily based in rhetoric.

Frequently, the arguments contain a kernel of truth but are correct only to a limited extent or tell only part of the story. Remember—you do not need a very sophisticated rationale to sell the policy. With a rationally ignorant public, a story that sounds good on the surface will usually carry the day. Likewise, such arguments lack objectivity by definition. Would you expect to get objective opinions about chiropractors from orthopedists? Do you blindly accept negative remarks about companies from their rivals? Firms *always* have an incentive to denigrate or restrict their competition.

Finally, proponents of government activism always have an incentive to tell you about only the best parts of their proposals. By nature, those who support a program will tell the public about the benefits of the policy while ignoring or downplaying its costs. Similarly, when people run for political office, they have an incentive to talk about the benefits of their policies and the costs of their opponents' proposals. Further, politicians have an incentive to make the costs as indirect and "long run" as possible—to make the costs more difficult to see.

James Schlesinger aptly describes the goal of the game: "to extract resources from the general taxpayer with minimum offense and to distribute the proceeds among innumerable claimants in such a way to

maximize support at the polls. Politics . . . represents the art of calculated cheating—or more precisely, how to cheat without being caught."[4]

Hazlitt's "Lesson"

Henry Hazlitt's *Economics in One Lesson* is a one-of-a-kind book. Writing
in 1946, Hazlitt hoped to dispel the myths behind Keynesian economics
and activist government policy.[5] Half a century later, the battle against
economic ignorance still continues. In Hazlitt's words, the "lesson" is
that "economics consists in looking not merely at the immediate but at
the longer effects of any act or policy; it consists in tracing the consequences of that policy not merely for one group but for all groups."[6] In
other words, Hazlitt stresses looking at long-term benefits and costs
when evaluating economic policy.

Let's start with a basic proposition, the familiar dictum "There's no
such thing as a free lunch." Everything government spends must be paid
for through some type of taxation—higher current taxes, higher future
taxes (to pay for deficit spending and debt), or inflation taxes (printing
money to pay bills, which makes current money worth less).

Of course, government often chooses to defer costs into the future
(deficit financing) or to make them less visible (by printing more money,
which leads to inflation). But to simplify things, assume that government programs are paid for with current taxes. Our $260 million pro-
gram from an earlier section will create 10,000 jobs. Meanwhile, government has taken $260 million away from taxpayers that would have been
used for consumption or saving. If spent, it would have created jobs in
many different industries—appliances, dry cleaning, movie rentals, and
so on. If saved, it would have been used to invest in capital and spur economic growth. At best, government's activism would amount to a shell
game: Government would create $260 million worth of jobs in the pub-
lic sector (or subsidized by government) while destroying $260 million
worth of jobs in the private sector. (Often, proponents of government
programs argue that those with the created jobs will spend their money,
creating more jobs. Of course, the same reasoning holds for the jobs
destroyed by taxing the public to pay for the programs. This returns us to
the shell-game idea.)

Given that the newly created jobs are subsidized or in the public sector, government will almost certainly destroy more than it will create. As
noted earlier, political markets and bureaucracies are not known for
their efficiency. An extreme case would be to pay people to dig holes and
fill them up again. Jobs will be created, but nothing useful will be produced by these make-work jobs. Meanwhile, the private sector suffers.
The bottom line is that (with a few exceptions) government cannot cre-

ate "net" jobs; it can create jobs through spending programs but will destroy more through the subsequent taxation.[7] We will revisit failures to understand Hazlitt's lesson throughout the book.

As Dave Barry notes sarcastically, "When the government spends money, it creates jobs; whereas when the money is left in the hands of taxpayers, God only knows what they do with it. Bake it into pies, probably. Anything to avoid creating jobs." Taking money from the general public creates jobs, but it destroys jobs that taxpayers would have created on their own.

Why are these policies so popular? Return to the tenets of public choice economics. The jobs that are created are relatively obvious. (If the jobs are in construction, workers even wear orange vests to help you see them.) The jobs that are destroyed are quite difficult to see. They are eliminated one dollar at a time (the amount taken from each citizen) and in many different industries. Who would attribute a particular job loss to the tax increase?[8]

Hazlitt also acknowledges the importance of interest groups in the political economy of a democracy. He opens his text with the idea that "economics is haunted by more fallacies than any other study known to man. This is no accident. The inherent difficulties of the subject would be great enough in any case, but they are multiplied a thousandfold by a factor that is insignificant in say, physics, mathematics or medicine—the special pleading of selfish interests."[9] The incentive to twist or omit information is not nearly as prevalent in other fields. And when information is distorted in these other fields, it is often done in the pursuit of government (political market) grants. Self-interested groups have an incentive to take advantage of the rationally ignorant public through political markets.

Government can redistribute income in a variety of ways. Direct redistribution to the non-poor would not be politically popular. So most of the time, politicians use indirect methods to transfer income to special interest groups. The indirect method involves restricting competition.

There is *Always* an Incentive to Restrict Competition

The story begins with the desire of a firm to charge higher prices and obtain greater profits. But since most markets are rather competitive, a firm's efforts to increase its prices are frustrated by other firms undercutting its prices and taking its customers. As a result, firms often look to restrict their competition by forming voluntary associations that restrict output, allowing incumbent firms in the industry to charge a higher price. The firms want to collude and behave as a monopoly. These are frequently called "cartels."

Thus, there is always an incentive to collude. But unfortunately for a fledgling cartel, once the firms have colluded to restrict output and increase prices, there is also an incentive to cheat on the cooperative agreement. It is now in each firm's best interests to produce and sell a few more units, since those would be very profitable—units for which the market price significantly exceeds the costs of production. In addition, outsiders also see a profitable opportunity and may decide to enter the market. If some of the firms cheat or if challengers enter, then we return to the competitive outcome we had before; the attempt to increase prices and profits is thwarted.

This is why so few voluntary cartels work. In recent times, only OPEC's (Organization of Petroleum Exporting Countries) control over oil and DeBeer's monopoly power over diamonds have been at all successful.[10] Usually, the cartel is unable to monitor and enforce the agreement properly. If cheaters cannot be inexpensively policed, the agreement falls apart.

Because they are unable to collude on a voluntary basis, frustrated industries then turn to government because it has the coercive power necessary to enforce such agreements. In the words of Walter Williams, "Free market competition is the most stringent, unyielding form of regulation there can be. That's precisely why so many sellers fear and abhor the free market . . . their common desire is to use government to lock out potential competitors—whether by import tariffs, minimum wages or airline regulation."[11] The use of government to restrict competition is a prevalent theme in subsequent chapters.

Two Examples of Redistribution

The next few chapters are replete with examples of the concepts explained in this chapter—public choice economics and Hazlitt's lesson. However, before we continue, I want to put these principles to work in looking at two examples of redistribution: a "direct" example involving a minimum wage for college professors, and an indirect example—sugar price supports.

My university has considered passing a minimum wage for its faculty. For those currently below the proposed minimum, the market has determined a value for their services, but some people believe these salaries are "too low" and want to use the political process to alter the market outcome. (As with any other "sellers," they would like their prices to be higher.) For teaching in the fall, spring, and summer semesters and doing some service and research, all assistant professors would make at least $34,800; all associate professors would make at least $43,200; and all full professors would make at least $51,600. Note that all of the professors would then have incomes greater than the median household income level for the population. If we assume that the money comes from expanding the university's budget, this policy amounts to redistribution from the taxpayers of Indiana to people in an upper-income class.[12]

Political markets have determined that we should protect our sugar farmers from foreign competition. The preferred tools are price supports and an import quota to prevent foreign suppliers from entering the market and creating a surplus. The resulting domestic price of sugar is often twice as high as the world price. As always, domestic producers benefit from the restricted competition. And as always, consumers are hurt by having to pay higher prices. The poor are hammered especially hard because a higher proportion of their budgets are used for food. But how much are consumers hurt by an artificially high price for sugar? How many bags of sugar does the average family buy in a year? Not many. So why is this important? The much more significant cost is that any product that contains sugar as an input will also be more expensive (soft drinks, fruit juices, and cereal, among others). So people get nickel-and-dimed at the grocery store through higher product prices—$50 per year for the average family of four and $3.2 billion for the entire country.[13] Jobs are destroyed because consumers have less disposable income.

Moreover, firms that use sugar (especially candy companies) are placed at a competitive disadvantage with foreign companies who have access to low-cost foreign sugar. A few years ago, citing higher sugar prices, Brach's Candy closed a plant in inner-city Chicago and moved overseas. Many other jobs in industries which use sugar have been lost as well. And what about foreign producers of sugar? Producers from countries such as Haiti are told they cannot sell their goods in our markets. It is less than friendly to turn away producers from a country with an average income of $440 per year.[14]

What about the politics of this redistribution? Its subtlety is a work of art. Who knows that a six-pack of soda costs more because of sugar price supports? Who knows why jobs are lost in firms that use sugar as an input? Whereas the costs are diffuse and extremely difficult to see, apparently the beneficiaries know what they are getting. The average U.S. sugarcane plantation received an additional $235,000 in 1991. In response, interest groups for sugar farmers spent $1.7 million in 1990 defending their subsidy in the farm bill.[15] Even corn producers contributed to politicians because their corn syrup (as a substitute) benefited from the restriction in competition as well.

After people understand the dynamics of redistribution, they want to know if income is transferred to the non-poor out of ignorance or deceit. Certainly, there are numerous examples of both, but it doesn't matter much; the results are still the same. The goal of these redistributive efforts is certainly not to hurt the poor, but self-interest outweighs any knowledge that the poor are harmed.

Given that the bulk of redistributive efforts go to the organized, we give lip service and a few programs to the poor, but the big dollars go to special interest groups. The problem for the poor is that once you rationalize the use of government to redistribute income, the poor may be harmed overall, because they do not organize as effectively.[16]

The principles developed here are responsible for the bulk of all government policy. They explain why policies exist when most would agree the costs outweigh the benefits, when the number of losers far exceeds the number of winners. The key is that the costs of the policy are small, diffuse, and very difficult to see. They also explain why children do so poorly and the elderly do so well in the redistributive game: The former cannot organize directly; the latter group can. Finally, they hold the key for implementing reform: making the difficult-to-see costs easy to see. In any given case, once the general public realizes its income is being transferred to those with above-average incomes, reform is inevitable.

Notes

1. Their seminal work was *The Calculus of Consent: Logical Foundations of Constitutional Democracy* (Ann Arbor: University of Michigan Press, 1962).

2. See also R. Wagner, *To Promote the General Welfare: Market Processes vs. Political Transfers* (San Francisco: Pacific Research Institute, 1989).

3. This also explains why politicians receive campaign contributions even when they are unopposed in an upcoming election. This type of "trade" is examined in greater depth in Chapter 8.

4. J. Schlesinger, "Systems Analysis and the Political Process," *Journal of Law and Economics,* October 1968, p. 281.

5. In a nutshell, the conclusions of Keynesian economics lead to the unfortunate premise that government intervention in the economy can frequently be optimal. The usually specious notion that "government can create (net) jobs" is a stubborn holdover from this theory. (See note 7 for a few exceptions.) See R. Vedder and L. Galloway, *Out of Work: Unemployment and Government in Twentieth-Century America* (New York: Holmes and Meier, 1993) for an excellent neo-classical Austrian treatment of the Great Depression and Keynesian economics.

6. H. Hazlitt, *Economics in One Lesson* (New York: Crown, 1946), p. 17.

7. In theory, government may be effective when markets are relatively ineffective. Expenditures on infrastructure are a notable example. For instance, it is difficult for the market to supply city streets because private firms would find it costly to collect payments or to exclude drivers who did not pay. The government has the license to use force to extract payments from people relatively inexpensively—through taxation. In the context of Hazlitt's lesson, the difference is that both recipient B and taxpayer A will directly benefit from the construction of a road that eases traffic congestion. Finally, note that the investment must be productive; merely digging holes in the ground is equivalent to the shell game.

In addition, if prices in an economy are slow to adjust (the key assumption for Keynesians), then government spending may be effective by channeling unemployed resources into productive uses. Finally, deficit financing of government spending can have short-term benefits (job creation) with long-term costs (higher taxes and subsequent job destruction).

8. H. Schlossberg draws an analogy to alchemy—the fictitious practice of turning lead into gold. Both give "the illusion of creating wealth where none existed before. But all [they do] is redistribute the wealth that is already present" (*Idols for Destruction: The Conflict of Christian Faith and American Culture* [Wheaton, IL: Crossway Books, 1990], p. 90).

9. Hazlitt, *Economics in One Lesson*, p. 15.

10. OPEC has had only limited success. DeBeer's has been effective because it controls both the supply and demand sides of the diamond market. Russia's vast store of diamonds and its emergence into Western markets may end this cartel as well.

11. W. Williams, *All It Takes Is Guts: A Minority View* (Washington, DC: Regnery Gateway, 1987), p. 68.

12. Whether the policy is fair is immaterial here. I merely seek to illustrate its redistributive element. Another option would be to take the money from the school's general operating budget. This would presumably decrease the quality of some other aspect of the students' education; it would constitute a transfer from consumers to producers, that is, from students to professors.

13. "Hidden Monopolies: Driving Up Prices for Consumers," *U.S. News and World Report,* February 3, 1992, pp. 42–48.

14. *The 1994 World Almanac and Book of Facts* (New York: St. Martin's Press, 1993).

15. Ibid.

16. See also D. Lee and R. McKenzie, "Helping the Poor Through Governmental Poverty Programs: The Triumph of Rhetoric over Reality," in *Public Choice and Constitutional Economics,* ed. J. Gwartney and R. Wagner (Greenwich, CT: JAI Press, 1988).

5

Redistributing Income Through Product Markets: Increasing Prices for the Poor

In Chapter 4, I developed the principles that allow redistribution to the non-poor to occur through political markets. Special interest groups pursue legislation that allows them to extract large and concentrated benefits while imposing small and subtle costs on members of the general public. The groups receiving government privileges have an incentive to support such activism with money and votes and to find rationalizations that make the income transfer more agreeable. The "rationally ignorant" public does not have much of an incentive to notice or protest such small costs. The result is a vast amount of redistribution that would probably not occur if it were done openly.

Income redistribution to the poor is usually direct and made easy to see because it is politically acceptable. However, the idea of transferring income to the non-poor is not as palatable; if it is done directly, people are more likely to complain. So indirect methods must be used if the incomes of the well-off are to be enhanced at the expense of everybody else. The most popular tool is to persuade government to restrict competition and grant producers a larger degree of monopoly power. This allows them to charge higher prices and obtain higher profits. In this chapter, I focus on how interest groups pursue those ends in product markets and specifically, how those outcomes hammer the poor.

Increasing the Price of Food

Like other special interest groups, farmers have goals they pursue through political markets. One way to achieve higher incomes is to persuade the government to artificially increase the prices of their products. A subsequent problem for government is that these subsidies encourage both existing and potential, and domestic and foreign farmers to increase the supply. Further, consumers are less interested in purchasing the goods at the artificially high price. The key question, then, is how to prevent the subsequent surpluses or, failing that, what to do with the excess.

The result is a mishmash of programs to accomplish both goals—higher prices and controlling surpluses. When surpluses exist, they are stored, destroyed, given away, or their purchase is subsidized. To prevent surpluses, government must limit supply by enacting import quotas, requiring licenses to enter the domestic market, or paying people not to plant crops or raise livestock. All these serve to eliminate or prevent surpluses of the products that government has encouraged farmers to produce in excess.

Although higher prices benefit farmers, they clearly hurt consumers. Artificially high prices are especially troublesome for the poor. Because they spend a higher proportion of their incomes on food, the costs of this redistributive effort are regressive. The transfers are regressive as well, since most of the farmers who benefit from these programs have incomes and wealth well above the national average.[1]

Some stories and a few numbers:

- Sugar price supports cost consumers an estimated $3.2 billion per year ($50 for an average family of four). The average U.S. sugarcane farmer receives $235,000 a year from such redistribution, prompting James Bovard to note: "Some people win the lottery, other people grow sugar."[2] Lobbyists for sugar and corn producers encourage the price supports with votes and money. With foreign sugar limited to as little as 8% of the market in the United States, corn syrup becomes more valuable as well.[3]

- Each year since 1937, by law, up to 40% of oranges have been destroyed, fed to livestock, or exported to prop up prices. Sunkist's influence with Congress has been particularly impressive. Over the years, it has been able to obtain $70 million from the U.S. Department of Agriculture (USDA) to promote foreign sales of products it would not sell here.[4]

- Since 1953, we have been allowed to import only about two peanuts per American per year. The U.S. International Trade Commission has estimated that the quotas are equivalent to a 90% tariff, nearly doubling the effective price of peanuts and peanut butter. Further, under penalty of law, one needs a license to grow and sell peanuts in the United States.[5]

- The annual subsidy per dairy cow is $700, an amount greater than the income of half the world's population.[6] The Commodity Credit

Corporation removed nearly 72 billion pounds of dairy product from the market between 1986 and 1993 to prop up prices.[7]

- In 1986 and 1987, direct payments to farmers exceeded earned income.[8] Although the number of farmers has declined since the New Deal, the number of farm bureaucrats has continuously increased. The USDA has 128,000 employees for 708,000 full-time farmers.[9]

A list of government's redistributive efforts would be far too long to cover in full; these "hidden monopolies" cover a wide assortment of farm products. Interested grocery shoppers and taxpayers are encouraged to delve into James Bovard's *The Farm Fiasco* or *The Fair Trade Fraud.*

These policies cause other problems for the poor. When we send subsidized or donated products to poor countries, we hurt their producers with "unfair competition." Further, our protectionism encourages reciprocation by other countries (and thus, higher prices for consumers) and allows others to point to American hypocrisy in trade policy. Finally, when prices are kept artificially high on products that are used as inputs for other products, those producers are put at a disadvantage. As we saw in Chapter 4, while protecting the sugar industry, our government inadvertently destroyed inner-city jobs in the candy industry.

When I developed the public choice framework, I noted that often, all it takes to win the day is a good story. The rationales for farm programs provide a diverse set of examples. Mohair subsidies originated because of concerns for "national security"—we needed wool to make our soldiers' uniforms. Frequently, proponents profess to be concerned about wildly fluctuating prices. Sometimes, soil erosion is used as a justification, but who more than the owner has a better incentive to take care of his land? Occasionally, the argument is that farming is riskier than most industries. Maybe so, but that's the purpose of (private) insurance. Some believe the country will potentially starve without financial support for farmers. Somehow we found a way to survive until farm programs debuted in the 1930s. Further, this belief grossly underestimates the productivity of our technology, the ingenuity of farmers, and the fertility of our farmland. But of all the rationales given, perhaps the most persuasive story has been the "need to save the family farmer." Of course, Hazlitt's lesson illustrates that saving the family farmer cannot save (net) jobs.

Until recently, I wondered why "ma and pa" grocery stores were not defended successfully using the same strategy. It turns out that Ma and Pa's defenders tried a similar technique in the 1930s; they wanted a tax placed on the new larger stores. But A&P hired a public relations expert to tell consumers about the cheaper prices and greater product availability they would have with larger stores.[10] In the context of our framework, A&P made the subtle benefits easy to see. If Ma and Pa had been protected, a small group would have received concentrated benefits at the expense of everyone else—from restricted competition. Instead, with a little education, consumers carried the day.

Increasing the Price of Clothing

The poor are also harmed whenever they purchase clothing. Despite the prevalence of foreign-made clothing, our domestic textile industry is greatly sheltered from foreign competition; in the absence of the existing protectionism, most U.S. clothing firms would be unable to compete. Protectionism causes prices to be significantly higher than they would be otherwise. Again, this policy is regressive in its costs, since the poor spend a higher proportion of their incomes on clothing. In addition, since many of the countries shut out of our markets have very low standards of living, this policy hammers the poor in other countries as well. Restricting competition in this market tells the people of Bangladesh to try to improve their $200 average annual incomes elsewhere.[11]

The textile industry is perhaps our most protected, benefiting from more than 3,000 tariffs and quotas on clothing and textile imports.[12] The U.S. Federal Trade Commission estimates that these policies increase the price of clothing by an average of 58%.[13] Gary Hufbauer calculated that Americans pay an extra $25 to $30 billion per year as a result of textile protectionism ($400–500 per year for the average family of four).[14] This constitutes both substantial redistribution to textile producers and a substantial penalty borne by all consumers, especially the poor.

This market also provides a vivid picture of how political markets function. Two of the most prominent Senators in seeking this protectionism are Jesse Helms (R–N.C.) and Patrick Moynihan (D–N.Y.). Helms is usually a big proponent of free markets and an avid opponent of civil rights quotas. Yet when it comes to textiles, he reverses those positions to support one of his constituencies. Somehow Helms finds central planning and quotas acceptable in this context. Moynihan is known as an advocate for the poor and has been consistently opposed to the use of force by the United States in less developed countries. Yet to protect textile workers, Moynihan betrays those ideas by voting to increase prices dramatically for the poor and to decimate the economies of poor countries.[15]

Hazlitt's Lesson Revisited: Does Protectionism Save Jobs?

Yes and no. It saves the jobs of those protected (or allows them to keep their wages artificially high), but it destroys more jobs than it preserves. Why? This is another application of Hazlitt's lesson. The common mistake is to look only at one group in the short run as opposed to all groups in the long run. It is easy to see the jobs saved, but a more challenging task is to see the jobs lost as a result of government's intervention.

Perhaps it is easier now because the costs of protectionism have been enumerated. Higher prices for consumers mean they will be unable to spend as much money elsewhere (or save and invest it). Lower disposable incomes mean that jobs that would have been created from the additional consumer spending and capital investment will not be realized. These job losses are more subtle, since they occur in many different industries.

Hazlitt illustrates protectionism with a numerical example: U.S. sweaters sell for $30, and English sweaters sell for $25.[16] If the United States protects its sweater industry with a $5 tariff, $30 worth of jobs will be saved in this industry. But those who buy sweaters are each $5 worse off; thus, $5 worth of jobs will be destroyed, since consumers have less income. Further, with protectionism, the English do not have the opportunity to sell their goods here and obtain dollars. They would have exchanged their dollars for goods; thus, $25 worth of jobs they would have created are also destroyed.[17] Again, the jobs saved are concentrated and easy to see; the jobs destroyed are widely dispersed and difficult to see.

Consider another hypothetical example: Alaskan banana farmers. Imagine that Congress wants to create jobs and end our dependence on foreign bananas. It might subsidize the construction of greenhouses and the incomes of banana farmers. Jobs would be created in Alaska, but they would be destroyed elsewhere in the country as disposable income decreases. The created jobs would be easy to see; the destroyed jobs would be difficult to see. Then, if someone tried to end the subsidy, one can imagine the opposition—arguments about job destruction, accusations about a lack of compassion for banana farmers, and nationalistic concerns about becoming dependent on foreign bananas. In the best case, this would amount to a shell game—redistribution to protected producers from consumers, special interest groups benefiting at the expense of all others. However, since we are protecting an industry that is relatively inefficient, these restrictions promote the inefficient over the efficient. The country as a whole is worse off.

It is ironic that people have no problem understanding that we all benefit when individuals within our own country specialize and then engage in trade. "Free trade" with other countries simply takes this principle a step further. Further, it turns out that our trade barriers are larger and more extensive than those of the European Community and our favorite "whipping boy" in this area, Japan.[18] Regardless of the numbers and how "unfair" another country's trade policy is, remember that domestic firms *always* have an incentive to restrict foreign (or domestic) competition. Finally, we usually understand that discrimination against buyers or sellers harms both parties. Trade restrictions are a mandated form of personal discrimination. Consumers and foreign producers are harmed by the government's arbitrarily preventing exchange (with quotas) or increasing the price of foreign-produced goods (with tariffs).

Advocates of protectionism should ask themselves: Why do we want to do to ourselves what our enemies would do to us during a war—enforce blockades that restrict trade? When we have boycotted Cuban goods and divested from South Africa, have we been helping or hurting them? Restricting trade and foreign investment may help certain groups, but it hurts the country overall.

Redistributing Income Using Political Markets

One could write an entire book on the use of government to restrict competition in order to increase the incomes of special interest groups.[19] Our government shelters industries from toys to steel, from wine to cheese, from dolls to the clothing that dolls wear. Each time, the result is the same: higher prices for consumers and higher incomes for protected producers.

Hufbauer estimates that U.S. trade barriers cost American consumers $80 billion per year (more than $1,200 for the average family of four).[20] These protectionist policies hurt all consumers, including the poor. However, since they do not harm the poor disproportionately (as with farm and textile policy), they are not as relevant in the context of this book. So I will leave these policies to the imagination of the readers who bear the brunt of these costs. The goal is not to provide an exhaustive list of governmental redistributive efforts but to develop the principles behind transfers to the non-poor and to provide some concrete examples.

Remember that special interest groups receive concentrated benefits at the expense of the general public, which bears small (per person), subtle costs. Protected producers are better off, but other firms face higher input prices, consumers pay higher prices, taxpayers pay higher taxes, and other countries are told to take their business elsewhere. No matter how good the rationale or how "unfair" another country's trade policy, producers *always* have an incentive to restrict competition. They cannot enforce cartels on their own, so they get government to do it for them.

One does not need to agree with the subsequent policy implications to simply acknowledge the redistribution of income that occurs under protectionism and its disproportionate impact on the poor. In addition, an understanding of the extent of redistribution in our economy provides the beginning of a basis for understanding why government intervention can be so damaging to the general public. The 18th-century historian Alexander Tytler said: "A democracy cannot exist as a permanent form of government. It can only exist until a majority of voters discover that they can vote themselves largess out of the public treasury." Many different interest groups have their hands in the till.

Finally, in some sense, it is amusing that some are so concerned with unearned transfers to the poor while being mostly blind to the larger welfare programs our government operates in support of special interest groups. And it is truly ironic that the public is so concerned with the poor being dependent upon welfare programs. From the protests that arise whenever reform is suggested, it would appear that the addiction to welfare programs for the non-poor is at least as strong. Until the costs of government intervention become easy to see, those protests will carry the day.

Notes

1. In 1991, the median net wealth for households was $36,623; the mean net wealth for farmers was $407,173 (U.S. Bureau of the Census, *Statistical Abstract of the United States* [U.S. Department of the Treasury], 1994, Table 742, and 1993, Table 1106). A more complicated case is when government buys the products at a high price or subsidizes producers' costs and then allows the public to buy them at low prices. Then, the redistribution is paid for with higher taxes instead of higher prices and thus is not as regressive.

2. J. Bovard, *The Fair Trade Fraud* (New York: St. Martin's Press, 1991), p. 71.

3. "Hidden Monopolies: Driving Up Prices for Consumers," *U.S. News and World Report*, February 3, 1992, pp. 42–48.

4. "End of the Citrus Cartel," *Wall Street Journal*, December 15, 1992. (This was an unfortunate choice of title, since the prophecy has not come true.)

5. Bovard, *The Fair Trade Fraud*, p. 96. There are more than 500 tariffs on food products.

6. J. Bovard, *The Farm Fiasco* (San Francisco: ICS Press, 1989), p. 103.

7. *Agricultural Outlook* (Washington, DC: U.S. Department of Agriculture, various years).

8. U.S. Bureau of the Census, *Statistical Abstract of the United States*, 1993, Table 1109.

9. Ibid., 1994, Tables 527, 1090. The Census Bureau defines a farmer as one who has farm sales of more than $1,000. "Full-time farmers" are defined here as those with sales of at least $40,000 per year. The net income for the $20,000–$40,000 category averages only $7,500 (and a third of that is from government).

10. L. Lord, "1940: America on the Eve of Conflict," *U.S. News and World Report,* August 27, 1990, p. 50. The "baskart" was the technological innovation that made large-scale grocery shopping feasible.

11. *The 1994 World Almanac and Book of Facts* (New York: St. Martin's Press, 1993).

12. Bovard, *The Fair Trade Fraud,* p. 36.

13. *Economic Report of the President* (Washington, DC: U.S. Government Printing Office, 1989), p. 172.

14. C. Oliver, "The Ghost of Christmas Presents," *Reason,* January 1990, pp. 37–39.

15. The same hypocrisy is evident in "left-wingers" concerning defense spending. They are doves in general, but they are adamantly opposed to shutting down military bases in their own districts.

16. H. Hazlitt, *Economics in One Lesson* (New York: Crown, 1946), pp. 75–79.

17. Expanding the example to more than two countries complicates the story but not the principle. Imagine what happens to your purchasing power when someone "restricts trade" with you on an individual level.

18. The *Economist* ("Japan's Troublesome Imports," January 11, 1992, p. 61) reports that in 1990 Japan's tariffs amounted to 2.6%, the European Community's were 2.9%, and America's were 3.0%. In addition, all three have "similar non-tariff barriers." Finally, in 1992, the Japanese spent more per person on goods from the United States than Americans spent on goods from Japan.

19. Bovard's *The Fair Trade Fraud* covers the topic well.

20. Oliver, "The Ghost of Christmas Presents," pp. 37–39.

6

The Minimum Wage:
Locking Unskilled Workers
Out of the Labor Market

Interest groups are proficient at convincing government to intervene in product markets to restrict competition and increase their incomes. The same is true in labor markets. For instance, domestic producers endeavor to restrict their competition by imposing tariffs on foreign products, artificially increasing the price of imports. Likewise, suppliers in labor markets (workers) seek legislation to artificially increase the price of their competition. In this chapter, we will look at one of the more harmful and the most misunderstood policies undertaken by government—the minimum wage.

An Introduction to the Minimum Wage

The minimum wage is a price floor that sets a minimum on the hourly wage rate employers can pay for labor services. It originated in the 1930s as one of the restrictive labor laws resulting from Franklin D. Roosevelt's New Deal. Although the law originally covered only 43% of workers, it now covers nearly 90%. (Food servers and agricultural workers are today's notable exceptions.) The minimum wage was $3.35 from 1981 until 1990, when it was increased to $4.25; the $3.35 was retained as a "training wage." The Clinton administration failed to renew the training wage in 1993 and has proposed increasing the minimum wage again to $5.15 and indexing it to the rate of inflation.[1] Although widely thought to help the poor, this law is in fact a great detriment to the most unskilled.

Its considerable popularity with the public stems from a failure to understand how markets function. Standard thinking on this is that if the minimum wage did not exist, firms could exploit workers by paying them exceptionally low wages. But if a labor market is relatively competitive, this will not happen. If my productivity is $5.00 per hour and a firm offers me $3.00 per hour (or cuts my pay to $3.00), I will go elsewhere. Given that the market is competitive, there are any number of firms who have an incentive to pay me $3.50. But even at $3.50, there is an incentive for someone to hire me at $4.00 per hour, and so on. The point is that as long as there are a number of firms around, I will not be paid a wage significantly different from my productivity.[2] (Similarly, firms cannot often charge "outrageous" prices.)

Moreover, if the minimum wage is $6.00, I will not be offered a job. Why would a firm want to hire workers who can produce $5.00 worth of output per hour if it has to pay them $6.00? The government can mandate that a firm pay workers $6.00 an hour *if* it hires them. But it cannot mandate that a firm hire particular people. Thus, unskilled workers will be unemployed.[3]

As in other areas, a market restriction that keeps prices artificially high creates a surplus because the quantity supplied increases and the quantity demanded decreases. In the context of a labor market, this surplus is called unemployment. As opposed to receiving "a living wage" or getting economic justice, workers trade jobs where they were earning income for the unemployment line and checks from the government.

How Do Firms Respond to a Higher Minimum?

Simple intuition and economic theory tell us that as the price of something goes up, consumers decrease the quantity they demand of the good. Consumers adjust by switching to close substitutes that have become *relatively* less expensive. The same is true for firms. If the price of labor increases, firms demand less labor and substitute other inputs.

Actually, we can be more specific. The minimum wage is not a binding constraint for those with greater skills. Firms required to pay a minimum wage will demand less *unskilled* labor. If your productivity is above the minimum, then you will not be affected—at least in labor markets. This policy directly affects only those with the most limited skills.

What else happens? Firms are likely to pass on the increased costs to consumers in the form of higher product prices. Alternatively, service may deteriorate somewhat—fewer baggers at grocery stores, longer lines at fast-food restaurants, more expensive full-serve gasoline, and so on. Another possibility is that firms would simply lower non-wage compensation and retain their low-skilled workers. For instance, they could reduce fringe benefits (for example, health insurance and free meals) and still find it worthwhile to employ a particular low-skilled worker.[4] But because low-wage workers frequently have few fringe benefits and government mandates on employers often make it impossible to reduce benefits, it is more likely that the firm will release the worker.

The same analysis also holds for other employer mandates (including health insurance, child care, family leave, Social Security "contributions," unemployment insurance, and plant-closing laws). These are particularly harmful to low-skilled workers. A firm simply cannot compensate a worker for more than he produces. Because countries in Europe have embraced some or all of these mandates, their unemployment rates are significantly higher than ours.

Although it is unfortunate that full-time minimum-wage workers have such low incomes, increasing the minimum wage is not the answer. If we want to help the unskilled, there are two ways to circumvent the problems caused by the minimum wage. Government can provide a wage subsidy for firms who employ unskilled workers or subsidize workers through the tax code (as with the EITC—earned income tax credit). Both methods have pitfalls, but at least they avoid locking the unskilled out of labor markets.[5]

Why Is the Minimum Wage Especially Troubling?

The minimum wage directly affects only those who are relatively unskilled. Further, the less skilled a worker is, the more likely he will be locked out of the labor market by the mandated higher wage. Ironically, these are the very people who are being targeted for assistance. The results are the opposite of the supposed intentions.

This policy is a barrier to entry for teenagers, whose skills tend to be relatively low. This is troubling, because it is precisely during these years that they need to be acquiring the training and experience that accompany employment. Such training involves not just attaining particular skills but learning the self-discipline of coming to work on time, the importance of treating customers well, and so on. Locking teenagers out of these opportunities robs them of valuable skills and knowledge they will need later. It also removes an important incentive that accompanies most minimum-wage jobs—the knowledge that "this is not what I want to be doing the rest of my life."

How Does the Minimum Wage
Harm Minorities in Particular?

For a variety of reasons—personal discrimination (past and present) and poor education, among others—blacks and other minorities are disproportionately represented among the relatively unskilled. Because of this, they are locked out of labor markets to a greater degree by a minimum-wage law.

Further, as we saw in Chapter 3, discrimination is made costless whenever the government creates a surplus. In this context, the minimum wage increases the pool of unemployed workers. If employers do not like a particular group, they can choose to hire one group of people over another without additional cost because there are so many unskilled people without a job at that wage.

The unemployment statistics support the contention that teenagers and minorities are especially harmed by the minimum wage. In 1992, black unemployment was 42.0% for 16- to 19-year-old males and 13.4% for males older than 20. For whites, the numbers were much lower: 18.4% and 6.3%, respectively.[6]

The Politics of the Minimum Wage

If the minimum wage is so harmful, why is it so popular, especially among those who supposedly have compassion for the poor? Again, to some extent, this can be explained by a failure to understand how markets function. With respect to the general public, we have another example of the rationally ignorant being persuaded by a good story and an appealing yet incorrect idea. Without an understanding of the costs of the policy, providing "a living wage" and economic justice for the poor sounds like something everyone should support.

But as we have seen, the intentions and the results are very different—the minimum wage does not have the desired effect. Instead of helping the poor, it hammers unskilled workers. In addition, the demographics (of those who earn the minimum) betray the notion that this policy primarily helps poor people struggling to survive. Unlike the stereotype around which the policy is built, only 2% of minimum-wage workers in 1988 were full-time employees and heads of households. One-third of the workers at or below the minimum were food servers who supplemented their incomes with tips. Finally, many are teenagers, in the middle-class, or part-time workers.[7] Wage subsidies and the EITC would reward work *and* more effectively target assistance to the poor.

Restricting Competition

If the unskilled are hurt by this policy, who benefits? The key is found in the change in behavior of firms—they will substitute other inputs, including more skilled labor, for unskilled labor. Skilled laborers—in particular, those who belong to labor unions—benefit because some of their competition is restricted. Indeed, the minimum wage originated under pressure from Northern textile manufacturers who wanted to be protected from their Southern competitors who had access to low-cost labor.

It would seem that unions would be mostly unaffected by a higher minimum wage, but a numerical example illustrates how this works. If the minimum wage is $4 and three less skilled workers can together do the work of a union worker, then the more skilled union workers will be hired only if their wage is below $12. An increase in the minimum wage to $5 allows union workers to demand up to $15 from the firm. By artificially increasing the wage of the less skilled workers, union workers can gain a higher income.[8]

Indeed, unions are the main proponents of a higher minimum wage. Instead of being concerned, as they say, for the welfare of all workers, they are almost exclusively concerned with the well-being of their own members. By limiting competition in their labor markets, these interest groups can enhance their incomes.

Public Choice Economics Revisited

The benefits of a higher minimum wage are relatively apparent to those who are made better off. Those who retain their jobs certainly appreciate the higher income.[9] And unions can see they are better off with reduced competition from less skilled labor.

But the costs are much more difficult to see. Who would attribute a particular job loss to a higher minimum wage? The costs are even more subtle when you realize firms are likely to respond before the increase even takes place. A firm cannot simply release all of its low-skilled workers on the day the higher mandated wage takes effect. Instead, it may look for reasons to fire workers or make the job more unpleasant in the weeks and months before the higher wage takes effect. In addition, who would attribute higher product prices to an increase in the minimum wage?

As with virtually all government intervention, the benefits are concentrated and the costs are dispersed and difficult to see. Those receiving the benefits respond with votes and campaign contributions. Those who are harmed remain rationally ignorant because the costs are too small and subtle to excite people.

Ignorance or Deceit?

If the minimum wage is detrimental to the poor—the group that is supposedly helped—the following question arises: Are politicians doing this on purpose or are they just unaware of the costs they are imposing on the poor? How can "caring politicians" vote to increase the price of food and clothing for the poor and lock them out of labor markets? Do they do it out of ignorance or deceit and self-interest?

Both. There are members of Congress who are well intentioned but do not understand the ramifications of the policies they advocate. Louis Brandeis warned against these "men of zeal, well-meaning but without understanding." There are also those who see the costs but believe the money we give the poor more than compensates them for any problems we cause with redistribution to the non-poor. As we have seen already, this is unlikely. When it comes to using government to transfer income, the organized are far more proficient than the poor. Finally, there are some who understand the costs but are more concerned with getting re-elected. Because the public does not understand the ramifications of the minimum wage, it looks bad for politicians to oppose it. Moreover, if they support a higher minimum, unions contribute to their election campaigns—in votes and dollars. Although these politicians probably have regrets about trampling the poor, the prospect of returning for another term is too enticing.

Regardless, it is important to realize that the results of the policies they advocate are at considerable variance with their supposed intentions. And whereas one might appreciate their "compassion," the results are much more important: Their policy prescriptions hammer the poor.

Ironically, South Africa also has a minimum wage. In an ominously similar manner, it serves to keep relatively unskilled blacks from competing with semi-skilled whites for union jobs. Is the motivation different in that country? Perhaps. But the results are the same. Regardless of whether the minimum wage is for economic or racial motives, the outcome has racial ramifications, since blacks are disproportionately represented among the unskilled. The outcome would make any racist happy.

Two Analogies to the Minimum Wage

Walter Williams uses a hypothetical "minimum steak law" to illustrate how a minimum wage works.[10] Suppose there are two types of meat available—chuck steak and filet mignon. Filet mignon is far better than chuck steak but is also more expensive. The only advantage of inferior meat is its price; it cannot compete on quality. If we were to pass a minimum steak law that equated the price of the two meats, chuck steak would lose its advantage. It would be priced out of the market; it would become "unemployed."

Also, we can imagine the impact of a "minimum babysitting wage." What would happen? Parents (firms) would consume less babysitting overall, particularly of the less-skilled variety. Lower-skilled workers (13-

year-olds) would be priced out of the market and would become "unemployed." Fifteen-year-olds would benefit from the restriction in competition and would even have an incentive to lobby for such a law. To complete the analogy, the minimum could be sold under the auspices of a concern for children—either "babysitter quality" or the need for a "fair wage" for babysitters.

If the minimum wage were any kind of solution for the problems of the poor, we should get down to business and legislate a $10 minimum.[11] However, when the policy is extended to that level, the costs become evident and the policy is revealed to be a farce. The fundamental problem with the minimum wage is that it does not address the key issue: the low productivity of unskilled labor. Instead of trying to mask this problem by mandating a higher level of compensation (which firms will not pay), we should focus on policies that enhance the abilities of the relatively unskilled—education and training that allow them to earn sufficient incomes in labor markets.

Notes

1. (Democratic) congressional proposals range as high as $6.50 per hour. The training wage (applied to the first six months of a 16- to 19-year-old's first job) was an exception to the standard minimum wage.

2. This explains why engineers do not work for $4 per hour. Note, however, that when firms have substantial degrees of market/monopoly power, the story can be different. Notable examples include government as the sole employer in a fully socialistic economy, the NCAA (National Collegiate Athletic Association) cartel concerning college athletes, professional sports in the absence of "free agency," and slavery.

3. People often ask, Who isn't worth $5 per hour? But they forget that firms must absorb other costs when hiring workers, including those of complying with many government mandates.

4. Even if the workers keep their jobs, they are still worse off because they are forced to be compensated in a way they had not already chosen voluntarily.

5. Note that fraud often accompanies wage subsidies. Subsidization through the tax code can be achieved using the negative income tax, the earned income tax credit, or a large standard deduction for taxpayers. These policies and their work disincentives are covered in Part 3.

6. U.S. Bureau of the Census, *Statistical Abstract of the United States* (Washington, DC: U.S. Department of the Treasury, 1993), Table 635. Note also that these numbers began to worsen in the 1950s when the real minimum wage and the proportion of jobs covered both increased. In the early 1950s, black and white teen males had quite similar labor force participation and unemployment rates.

7. R. Samuelson, "Minimum Wage Politicking," *Newsweek*, July 11, 1988. Today, only 1.8% of all full-time workers and 2.7% of those at least 20 years old make the minimum wage. (See U.S. Bureau of the Census, *Statistical Abstract of the United States*, 1994, Tables 670, 665.) Moreover, only a fraction of those are sole breadwinners trying to support a family.

8. Obviously, this is a simple model. Although the real world is more complex, this basic principle remains.

9. With the number of workers decreasing, the (marginal) productivity of the remaining workers will be higher, allowing wages to increase (to the level of the minimum wage) for those who keep their jobs.

10. W. Williams, *The State Against Blacks* (New York: McGraw-Hill, 1982), pp. 40–41.

11. M. Reynolds notes that Puerto Rico experienced something similar to this in 1938. The original minimum wage covered Puerto Rico as well, where the *average* wage was less than the mandated minimum of $0.25. As a result, employment fell by half before Puerto Rico was granted an exemption two years later. (*Economics of Labor* [Cincinnati: South-Western, 1995], p. 95.)

7

Other Labor Market Interventions: Locking Out Relatively Unskilled Workers

Interest groups specialize in mutually beneficial trade with politicians who intervene in product and labor markets. The goal is to increase their incomes, often by restricting their competition. In addition to the minimum wage, labor interest groups use other methods to artificially increase the wages of their competitors, as well as an assortment of barriers to entry. As before, because compelling stories accompany these issues and because the direct costs are so small per person, many people inadvertently accept poor policies, hurting themselves and especially those who are relatively unskilled.

Davis-Bacon Laws

These laws—also known as comparable worth laws—are very similar to the minimum wage law. In 1931, the federal version of these laws (in 35 states by 1995) began to mandate that for government contracts, workers would be paid at least the "prevailing wage," which is generally set at the local union's wage rate. One problem is that these laws increase the cost of government activity in public works by nearly $1 billion per year. But for our purposes, the main problem is that they restrict competition from relatively unskilled labor.

Imagine you are a relatively new carpenter whose skills are worth $14 per hour compared to a veteran carpenter whose skills are worth $18. You're not as quick as your competition; you haven't learned "the tools of the trade." But if you are allowed to compete on the basis of price, you may get a job. If the price is mandated to $18, the game is over and you lose. The purpose of these laws is to preserve the status quo, to protect the incumbent from the challenger, to promote union over non-union workers. Ironically, Davis-Bacon laws often prevent inner-city residents from working on inner-city construction projects.

Davis-Bacon laws are discriminatory for the same reasons as the minimum wage—these laws restrict relatively unskilled laborers, who happen to be disproportionately minorities. Unlike the minimum wage, this law's origins were overtly racist. For instance, in debate over the bill, Representative Clayton Algood said, "That contractor has cheap colored labor . . . and it is labor of that sort that is in competition with white labor."[1] These laws also exist in South Africa as part of the strategy to keep relatively unskilled blacks from competing for white union jobs. It is truly ironic that we have spent so much energy condemning South Africa while using the same policies and getting the same results. Again, whether our motivations are different or not, the outcome is the same.

Mandatory Occupational Licensing

Another way to restrict entry into a field is to require a permit or license to work in a particular occupation. With fewer legal practitioners, consumers face higher prices for their services. The restricted competition allows those with licenses to benefit at the expense of consumers. With artificial barriers to entry, incumbents are protected at the expense of challengers in the labor market. As before, a relatively small special interest group extracts concentrated benefits while the general public bears diffuse and subtle costs.

Remember that the rationale given to the public cannot be to achieve higher incomes—that would not be popular. Proponents of government intervention need to find stories that make it seem as if mandatory licensing benefits consumers. So we hear about the supposed intent of the laws: to improve quality or safety, to provide stability in the market, and so on.[2] But as in many previous examples, the spoken intents are at considerable variance with the results of the policy and the probable motivations.

Concern for the Consumer?

It is easy to support the contention that those who pursue licensing primarily have their own interests in mind and not those of consumers. First, we know that people generally behave in self-interested ways in political as well as economic markets. However, in economic markets, my self-interests usually benefit other people because I strive to increase my income by pleasing others; in political markets, my self-interests would increase my income at the expense of other people.

Second, as we have seen in previous chapters, people *always* have an incentive to restrict competition. Third, licensing arrangements are often the result of lobbying by producers, not consumers. Fourth, the incumbents in the field to be licensed inevitably seek "grandfather clauses," exempting themselves from the new standards. If concern for the consumer were paramount, all practitioners would have to comply with the higher standards. Finally, violations of licensing laws are often reported by producers, not consumers. Note that once the mandatory licensing arrangement begins, some consumers and producers have an incentive to engage in black market activity, since it is mutually beneficial trade. In sum, it seems likely that producers seek restrictions for their own interests, not those of consumers.

The Impact on the Relatively Unskilled

At least the majority of consumers get a good story; the relatively unskilled, who have fewer employment options, are mostly ignored. As with the other labor market restrictions we have looked at, mandatory licensing hurts those who are relatively unskilled. And since these workers are disproportionately minorities, they are especially harmed.

Getting the required license often entails taking written, oral, and performance exams. To the extent these exams are unrelated to productivity, the practice is inefficient and individuals are hurt by the need to "jump through hoops." In addition, there are usually significant fees attached to acquiring the license. In sum, people are forced to spend scarce resources (time and money) to pass exams that are (in varying degrees) irrelevant to performing well. For the country, it is inefficient to have people making investments in human capital (training) that are not productive. For the affected individuals, such barriers to entry can limit access to certain labor markets and cause lower standards of living.

Mandatory Versus Voluntary Licensing

The main problem with licensing is that it is often mandatory. If economic markets were allowed to work properly, one would still see licensing of some sort in many fields, serving as a signal of quality. But in that case, consumers would still have the freedom to legally choose someone who was unlicensed, and workers would have the option to avoid the licensing process if they could prove they were competent by other means. It works this way in some occupations. For example, you are not required to have a certified public accountant (CPA) file your tax returns for you. And you do not have to pass the CPA exam to file tax returns for others.

Instead, imagine that a state passed a law requiring people to have "qualified" tax consultants prepare their returns. The story could be that the legislature wants to prevent people from receiving low-quality tax returns. Clearly, accountants in the state would benefit from the restricted competition. Also, consumers would be worse off by being forced to consume "Cadillac service" or none at all. And the *relatively* less skilled people who prepare returns would be eliminated from this labor market.

Although some low-quality service or products may be eliminated, people should not have their choices restricted to accomplish this. A range of quality is important to the poor in many markets. The effects of mandatory licensing are analogous to those of the minimum wage and rent controls, which hurt the poor by eliminating low-productivity workers and low-quality housing. Although average quality in licensed markets may increase, the improvement is costly; prices will rise due to the restricted competition. This may limit the ability of the poor to obtain any service at all.

Moreover, quality might diminish. If barriers to entry are large enough, incumbents may be relatively unconcerned with providing high-quality service. Many government enterprises serve as excellent testimony to the impact of limited competition on quality.

Because of the way producers pursue occupational restrictions through licensing, they reveal that their intent is not to help consumers but themselves.

Some Examples of Restrictive Labor Laws

In *The State Against Blacks,* Walter Williams's theme is that the "state" (the government) harms blacks in particular and the unskilled in general with restrictive labor laws.[3] Much of his book is devoted to examples of mandatory occupational licensing and its effects.

The first chapter on a specific occupation is devoted to operating taxicabs. Williams focuses on this occupation because these jobs would normally be quite attractive to those who do not have many other marketable skills. There are very small economic barriers to entry, since the "fixed costs" are so low. All one needs to provide taxi service is a vehicle, a sign, and perhaps a meter. Since the vehicle could be used outside of work, the cost to enter this market is negligible. In addition, the skills required to drive a car and negotiate city streets are relatively limited. This would seem to be a natural opportunity for the relatively unskilled to earn a living.

But despite small natural or economic barriers, the artificial or political barriers are often tremendous. In many cities, a special occupational license (a "medallion") is required to operate a taxicab. Further, in many of these cities, the number of medallions does not increase over time, thus failing to keep pace with expanding populations. For instance, in 1937, New York City issued 13,566 medallions for $10 apiece; the number of medallions decreased to 11,772 during World War II and has not changed since then. In a free market, the price of such a medallion would be zero. However, with additional competition frozen out (which allows higher rates of return), the value of the medallion can be quite high. In recent years, the price has been above $100,000 in Boston and New York. As opposed to "protecting consumers," licenses allow a life-time right to monopoly profits for cab companies. The medallion makes it prohibitively expensive for individuals to operate a cab legally and privately. Instead, they typically work for one of a few cab companies in a city.

What are the results? With less competition, fares are higher and there is an incentive to provide lower quality. Licensed cab drivers tend to discriminate by staying in "nice neighborhoods," where the tips are greater and the trips are safer. And despite the greater risks, the high rate of return serves as an incentive for illegal cabs or "jitneys" to operate and provide mutually beneficial trade to people looking for rides, especially those in the under-serviced inner-city areas.

Most important, the poor are harmed in two ways: Their ability to consume cab service is compromised, and the unskilled are locked out of a "natural" labor market. Williams notes that the market in Washington, D.C., for cab services operates relatively freely, and as a result, fares are lower, quality is higher, and minorities operate 70% of the cabs (compared to Philadelphia's 3%).[4]

Miami bans the non-licensed operation of vans for the purpose of transporting people who pay for the service. The intent is to restrict competition and allow cabs and Dade County's buses to have greater monopoly power in the market for transportation.[5] Again, the poor are hurt disproportionately—consumers face higher prices and lower quantity and quality of service; relatively unskilled laborers are locked out of another "natural" market.

The same is true in a variety of other markets, including the provision of personal services:

- Monique Landers is a 15-year-old who started her own small African hair-braiding business. After she returned from New York, where she was honored as one of five outstanding high school entrepreneurs, the state licensing board in Kansas shut her down. There were no complaints from customers, only incumbents. But the board threatened her with "fine, imprisonment or both" if she continued to operate without a license.[6]

- The desire to stifle competition is so strong that even free haircuts are opposed. In Duluth, Minnesota, Velma Richardson and Theresa Taylor were threatened with 90 days in jail and a $700 fine if they didn't stop a 10-year practice of giving free haircuts to the needy.[7]

- Texas (along with other states) requires written, oral, and performance exams to test for "quality" hair cutting. This often excludes immigrant Hispanics and others who do not speak or write English particularly well.

- Officials in Berkeley, California, assessed fines of $11,320 on "street artist" Phillip Roundtree for "charging people to tie colored and beaded strips in their hair." His behavior is illegal because it constitutes vending and practicing cosmetology without a license.[8]

- In 1984, Ego Brown decided to start a shoe-shining business on the streets of Washington, D.C. He hired 50–60 teenagers and homeless people and was soon doing a brisk business. But in summer 1985, he was shut down for using public space, despite the fact that virtually all other types of vendors were allowed access. After four years of legal battles, he was finally able to re-establish his "right to work."[9]

Williams devotes other chapters to plumbers, electricians, truckers, and the railroad industry.[10] Different tools are (or were) used in each area—licensing exams, overt racial discrimination by unions with monopoly power, comparable worth laws to make less expensive black or unskilled labor too expensive, grandfather clauses, and quotas to limit new entrants, among others. In some cases, the primary motivation seems to be economics and restricting competition; in other cases, it seems to be racial animosity. Regardless, the results are the same. In each case, prices are driven up for consumers and relatively unskilled laborers are locked out of labor markets for which they would be well suited.[11]

Williams concludes by distinguishing his ideas for reform with the prescriptions of others. The primary distinction between the two camps is whether the poor would be helped by more or less government intervention. Williams argues for less, saying that minorities (or in our primary context, the poor and the unskilled) are better off allowing economic markets to work instead of political markets.

This certainly seems to be the case in the issues developed thus far. In each case, the "organized" have pursued their own goals and inadvertently hammered the poor. Apparently the organized are better at using political markets than the poor. Williams also makes the point that in ghettos, people have some "nice" belongings—things provided through economic markets despite low incomes. In contrast, the government provides few if any "nice" things in inner cities. There, its public housing, education, roads, and other projects are almost uniformly pathetic. Williams concludes that minorities and the poor would be best served by a proliferation of economic markets and the stifling of political markets.[12]

The Role of Labor Unions

Labor unions are simply cartels in labor markets. As with cartels in product markets, they have an incentive to collude and restrict quantity in order to earn higher "prices" (wages and other compensation). But with wages artificially high, potential non-union entrants have an incentive to enter the market and underbid the incumbents. Thus, like virtually all other cartels, unions would be unable to gain above-market wages and compensation without government help.

The government has enforced and strengthened these cartels in a number of ways. With the Wagner Act (commonly known as the National Labor Relations Act) of 1935, unions gained substantial bargaining strength in dealing with firms. And the fact that only one-third of the states have Taft-Hartley ("right-to-work") laws increases the monopoly power of unions. In the absence of these laws, all workers must join the representing union *and* pay full dues.

In addition, government has been used by labor unions to restrict competition from other forms of labor. The goal is to gain market power and increase the incomes of union members. As we saw in Chapter 6, unions benefit from a higher minimum wage because less skilled labor is priced out of the market. Earlier in this chapter, we saw how Davis-Bacon laws and mandatory occupational licensing serve to restrict competition from relatively unskilled labor.

Unions also pursue stringent immigration policies as well as quotas and tariffs on foreign products. The former obviously eliminates a source of potential labor market competition. The latter restricts competition for the products made by union labor and thus increases the demand for union labor. Finally, the incentive to restrict competition also explains avid union interest in "strike-breaker" laws, which prevent firms from hiring permanent replacements, further restricting competition from non-union workers.

The historical union penchant for violence is simply a variation on the same theme. Physical harm (or the threat of it) serves to make non-union members think at least twice before competing for a union job or replacing a striking union member. In order to be effective, a union must prevent non-union workers from taking jobs (with above-market levels of compensation) that would clearly benefit the non-union workers.

The Landrum-Griffith Act of 1959 actually condones the use of intimidation through picketing during strikes as long as it is in pursuit of a "bona fide increase in wages or other employee benefits."[13] In other words, if the cause is "just" (however defined), then the ends justify the means. And since police forces are frequently unionized, they are likely to be sympathetic to the means and ends of other unions. This may explain why one rarely hears about prosecutions resulting from violence along picket lines.

Taken together, these policies constitute an agenda that restricts competition for union laborers, allowing them to earn greater incomes. (Union leaders do particularly well: One hundred and twenty-nine teamsters' union officials were paid over $100,000 in 1994.[14]) Again, a relatively high income group receives indirect transfers from the general public. As always, the benefits are concentrated and go to a relatively small group that supports its politicians with a solid block of votes and significant campaign contributions. Moreover, relatively unskilled labor is prevented from competing and earning income in various labor markets.

The result is a wage (and compensation) premium of 10%–20%. But the union share of the labor force is falling. In the private sector, the key is competition. With an economy moving toward a greater proportion of service industries, more women in the labor force, and greater international competition, the monopoly power of unions in the U.S. labor market is becoming less and less relevant. Absent a dose of heavy protectionism, one would expect this trend to continue.

However, the opposite is true in the public sector; with respect to government jobs, unions are booming. Again, the key is competition—or rather, a lack of competition. Without competition and with the deep pockets of taxpayers as well as the incentives of budget-maximizing bureaucracies, public-sector unions could continue to grow well into the future, increasing the transfer of income from taxpayers to middle-class union workers—the non-poor. As before, a special interest group receives concentrated benefits at the expense of a general public that bears subtle and relatively small per-person costs.

Notes

1. *Freeman,* February 1994, p. 67, citing "Rates of Wages for Laborers and Mechanics on Public Buildings of the United States," 74 Congressional Record 6504, 6513 (1931).

2. Sometimes, appeals to emotion are used to promote more direct redistribution—to allow a "fair" rate of return to those in the field, for example.

3. W. Williams, *The State Against Blacks* (New York: McGraw-Hill, 1982).

4. Ibid., pp. 81, 84, 86.

5. G. Garvin, "Van Bans," *Reason,* December 1992, pp. 53–55.

6. "Monique in Tangles," *Wall Street Journal,* June 18, 1993.

7. C. Oliver, *Reason,* December 1994, p. 13.

8. C. Oliver, *Reason,* March 1994, p. 15.

9. M. Olasky, *The Tragedy of American Compassion* (Washington, DC: Regnery Gateway, 1992), p. 229.

10. The medical profession also uses mandatory licensing. Although this is not much of a labor market issue for the poor, there is still the "Cadillac effect," higher health care costs and redistribution to upper-income doctors. This is covered further in Chapter 11.

11. On certificates in trucking, Williams notes that the requirement for entry was to prove to a (less than sympathetic) regulating board "whether [the petitioner] will serve a useful public purpose . . . without endangering or impairing the operations of existing carriers." (*The State Against Blacks,* p. 112).

12. Ibid., p. 142.

13. Section 602a (cited in M. Reynolds, *Economics of Labor* [Cincinnati: South-Western, 1995], p. 348).

14. *American Enterprise,* September/October 1995, p. 4. Public-sector unions are covered further in Chapter 8.

8

Other Types of Redistribution to the Non-Poor: Let Me Count the Ways . . .

So far in Part 2, we have looked at indirect ways to redistribute income. Because openly transferring income to the non-poor is usually not acceptable, it is generally done as indirectly as possible. However, there are some policies that are more direct. There are also a number of policies that inadvertently but directly redistribute income; seemingly, the primary goal is something other than enhancing the incomes of a special interest group. I cover both types of policies in this chapter.

Paying Congress and Public-Sector Unions Too Much

Despite considerable public outcry, Congress passed a substantial pay raise for its members in 1989 (40%—from $89,500 to $125,100).[1] Members of both parties had complained that their compensation was too low. But was this true? Their objectivity is not at all guaranteed; people always have an incentive to pursue higher prices for the things they sell.

More objectively, labor economists say you need to look at two things to determine if people are paid too much or too little: the rate at which workers quit and how many people line up to pursue available jobs. If people rarely leave certain jobs or many people respond to a job opening, the rate of compensation is probably too high.[2]

For example, by these criteria, U.S. Postal Service workers are paid too much: Their "quit rates" are extremely low, and typically, hundreds of people apply for openings when they become available. USPS workers are the beneficiaries of the deep pockets of consumers and taxpayers footing the bill for an inefficient government monopoly. (Compensation for the average blue-collar USPS worker was $44,342 in 1994.)[3] Other public-sector unions are also consistently compensated at above-market rates. Yet again, an organized group of middle-class workers receives an income transfer from the general public.

Similarly, from 1960 to 1990, quit rates for our nationally elected representatives were very low.[4] By their behavior, they revealed that the previous combination of pay, power, and perquisites was sufficient to satisfy them. In addition, the willingness to spend so much money to pursue elective office reflects the value of the seats.

A few other details make "the pay raise" a particularly ugly story. Until 1989, Congress had a mechanism by which salary increases could pass without a floor vote; the only way a raise could be avoided was if both chambers of Congress and the president passed a bill refusing the pay increase. In 1987, members allowed their raise to go through and then voted against it the day after it could be repealed. So although the pay raise went into effect, many members of Congress could be represented in the Congressional Record as opponents of the measure. They used the same strategy in 1989 but were stymied by public opposition.[5]

In addition, if members were elected before 1980 and retired before 1992, they were allowed to keep any excess campaign contributions. For those eligible, this amounted to over $40 million.[6] Further, congressional pensions are determined by the number of years in office and salary over the last three years. With the pay raise taking effect in 1990, pensions for those retiring in 1992 were determined by the higher salaries for those three years. Thus, pensions were (and are) more than 40% higher than if they had retired before the pay raise went into effect.[7] The many retirements from Congress in 1992 and 1994 should come as no surprise.[8]

People are becoming more disenchanted with the performance of Congress. With respect to public choice theory, the difficult-to-see costs are becoming more obvious. However, re-election rates remain high either because there are significant barriers to entry into the congressional labor market or because it is not in an individual district's best interests to defeat its incumbent while other incumbents remain. If challengers triumph, they go to the bottom of Congress's seniority ladder and subsequently have little power to bring pork back to their constituents. This explains Dave Barry's observation that representatives are like body odor—people don't mind their own, but they can't stand anybody else's. Instead, voters have responded in other ways to express discontent with their elected representatives: the growing term-limits movement and the "successful" independent presidential candidacy of Ross Perot in 1992.

Redistribution to the Elderly

Redistribution to the elderly can be done openly because it is perceived to be deserved. However, determining the extent of need for this group is difficult because income transfers to the elderly are replete with normative issues. On the one hand, the elderly have a below-average poverty rate. Moreover, this particular poverty rate does not reflect the usual bias in the poverty statistics as discussed in Chapter 1. On the other hand, elderly individuals are the least able to fend for themselves. This and the normative idea that society owes them a debt moves this issue beyond quick resolution. Further, income transfers to elderly individuals are vigorously defended by what many consider the most politically powerful special interest group.

With that said, there are many interesting points about current (and future) efforts to redistribute income to the elderly. First, like most government programs, Social Security has grown tremendously in terms of scope and budget. It began in 1935 as a supplementary income for retirees. In 1939, its benefits were extended to survivors of retirees and in 1954, to the disabled; in 1965, it was extended to include Medicare.[9] Spending on Social Security programs was $0.3 billion in 1945 and $352.4 billion by 1990. In addition to Social Security's broader scope, there are more elderly people because of longer life spans, a higher proportion of the elderly are now eligible, and the programs pay greater benefits than before.

Second, there is a misconception about who pays the 15.3% Social Security tax. The government has *imposed* it equally on employees and employers (7.65% each). But if you believe firms pay half of your Social Security tax, you should also believe gas stations pay the excise taxes on gasoline instead of passing them on to consumers. In fact, employees pay most or all of the Social Security tax. Repealing the tax would allow wages to rise as much as 15.3% when labor markets adjusted.[10] Imagine receiving a 14%–15% raise. Better yet—imagine how a 14%–15% raise would increase the living standards of the poor and diminish the temptation of welfare.

Third, Social Security is a pay-as-you-go system. Thus, current benefits are paid out of current taxes; it is not a retirement account where an individual's benefits accrue. As such, it redistributes money from workers to retirees. A pay-as-you-go system yields excellent rates of return to its earliest beneficiaries: these retirees received full benefits from Social Security after contributing to the system for only a few years. Now, in a fully mature system (after a generation of workers has passed through), the rates of return are anemic—an estimated 1%–2% per year.

Fourth, because Social Security is funded by current taxes, it is subject to financial difficulties if the number of retirees increases or the number of workers decreases. With the retirement of the baby boomers in the next century, financial problems will begin in earnest. Under the most reasonable assumptions about fertility rates and economic growth, Social Security tax rates will have to increase to 25.2% in 2030.[11] Clearly, something will have to change.

Of potential short-run reforms, the government could further tax the benefits of retirees with higher incomes or increase the age of eligibility. Either of these would have to be pursued slowly to avoid inconveniencing those in or near retirement. The most reasonable long-run solution is to privatize Social Security.[12]

Fifth, Social Security redistributes a significant amount of money among the states. Taxpayers in New York and California pay $16.3 million more than recipients in their states collect; Floridians net $10.3 billion from this income transfer.[13] Finally, Social Security and Medicare redistribute income across generations but also across income classes. For instance, Medicare benefits go to many members of the middle and upper classes. Nearly 20% of families with incomes above $20,000 receive benefits, including 20% of those earning more than $150,000 per year.[14] In sum, because the elderly have such a low poverty rate and because Social Security taxes are regressive (they are capped for higher income levels), these programs also redistribute vast amounts of money from the working poor to the non-poor elderly.

The Health Insurance Subsidy
for the Non-Poor

Our tax code provides a subsidy to those who have employer-provided health insurance. Because fringe benefits are not subject to taxation, workers may elect to receive this non-cash (untaxed) compensation. In some cases a job that offers more in such benefits may be preferable to a job paying more in post-tax income. At a tax rate of 40%, $1,000 worth of health insurance, if converted to $1,000 in additional salary, would be worth only $600 ($400 having gone for taxes). Allowing workers to avoid taxation serves to redistribute income to those who take advantage of the tax-free nature of employer-provided health insurance (and other fringe benefits). Unfortunately, the uninsured do not receive this subsidy. Although the poor are subsidized through Medicaid, the (uninsured) working poor are hammered twice: they pay taxes but do not receive Medicaid or the health care subsidy. Thus, the working poor are harmed immensely.

Further, the amount of the subsidy increases with the level of income. Assume that a rich person (with a 36% marginal federal tax rate) and a poor person (with a 15% marginal tax rate) each have a $3,000 health insurance policy through their employer. The rich person's tax burden is reduced by $1,080 (36% of $3,000), but the poor person's tax burden is reduced by only $450 (15% of $3,000). And if the wealthier person gets a more comprehensive (and more expensive) policy, his subsidy will be even larger.

John Goodman and Gerald Musgrave calculate that the average subsidy for health insurance amounts to $600 per family—for a total of $60 billion. However, for the top quintile of income, the average subsidy is $1,560 per family; for the lowest quintile, it is $270 per family.[15]

In this case, our tax code serves to redistribute income in a highly regressive way—by sheltering fringe benefits from income taxation. Note that other tax loopholes and income deductions yield the same result.[16]

Public (Subsidized) Television for the Non-Poor

In 1992, the Public Broadcasting System (PBS) received a three-year subsidy of $1.1 billion. Its popular shows—*Sesame Street*, Ken Burns's *Civil War*, the *MacNeil-Lehrer Newshour*, and others, would clearly survive the "test of the market." They would be profitable and would not require financial assistance to remain on the air. However, for the shows with more limited audiences, a subsidy is necessary to ensure their survival.

Why is PBS subsidized? We can tell the standard public choice story of diffuse costs for taxpayers and concentrated benefits for viewers, the bureaucrats who administer the agency, and corporate donors who receive advertising and tax breaks. The bureaucrats are often paid well; for example, in 1989–1990, a public television station in New York City (WNET) had 15 officials with compensation packages of more than $100,000.[17] When culture is involved, there is probably a little paternalism mixed in, and occasionally one will hear about its necessity for "the social good." But regardless of the merits of these arguments, taxes from the working poor and middle class subsidize programming for the wealthy and the salaries of well-paid bureaucrats. This policy redistributes income to those in upper-income brackets.

Public (Subsidized) Insurance for the Non-Poor

Government provides subsidized insurance for a number of natural events—earthquakes, hurricanes, beach erosion, and floods. Frequently, proponents claim there is "market failure" in these arenas. In other words, the private market's price for providing such insurance is too high, so government decides to provide the insurance at a reduced rate. In fact, the market works just fine in those contexts—it is saying, "Don't build there!" Public insurance policies subsidize undesirable behavior—building in risky locations. Further, they transfer income from taxpayers to those who build in dangerous areas. Often these people are wealthy—how many poor people own beachfront property? Independent of whether we agree with these policies in principle, we should at least recognize the redistributive nature of the subsidies.

In addition to providing insurance, the federal government often pays for rebuilding after natural disasters. Following the Mississippi River flood of 1993, the government paid out $6.4 billion. Unfortunately, 12 different agencies and 38 different programs were involved. From 1989 to 1993, the federal government provided more than $34 billion in disaster-relief aid. This amounts to over $500 per each average family of four.[18]

Private insurance should be sufficient, particularly in higher-risk areas. But if the public decides government should be involved, it should be at the state or local level instead of a federal responsibility. Why should the working poor in Ohio pay for earthquake damage in California?

Farming (the Government) Revisited

In 1994, agribusiness received $29.2 billion in direct subsidies, earning the title "the most costly form of corporate welfare."[19] This amount compares with a combined $50 billion for food stamps and AFDC, two commonly criticized handouts. In addition, the Bureau of Land Management rents public lands to ranchers at greatly subsidized prices. In 1992, their annual grazing fee was $1.92 per animal; private landowners charged $9.26. These programs redistribute income to the non-poor.

In addition to outright grants, subsidized loans are provided to farmers. At below-market interest rates, they can borrow $200,000 to buy a farm, $200,000 to operate it, and up to $500,000 at 4.5% interest in counties that have been declared disaster areas.[20] These loans are often equivalent to grants, since they have such high default rates. From 1988 to 1992, the Farmers Home Administration wrote off $11.5 billion in bad loans—an incredible amount considering that the principal on loans outstanding in 1992 amounted to $13.8 billion.[21]

California subsidizes farmers for their purchases of water (they use 80% of the state's water at prices discounted up to 94% of cost). The result is rice and alfalfa grown in deserts, asinine restrictions on residential users (who consume only 10% of the state's water—at full price), a water shortage in the state, and higher incomes for farmers.[22]

Subsidies and Labor Market Exploitation
in Higher Education

College students at public universities receive vast subsidies in the form of reduced in-state tuition rates. In 1991, the average tuition at four-year state colleges was less than $2,200, but the average expenditure per student was about $8,000.[23] In addition, many students have access to a variety of student grants and subsidized loans. Proponents usually put forth an equity argument—that these subsidies enable disadvantaged young people the opportunity to attend college, especially poor people, who would otherwise be unable.[24] Although this is true in certain circumstances, the low quality of public education at the elementary and secondary level makes concerns about college attendance seem misplaced. (I will cover this topic in the next chapter.) Also, these subsidies are mostly pocketed by the middle class, whose kids constitute the bulk of college students.[25] Subsidized tuition, grants, and loans for those in the middle and upper classes or those who attend graduate school often amounts to an income transfer to people in upper-income brackets.

In order to systematically pay employees less than their productivity (their worth in a labor market), an employer must have substantial bargaining power over prospective workers. A few notable examples are professional athletes without "free agency," those with limited "job mobility," slaves, and government as the sole employer in a country. Another notable example is the NCAA labor market cartel—a collusion to prevent payments to college athletes. Although students receive in-kind payments, many are paid far less than the revenues they generate for universities. In a competitive market (or in the case of "cheating" against the cartel), compensation would be significantly higher. And even though one might be sympathetic to the notion that collegiate athletics should have amateur standing, the fact remains that universities have conspired to "pay" many of their "employees" far less than what they produce, resulting in an income transfer away from talented athletes.

Bailouts, Public Monopolies, and Stadiums

In 1993, Kentucky decided to reduce a large manufacturer's tax burden by $20 million over ten years. The manfacturer argued that to keep the jobs in Louisville, it needed to decrease costs by that much in order to keep its plants open. Keeping jobs in a city is a laudable pursuit, but other strategies would have reached the cost-cutting goals. For instance, the firm could have lowered labor costs by $20 million. This would have entailed wage cuts of $.11 per hour for the average union worker (who made $28,000 in 1992 plus sizable fringe benefits). Mysteriously, such a solution was not considered publicly. Instead, the state decided it would be easier to take a little bit from each taxpayer rather a bit more from a unionized (and politically organized) workforce. Again, income was transferred from taxpayers to a middle-class special interest group.[26]

Until the 1980s, telephone companies, railroads, and airlines were "regulated"—granted cartel-monopoly power at the expense of consumers. Today, most cable companies have monopoly rights to be the sole provider of cable services in a locality. The result in all of these examples is higher prices and lower quality—an income transfer away from consumers. Telephone rates are still regulated and subsidized with certain groups receiving favorable treatment. Wayne Leighton estimates the following income transfers for 1993: (1) an urban-to-rural transfer of more than $9.3 billion in subsidized rates and $381 million in government expenditures; and (2) a long-distance-to-local transfer of more than $2.3 billion in subsidized rates.[27] Even if we ignore the impact of inefficient market structures enforced by governments, these subsidies cost the average family of four almost $200 per year.

Further, many public-sector enterprises (for example, airports, universities, and toll roads) frequently sell exclusive rights to provide a service. (In a competitive market, such "rights" are worthless.) For example, in 1994, Pepsi-Cola Company signed a ten-year, $3.4 million deal with the University of Cincinnati for exclusive vending rights on campus. This monopoly power allows the company to charge higher prices and "earn" higher profits (presumably at least $3.4 million more).[28] Mutually beneficial trades between the public sector and the acting monopoly are made at the expense of consumers.

Two federal agencies—the Appalachian Regional Commission and the Economic Development Administration—are scheduled to provide $1.25 million to help finance a football stadium for Wofford College (a private school with yearly fees of nearly $17,000 for tuition, room, and board) and the Carolina Panthers (a professional football team).[29] Often, local governments build stadiums with public funds. Given the incomes of the standard sporting-event audience, this amounts to redistribution to those with good incomes and a transfer of income to sports fans.[30] Other examples abound. As before, the point is not to provide an exhaustive list but to allow readers to see how income transfers permeate our public policy and how redistribution targets non-poor interest groups at the expense of the general public and, unfortunately, the poor.

Seemingly Inadvertent Direct Redistribution

There are many other government activities that would seem to be unrelated to income redistribution. This is because their primary purpose is to provide some good or service. Regardless, these policies transfer income as well.

For example, redistribution takes place in the government's provision of national defense. First, there is a distinction between what Congress and the Pentagon want for the military. Often, those differences are based on politics, not honest disagreements over the best way to defend the country. Often, the workings of political markets supersede concerns about national defense. The Pentagon may choose one weapon system over another, but its decision may be rejected because a powerful member of Congress represents the district that makes the "undesirable" weapon. This influence is also evident with the placement of troops: Even the most ardent pacifists are incredibly militant about keeping military bases operating in their districts.

Second, income transfers occur even with the optimal provision of national defense. For instance, during the 1980s, California benefited from the "Reagan defense buildup": Federal money flowed into the state through defense contracts. Some of the economic problems California has faced in recent years have been caused by reduced defense expenditures because the Soviet threat has faded. In addition, defense contracts enhance the career opportunities of engineers, scientists, and others. National defense is crucial, but its provision redistributes income to certain groups of people.

Redistribution also takes place in the government's provision of education. Public schools at the secondary level—their effect on the poor and their redistributive elements—are the subject of the next chapter. Income transfers also occur with the subsidization of higher education through reduced tuition and fees. Although cheaper tuition might allow the poor to attend school, most of the poor never make it that far. This redistribution mostly subsidizes the middle class, whose children attend public universities at such a high rate.

Government employees are also beneficiaries of public-sector spending, and they generally have above-average incomes. Because of the relatively deep pockets of taxpayers and the absence of the efficiency promoted by economic markets, they are able to unionize at a much higher rate than the private sector and obtain greater incomes. The existence of unnecessary bureaucrats and military personnel is also a needless transfer of resources from taxpayers to interest groups.

Finally, complicated laws and regulations increase the demand for the services of lawyers, consultants, and accountants. Unnecessarily onerous tax codes and regulations are wasteful for the economy and transfer income to relatively wealthy people. Most spending in the public sector (whether for NASA, supercolliders, or public works projects) increases the demand for the services of planners, bureaucrats, engineers, consultants, and so on. Even programs designed to help the poor are a boon to many with incomes well above the national average.[31]

Job Creation?

It would seem these policies could be easily defended as a means of "job creation." However, Hazlitt's emphasis on looking at the whole picture allows us to understand that the costs for all groups (higher taxes and subsequent job destruction) outweigh the benefits of the jobs created by government. Besides, the created jobs would not have appeared in economic markets; they are inefficient and (on net) wealth destroying.

It is not necessary to disagree with any of these policies to understand that income redistribution takes place. As before, this is not an exhaustive list of the relevant policies. The main point is to illustrate the principles behind the operation of political markets. Again, we have seen special interest groups receiving concentrated benefits at the expense of the general public, which bears diffuse and subtle costs. Too often, these policies transfer income from the poor to the non-poor.

Notes

1. *Congressional Quarterly Weekly Report* (Washington, DC: Congressional Quarterly, July 20, 1991), p. 1956.

2. An exception would be what economists call "efficiency wages"—when it is in a firm's best interest to voluntarily pay above-market wages. If turnover is particularly costly or troublesome (because of company secrets, for example), extra compensation may be the optimal strategy.

3. *American Enterprise*, September/October 1995, p. 4.

4. Quit rates averaged 4.4% per year from 1960 to 1990. In the same period, the quit rate in the manufacturing sector averaged about 2% per *month*. (D. Eric Schansberg, "An Analysis of Congressional Quits: Moving Out of the House," *Economic Inquiry*, July 1994.)

5. *Congressional Quarterly Almanac* (Washington, DC: Congressional Quarterly, 1989), p. 51. In *The Ruling Class: Inside the Imperial Congress* (Washington, DC: Heritage Foundation, 1993), E. Felten reports that Democrats and Republicans signed a "non-aggression pact" that neither party would fund opponents who tried to use the pay raise as an issue against incumbents in the 1990 campaign (pp. 7–9).

6. Public Citizen's "Congress Watch" (Washington, D.C.), cited in *What Counts: The Complete Harper's Index* (New York: Henry Holt, 1991).

7. "More than 40%" because salaries increased by 40%, and they would have served three additional years. According to the National Taxpayers Union, 303 of the 535 representatives serving in 1994 could have become "pension millionaires"—their expected lifespan would allow them to receive over $1 million in pension income.

8. There were 114 new representatives elected to the U.S. House in 1992. Many were elected to open seats following the retirement of an incumbent. This

exceeds the number of those entering the House following Watergate and is nearly equal to the combined turnover of the preceding three elections. The relatively large number of retirements in 1994 may also have stemmed from the security of substantially higher pensions.

9. The acronym for Old Age Insurance (Social Security) was OAI in 1935 and OASDHI (Old Age, Survivors, Disability and Health Insurance) thirty years later, after its scope had expanded.

10. Of course, this number is dependent on the elasticity (flexibility) of labor supply and demand. Since labor supply is inelastic and labor demand is fairly elastic, economists estimate that workers bear most of the burden of the Social Security tax—whether imposed on firms or employees.

11. E. Browning and J. Browning, *Public Finance and the Price System*, 4th ed. (New York: Macmillan, 1994), p. 234. See also H. Aaron, B. Bosworth, and G. Burtless, *Can America Afford to Grow Old?* (Washington, DC: Brookings Institution, 1989).

12. Those interested in the details are encouraged to read P. Ferrara's *Social Security: Averting the Crisis* (Washington, DC: Cato Institute, 1982). E. Kingson and E. Berkowitz provide a "more balanced" analysis and conclude by advocating relatively minor reforms (*Social Security and Medicare: A Policy Primer* [Westport, CT: Auburn House, 1993]).

13. J. Goldstein, "Hills and Valleys on the Social Security Interstate," *Wall Street Journal,* May 31, 1995.

14. S. Collins, "The Budget Monster," *U.S. News and World Report,* November 21, 1994.

15. *Patient Power: The Free Enterprise Alternative to Clinton's Health Plan* (Washington, DC: Cato Institute, 1994), pp. 37, 40–41.

16. Dave Barry describes "tax breaks" as "when the government, amid great fanfare, generously decides not to take quite so much of your income. In other words, these candidates are trying to buy your votes with your own money."

17. Ibid., p. 49.

18. W. Cohen, "Uncle Sam's Open Wallet," *U.S. News and World Report,* August 22, 1994, pp. 54–55.

19. J. Donahue, "The Corporate Welfare Kings," *Washington Post National Weekly Edition,* March 21–March 27, 1994 (numbers are cited from the Office of Management and Budget and the Joint Committee on Taxation).

20. S. LaFraniere, "Though They Owe, Still They Reap," *Washington Post National Weekly Edition,* February 28–March 6, 1994.

21. Ibid.

22. S. Hayward, "Muddy Waters," *Reason,* July 1991, pp. 46–47.

23. M. Reynolds, *Economics of Labor* (Cincinnati: South-Western, 1995), p. 175.

24. One can also argue that government should have an active role in education (however defined) because of two market imperfections—the positive externalities associated with obtaining an education, and limitations in human capital investment markets. On the former, because education provides additional benefits to society that are not taken into account directly by individuals,

society will tend to produce "too little" education. On the latter, because people cannot often use themselves as collateral for loans (many forms of "indentured servitude" are prohibited), the capacity to finance education through debt is limited. Regardless of the extent of these factors, this policy is still redistributive.

25. D. Lee and R. McKenzie note that at the inception of the loan programs in 1957, assistance was limited to low-income families. But over time, interest groups for higher education asserted themselves and the programs were expanded. For example, from 1977 to 1981, guaranteed student loans rose from $1.5 to $7.8 billion. (*Failure and Progress,* [Washington, DC: Cato Institute, 1993], pp. 127–128.)

26. R. Manning, "GE Jobs Saved If Workers Accepted the Rescue Package," *Louisville Career Journal,* February 3, 1993.

27. Citizens for a Sound Economy (Washington, D.C.), "Telecommunication Subsidies: Reach Out and Fund Someone," *Issues and Answers,* January 1995.

28. Associated Press, as published in *Horizon* (the Indiana University Southeast student newspaper), February 1, 1994.

29. Mike Brown, "Agency's Use of $750,000 Gives Critics Ammunition," *Louisville Courier-Journal,* April 25, 1995.

30. See R. Keating, "Pro Sports on the Dole," *Freeman,* February 1995, pp. 114–118.

31. This will become more evident in Part 3, when I analyze the implementation of welfare programs.

9

Mandating a Pathetic Level of Education: A Way to Ensure Lifetime Poverty

To my mind, education is the most important issue facing our country.[1] On a national level, it is intricately related to our productivity and economic growth. On an individual level, it is a crucial determinant of a person's earning potential, especially the inner-city poor.[2] The surest way to ensure a lifetime of abject poverty is to not complete high school or to receive an otherwise less than quality education. Of those under the poverty line in 1992, 38.1% were in households headed by someone with less than a high school education. The poverty rate for that group is 24.1%.[3]

Our public (elementary and secondary) school system is a combination of one of the worst economic systems (socialism—government control of resources) and the worst market structure (monopoly—one dominant firm in a market). It should come as no surprise that schools run by the government with little competition exhibit the same characteristics as other socialistic or monopolistic endeavors.

The key question in this chapter is, Do institutions matter? Specifically, are incentives and performance significantly worse in a monopolistic and socialistic system? If not, the best solution would be to effect minor reforms. But if institutions matter, propping up the current system with more money will not help. In that case, the only effective solution would be to overhaul the system. How? By injecting the private sector and competition into the market for education.

As before, we will see that considerations from public choice economics are the biggest impediment to reform. In education as elsewhere, producers use the government to restrict their competition, enhancing their well-being at the expense of the general public. Unfortunately, the inner-city poor are harmed most by this use of government power.

Minorities and the poor overwhelmingly want competition introduced into the market for education through educational choice or vouchers, but incumbents in the educational establishment continue to try to protect their privileged market position.[4]

Some Numbers

Expenditures on education have risen dramatically since World War II. In 1946, we spent $900 per student (in 1992 dollars); by 1994, the amount had risen to nearly $6,000 (costing the average family of four more than $4,000 in taxes).[5] In New Jersey and many cities, per student spending has increased to more than $10,000.[6] What about performance? SAT scores have decreased, our children's aptitude is lower than many other industrialized countries (especially in math and science), and there is more violence in the schools.[7] From any measure of our government's educational system, it is clear that despite dramatically higher spending, there has been, at best, no overall improvement. For those in the inner cities, the situation is obviously bad and getting worse.

Independent of the numbers, most people perceive that the quality of public education has been declining for some time and that it is almost a universal failure in the inner city. This impression is enhanced by the movement toward private schools and home schooling. Even those who operate the schools know their product: Public school teachers send their kids to private schools at more than twice the national average (22% versus 10%).[8] This would be akin to employees refusing *free* products or services at their place of employment to pay full price elsewhere. And elected officials are infamous for fighting against educational choice while sending their kids to private schools.[9]

The Analogy to Socialism

Socialism is an economic system where the production and distribution of resources are controlled by government. It is often said that the West was "victorious" over the Soviet Union and that capitalism has defeated socialism, but this view is far too simplistic. Ironically, the United States has a large and growing government sector, and people still have great faith in government's ability to "deliver the goods." In education—one of the most important areas of life, we have placed nearly complete faith in government and thus, the efficacy of socialism.

Our market for education parallels the characteristics of a socialistic economy in many ways. Administrators abound and bureaucracy is rampant. In New York City, public schools have 10 times more employees per student and more than 60 times the number of administrators per student than Catholic schools.[10] This contributes to much higher costs in the public sector. As opposed to nearly $6,000 in costs per student for public schools, private school tuition averages half that much.[11] In general, outside the rigors of economic markets, government enterprises are relatively unconcerned with costs and the bottom line. They can usually dig deeper into the pockets of taxpayers.

As with a socialistic economy, public education focuses on the "production side" and is relatively uninterested in the desires of consumers. Funding from the government is often based on enrollments, not quality or even attendance. This is similar to the goal of reaching production quotas in command economies: The motivation is not to maximize profits, minimize costs, and maintain quality but to maximize quantity or to reach the defined quota.[12]

The parallels in reform efforts are also noteworthy. Mikhail Gorbachev's perestroika was an attempt to fix socialism, to make it work better, to tinker with it instead of pursuing structural reform.[13] But if institutions matter, such peripheral efforts are doomed to fail. If socialism is inherently flawed, if its economic incentives are inadequate, then the only true reform is to change the system—not to throw additional money at it, not to try to make socialism work better.

Finally, who fights for socialism in both cases? The status quo. In Russia, it is the party chiefs, the apparatchiks, the bureaucrats, and certain groups of workers who have much to lose. They are the only winners in the current system; likewise, they will be the only losers under substantial reform. Thus, they will do anything to avoid it—distort information, lead coups, and so on. The same is true in the U.S. market for education. Only the educational establishment loses with the introduction of competition and private markets into this arena. If you allow educational choice, many would leave the public school system—similar to the results after the Berlin Wall came down in 1989.

Am I saying there is no role for government in providing education? No. But it is a question of the extent to which government should be involved. In the market for food, the government empowers poor people to buy food (with food stamps and other income supplements) but does not operate the grocery stores. This is left to the private sector. In that case, the degree of socialism is much smaller; government is not involved in the production of grocery services. The same should be true in education.

The Analogy to Monopoly Power

Government-run (public) schools also have a large degree of monopoly power in the market for education. In contrast, it is competitive markets that are known for efficiency, flexibility, quality, and the best products at the best prices. Monopolies represent the other end of the spectrum.

This monopoly power can be understood in two ways. On the production side, it derives from the vast subsidy that government (public) schools receive—on average, nearly $6,000 per student in 1994. Of course, private schools are not eligible for those monies. This gives government schools a huge advantage. This also explains why most existing private schools are "religious." They are often subsidized directly by churches and indirectly by teachers and staff willing to accept lower salaries.

On the consumption side, parents are hamstrung by the all-or-nothing nature of the subsidy. If they choose to enroll their kids in government schools, education is provided at no additional charge. If not, they enroll their children in private schools and the education must be paid for completely by the parents. In this case, they must pay taxes to support the government schools *and* pay private school tuition. Even if parents want more education for their children, they must be willing to incur large opportunity costs to turn down the subsidy.

Thomas DiLorenzo has made the case that the government schools also act as a cartel, gaining greater monopoly power.[14] As has been established, producers do not like competition. In this context, the primary threat to producers comes from other local governments—the other producers of (subsidized) education. There are two ways to limit this threat. First, they try to prevent parental choice among different government schools. Having all the students in a given geographic area as a "captive audience" allows greater monopoly power. Second, they try to arrange funding from the state or federal government rather than at the local level. The idea here is that if one district had to increase local taxes to pay for greater bureaucracy, it would be relatively easy for people to vote with their feet and move to another district. In the current system, educational budgets are usually funded by state taxes, so that voting with one's feet involves changing states—a more costly proposition. The state collects taxes from the locals, pockets some, and then sends it back to the locals, enforcing and enhancing the cartel's monopoly power.

An Analogy to Restaurants

James Gwartney has a thought experiment that illustrates why a system that features socialism and monopoly power is not a good idea.[15] Imagine that government decides to operate all restaurants. Further, your geography determines your restaurant; you will eat at the government ("public") restaurant in your neighborhood. (To make the analogy more accurate, also assume home cooking—like home schooling—is very costly.) What would the incentives be for the person who manages the restaurant? Why does the fact that the clientele is captive make a difference?

Of course, the economic incentives are not at all favorable. Consumers are likely to receive low-quality food. In addition, costs (taxes and government spending) are likely to be artificially high and to increase further. But since customers still pay a "price" of zero for the service (government education is "free"), people are less likely to notice the relationship—the subsequent tax increases are much more subtle than price increases in the private sector would be.

In addition, you will be forced to eat the type of food your particular restaurant serves. If it's Mexican food and you don't like burritos—too bad! The point is not that Mexican food is "right or wrong" but that by definition, the menu will offend or disappoint someone. The same is true in the menu of issues provided by government schools—whether to use corporal punishment, when to teach sex education, whether to use phonics, whether to focus on academics or on building self-esteem, and so on.

If you decide to eat at a private restaurant to get better quality or because your tastes and preferences differ from what your government school provides, you will have to pay taxes for the government restaurant as well as the prices at the private restaurant. Clearly, your ability to do this would be a function of your income level. In the same way, educational choice is restricted, especially for the poor.

If the System Is Bad, Why Is My Child's School Good?

Many of you are probably wondering how the foregoing can be true if the government (public) school you or your children attended was good. Or maybe you're thinking that other social factors are the primary explanation of the problems with contemporary schooling, especially in the inner city. Although family structure, crime, and drug use are important, they are also more difficult to change. Much can be done by simply changing the structure and incentives in the market for education.

An analogy to marriage is instructive. From a strictly economic perspective, compared to dating, marriage is not a very good institution. The trouble is that marriage limits competition and thus discourages incentives for good behavior.[16] Often, after the wedding, people gain weight, don't buy flowers or shave as often, and so on. These are behaviors that would probably not be tolerated in a dating relationship. Why the difference? Because when a couple is just dating, there is still substantial competition.

If the incentives are all wrong, how does a marriage work? It can still be successful if the spouses behave as if there is competition. To generalize, if a bad institution has "good" people, it can still function well. But if a bad institution has "bad" people, its deficiency will be revealed. The same is true of government schooling, particularly in the inner cities. With the decline of the family and the increase in crime amd illegitimacy, the bad institution (socialistic and monopolistic schools) is revealed. Since there is not as much socioeconomic upheaval in the suburbs, the institution still works fairly well there (although at higher costs than necessary).

Furthermore, anecdotal evidence will never solve this debate. Well into the future, there will be many people who are perfectly satisfied with their government schools. On the basis of their experience, they will be unable to understand why systematic reform is necessary. It is only when the debate moves to discussing institutions that the need for dramatic change becomes evident.

Standard "Reform"

Reform efforts usually have the following characteristics in common: They originate with the educational establishment, involve greater expenditures, and provide no structural change. With rare exceptions, they are also failures. Why? Trying to improve an inherently flawed system is a recipe for futility. Why do we continue to try this general approach? There are three possibilities: ignorance, deceit, and paternalism.

There are some who earnestly believe the latest reform will improve the situation. However, they fail to understand the importance of economic institutions and their effect on human behavior. Although it is conceivable these "reforms" might help somewhat, it is unlikely that a socialistic and monopolistic system will ever provide optimal results.

Certainly there are others who know the proposed reforms are a smoke screen to avoid true reform. The issue here is the pursuit of greater funding and maintaining the largest possible degree of monopoly power. When special interests pursue the supposed reforms, the idea is to keep the public thinking they are trying to improve the system. When the attempts fail, they point to racial issues, the breakdown of the family, the need for more funding, or the latest educational reform proposal. As before, consumers bearing relatively small and diffuse costs are rationally ignorant and prone to being convinced by "good stories." As such, they will always lose out to a politically organized group protecting large benefits.

Some people believe that others, especially the poor, are not particularly capable of making decisions for themselves. Such paternalism stems from an elitist mind-set. But even if it is true that some are less capable than others, it does not necessarily follow that their decisions should be made by others. First, presumably we put a positive value on freedom in and of itself. Second, it is unlikely that the paternalist knows more about what is best for the person. This is especially true when the decision-making body becomes less and less localized. And even if the paternalist does know more, another option would be to merely educate people about the better choices rather than making the decision for them. Third, it is unlikely that the paternalist cares more about the other person's best interests than his own. Fourth, such paternalism may further deteriorate an already-limited ability to make competent decisions. Finally, the concern about consumers being uninformed is over-rated, since there is far from full information in other markets as well. (What does the average person truly *know* about cars, TVs, computers, and many other products?) Given any level of concern and effort, consumers can pay attention to the behavior of others and make relatively informed decisions about a variety of products, including education.

True Reform

If a socialistic and monopolistic system is the problem, true reform is easy to identify: a move toward the economic markets of capitalism and a fostering of competition in the market for education. The advantages would be the same as in any other free market: Consumers get higher quality, greater choice, and greater responsiveness to their desires—all at lower costs. In addition, schools would have greater incentives to find innovative teaching techniques, especially for promoting vocational training and dealing with "difficult" students. Teachers would not have to deal with the long delays and immense paperwork of an overblown bureaucracy. The losers would be the educational establishment, those who currently benefit from the status quo.

A number of cities are currently experimenting with privatization or "educational choice" programs. "Public" schools are operated by private-sector firms in Baltimore, Hartford, Dade County (Florida), Minneapolis, and Massachusetts.[17] This results in more efficiency, if not an improvement in quality. In addition, many state and local governments allow choice between various government-run schools. At times, the results have been impressive. For example, East Harlem's District 4 split into 44 different schools, allowing parents a choice. The result was an increase in its reading scores from last to the middle of the pack in New York City.

Privatization of public schools retains the monopoly but moves it to the private sector; educational choice eliminates the monopoly but retains the socialism.[18] Privatization or choice would be an improvement, but allowing the private sector to compete freely would be even better. (Unregulated private monopolies are little better than public monopolies; educational choice under such a system would be akin to choices involving use of the U.S. Postal Service—the government operates it, but at least you can choose whichever branch you prefer.) Vouchers are the vehicle for leveling the subsidies between private and government schools; they are the best way to ensure that poor children receive a quality education.[19]

Milwaukee has the most famous educational voucher program. In 1991, Polly Williams—a former welfare mother of four, the Wisconsin campaign manager for Jesse Jackson's two presidential campaigns, and a current state legislator—spearheaded the movement, representing the inner-city poor in Milwaukee. To do so, she had to fight tough legal opposition from bureaucrats and the state teachers' union, which did not want to face greater competition. The arrangement allows low-income parents to use $2,700 in vouchers at the private school of their choice. Although it is too early to determine academic results, the parents are pleased. Further, the voucher program saves taxpayers $3,300 per student (since the Milwaukee public schools spend $6,000 per student).[20]

True educational reform has appeared in a variety of places, but mostly in cities. It is in the cities that the costs of the current system are most evident. Thus, reform is easier to sell. For example, in 1993, Bret Schundler, a white Republican, was elected mayor in the predominantly Democratic and minority city of Jersey City, New Jersey. One of his primary issues was a school-voucher proposal.

In statewide reform attempts, the costs of the current system are not as obvious. Attracting a large enough proportion of the population to win is more difficult. In 1993, California defeated a voucher proposal by more than a 2 to 1 margin. It was difficult to convince people in the suburbs—where government schools are still adequate—to take a chance on significant reform. In addition, the state teachers' unions spent over $16 million to defeat the referendum.[21] However, although less likely, reform at the state level is still possible. Michigan is considering educational vouchers in the face of higher taxes and complaints about poor-quality education. And in September 1993, Puerto Rico established a voucher program for students whose family's income is less than $18,000 per year.

Other attempts at institutional reform have been more creative. In Indianapolis, the Golden Rule Insurance Company established the first of many privately funded voucher programs for poor children.[22] Although these programs are more difficult to maintain because they require voluntary contributions, private vouchers have an important advantage: They cannot be challenged in the court system, since the money is donated. The teachers' union and government school bureaucrats complain about this *charity* to poor parents and students— because it subsequently reduces their funding. Every time Golden Rule empowers a parent to send her child to a private school with a voucher of $800, the government school system's enrollment drops by one and its funding (and the burden on taxpayers) drops by $5,000.

Finally, the poor and minorities overwhelmingly support choice and educational vouchers. Why should taxpayers spend additional thousands of dollars per student to stand in their way, especially regarding a decision that concerns poor parents more than the average bureaucrat? Why should we condemn them to pathetic schools and a life of low productivity and income? Why should we allow relatively wealthy people to have choice about where they send their children to school but allow the poor to attend only government-run fiascos? Why is government in the business of running schools instead of merely providing the poor with the ability to attend the school of their choice? The solution is to subsidize schooling (at least for the poor), not schools.[23]

What Stands in the Way of True Reform?

Once again, we have an example of principles of public choice economics at work. The government-sponsored monopoly redistributes income to the educational establishment (whose incomes are well above the national average) at the expense of taxpayers and consumers (parents and students).[24] Given that choice in education is mostly determined by income level, the poor are left with the fewest and least desirable choices. They are the most restricted and end up with the least competitive outcome and the worst schools. The social problems troubling inner cities add to the educational disaster.

In the cities, there is clearly hope for systemic reform. Because the costs have become so obvious, because inner-city parents have become so desperate, because embracing competition and market solutions is fairly intuitive, we can expect to see the current movement toward vouchers and choice extended in the future.

In addition, true reform receives bipartisan support. As noted before, Polly Williams is a liberal Democrat; both the liberal Brookings Institution and the conservative Heritage Foundation support voucher reform; and minorities and the poor support it overwhelmingly. The problem is that choice and especially vouchers would be a disaster for the educational establishment. Like the apparatchiks in Russia, incumbents will likely fight both of them tooth and nail. This is not a Republican versus Democrat issue; this is an issue of general versus special interests.

Given that the poor want this reform so badly, turning down their request amounts to ignorance, rampant paternalism, or an attempt to protect the status quo. Public school teachers and especially politicians send their kids to private schools at a very high rate. But in the words of Polly Williams, they "just don't want choice for poor people."

Some Final Concerns

There are those who are concerned that if private schools spend public money foolishly, taxpayers will have no one to complain to. This notion can be addressed simply by noting the greater accountability required from private schools through the market system and the lack of incentives in government schools. If inner-city *public* schools are inadequate, to whom can taxpayers complain?

Others are worried that vouchers will amount to state support of private religious schools—the mixture of church and state. But the GI Bill did the same thing for colleges without complaint. In addition, students spend government grant and loan money at church-supported universities with regularity. Hospitals run by churches also receive government funds. If we are consistent in our thinking, this is not a significant complaint.[25]

The most frequent argument is that government schools will become a "dumping ground" for poor students. This concern is misplaced for a number of reasons. First, inner-city government schools are *currently* a dumping ground for the poor. Those who can afford private school tuition have a choice and often exercise it by leaving the government school system. Second, it misses the goal of education—not to reach an absolute goal but to improve the skills a student brings to the classroom. The private sector is better equipped to help students of any type. Third, the education of over 100,000 handicapped and special education students is already contracted out to the private sector.[26] Such students require larger vouchers to cover greater costs, but the market is well able to deal with the challenges involved in their education. Fourth, this concern reveals the inferior quality of government-provided education. If public schools would collapse from injecting a little competition, they must be inefficient and inept. Finally and most important, concern about dumping grounds shows a complete lack of understanding about how markets function. If a set of parents approach an educational entrepreneur with $2,500 vouchers in hand, that person will figure out a cost-effective way to teach their children even if the students are "difficult."[27]

Some argue there will be greater inequality. But can it be any worse than the differences between inner-city and middle-class schools today? Polly Williams claims that in Milwaukee, only 40% of entering high-schoolers graduate and only 10% can read. (And 62% of its public school teachers send their kids to private schools.)[28]

Some argue that segregation will worsen. But again, to a greater degree than today? In Washington, D.C., government schools are 98% minority. In Houston and Dallas, the proportion is greater than 90%. Nationwide, one in three black and Hispanic students attends a school with more than a 90% minority enrollment.[29] Besides, what is the goal? Polly Williams argues that people in the inner city "want education and then integration will follow."

An enjoyable aspect about debating this issue is that the opposition has no ground to stand on. There are no significant reasons to avoid this reform except that a special interest group will be made worse off. The benefits are potentially enormous on a national and an individual level: The country would become much more productive and a whole set of people would be empowered to earn a decent education, build skills for life and the job market, and lead more prosperous lives. The only losses would be borne by some members of the special interest group with monopoly power—the public school establishment.

Anecdotal evidence is not sufficient. This argument comes down to economic institutions. Do you believe socialism and political markets are more equitable or more efficient than capitalism and economic markets? Do you think we should pursue monopolies at the expense of competition? Can we ignore the poor and minorities who desperately want this reform—a reform that would also save so much money? Finally, can educational vouchers be any worse than the current system for the inner cities?

Notes

1. Despite its importance, this issue appears later in the book because it begins to take us away from public choice issues to other policies that hurt the poor.

2. One of the staggering observations to emerge from M. Bernick's *Urban Illusions: New Approaches to Inner-City Unemployment* (New York: Praeger, 1987) concerns the level of skills he encounters in trying to train young people in the

inner city. He found that 20% of his clients could not read, most had numerous spelling and grammatical errors in samples of writing, and fewer than half could pass competency exams that reflected ninth-grade reading and math skills. Bernick cites high dropout rates but then notes that the dropouts were *more* proficient than those who graduated.

3. U.S. Bureau of the Census, *Statistical Abstract of the United States* (Washington, DC: U.S. Department of the Treasury, 1994), Table 734.

4. *World*, May 20, 1995, p. 14, citing a study by the Heritage Foundation; "Education Reform Breakout," *Wall Street Journal*, December 17, 1993; J. Norquist, "A Ticket to Better Schools," *Reader's Digest*, July 1993, p. 69; *Imprimis*, March 1992.

5. U.S. Department of Education, *Digest of Education Statistics* (Washington, DC: Department of Education, 1994), Table 165.

6. G. Will, "Quality and Proximity," *Louisville Courier-Journal*, September 12, 1993.

7. P. Brimelow, "American Perestroika?" *Forbes*, May 14, 1990.

8. In "The Educational Octopus" (*Freeman*, February 1995, p. 128), M. Perry reports this statistic and notes that no member of the board of education or city-wide elected official has had children in the New York City public schools since 1988. See also *Imprimis*, March 1992; and "Education Reform Breakout," *Wall Street Journal*, December 17, 1993. The latter article quotes National Education Association president Keith Geiger saying that "about 40% . . . of urban-area public school teachers with school-age children send their children to private schools."

9. President Clinton, Ted Kennedy, and Jesse Jackson are just a few famous opponents of educational vouchers who have chosen private schools for their children. In the U.S. House of Representatives, 70% of the Hispanic caucus and 30% of the black caucus send their children to private schools while mostly opposing educational vouchers. Nationally, 6% of Hispanics and 4% of blacks send their children to private schools (*World*, May 20, 1995, p. 14, citing a study by the Heritage Foundation).

10. M. Perry, "The Educational Octopus," *Freeman*, February 1995, p. 127.

11. U.S. Department of Education, *Digest of Education Statistics 1994*. For public school costs, see Table 61; for private school tuitions, see Table 165.

12. There is a great example of this in Great Britain's plans to compensate its dentists. For a while, the British National Health Service paid dentists on the basis of the number of cavities filled. Not surprisingly, the amount of tooth decay "found" by dentists increased dramatically and the time to fill the average cavity fell from 18 to 6 minutes. (R. Ehrenberg and R. Smith, *Modern Labor Economics*, 4th ed. [New York: Harper-Collins, 1991], p. 418.)

13. Brimelow, "American Perestroika?"

14. T. DiLorenzo, "America's OPEC: The Public School Cartel," *Freeman*, July 1991, pp. 244–247.

15. J. Gwartney, "A Positive Proposal to Improve our Schools," *CATO Journal*, Spring/Summer 1990, p. 166.

16. Clearly, divorce allows greater competition. But it is still costly for many reasons and thus is not as competitive as the pre-marriage state.

17. In 1993–1994 in Washington, D.C., School Superintendent Franklin Smith wanted to give control of 15 struggling government schools to a private firm, but his idea was rejected by the school board. In fall 1995, the school board adopted Smith's plan for 11 schools.

18. "Charter schools," another commonly discussed reform, can fit into either category. In other attempts at reform, parents in Chicago and Los Angeles, with the help of the Institute for Justice (in Washington, D.C.) have brought lawsuits against their government school systems for "educational malpractice." The litigation has not been decided but is another potential vehicle for pursuing systemic reform.

19. Vouchers can also be designed to cover transportation costs to the school. Educational vouchers were proposed by Milton Friedman over 30 years ago. (Friedman also coined the phrase "government schools.")

20. See "Education Reform Breakout" and Norquist, "A Ticket to Better Schools."

21. *Reason*, February 1994, p. 8.

22. CEO America in Bentonville, Arkansas, has organized private voucher programs in a number of other cities, including Albany, Atlanta, Austin, Buffalo, Dallas, Denver, Detroit, Houston, Knoxville, Little Rock, Los Angeles, Milwaukee, Oakland, Orlando, Phoenix, San Antonio, and Washington, D.C.

23. To implement this program, one could give equal vouchers to all parents. Alternatively, the poor could receive "full" vouchers while those with higher incomes received smaller vouchers.

24. In 1992, the average salary of elementary and secondary teachers was $34,100 (*U.S. Bureau of the Census, Statistical Abstract of the United States* [Washington, DC: U.S. Department of the Treasury, 1993], p. 161, Table 245). Of course, administrators and union leaders have considerably higher salaries.

25. There are those who are concerned that government regulation of private schools will follow government dollars. Although this is potentially problematic, it is a separate issue that can be handled.

26. "Special Choices," *Wall Street Journal*, December 30, 1993.

27. With pre-fabricated buildings and trailers, a school could be "built" very quickly. In addition, existing buildings could easily be used to educate children.

28. *Imprimis*, March 1992.

29. *U.S. News and World Report*, December 12, 1993, p. 12.

10

Prohibition II: The Sequel

Kurt Vonnegut has a character in *Hocus Pocus* who never swears. People in the story think it is because he is a religious man, but in fact, he is an avid atheist. When his grandson is old enough to understand the irony, he asks his grandfather why he never swears. The wise old man replies that he doesn't want to give people an excuse not to listen to what he has to say.

To some, the words "drug legalization" (or "revoke the minimum wage") are akin to swearing. But given the effects of prohibition, particularly the devastation of the inner-city poor as a result of current drug policy, it is imperative to analyze all the benefits and costs of our policy alternatives. Throughout, I will be careful to avoid a "false-cause fallacy"—the confusion between the negative things caused by drugs and those caused by drug prohibition.

Drug Prohibition and Violent Crime

Probably the biggest problem with prohibition of drugs is that it dramatically increases violent crime. Drug *laws* are directly responsible because they create extremely high profits. As a result, gangs engage in turf wars to protect and enlarge their share of this highly profitable market.

This situation is directly analogous to the warfare among those in organized crime during the prohibition on alcohol in the 1920s and early 1930s. It is disappointing to see so few people make the connection between Prohibition II and the extent and violence of today's gangs. Under legalization, extra-normal profits would disappear and subsequent crime would diminish greatly. How much violence is there today surrounding the sale and purchase of alcohol and tobacco?

Similarly, when Prohibition I ended in 1933, the resulting urban warfare and crime wave dissipated as well. With the repeal of Prohibition I, the murder rate declined for 11 consecutive years, falling by more than one-third. The rate of assaults with firearms declined for 10 consecutive years, falling by more than 40%.[1]

Violence is also more likely in this context because dealers do not have a non-violent way to settle disputes; the judicial system is not available to mediate. Currently, the only way to resolve differences is by the point of a knife or gun. As mayor of Baltimore Kurt Schmoke notes: "Drug dealers fear other dealers more than cops."[2] The perpetrators of violence may also consider it to be an acceptable way to limit competition in this arena. Here, people use guns while others use the coercive powers of the state to restrict their competition.

The end result is a much more dangerous environment for those in the inner city. Innocent children die in cross fires and from stray bullets. Some people sleep in their bathtubs because it is the safest place to spend the night. As noted earlier, doing business is more expensive in the inner city; this violence contributes to those costs. In sum, the crime and violence that stem from Prohibition II make the inner city a much less pleasant place to live. David Boaz notes with some irony, ". . . and some people still say that ending drug prohibition would be a dangerous social experiment!"[3]

The costs of prohibition of drugs are difficult for middle-class America to see. The victims of crime are disproportionately inner-city blacks. This is a class issue and thus a race issue, driven to a large extent by Prohibition II. Kurt Schmoke has commented that "it is very easy for people living in communities where drugs are not a problem to argue that drug-related violence cannot justify decriminalization. But if you have to live with that violence day in and day out. . . "[4] For Mayor Schmoke and those in the inner city, the costs are large and easy to see.

The key here is that drugs per se do not cause this problem; drug prohibition is responsible. With respect to ending Prohibition I, Ethan Nadelmann says that the "repeal of Prohibition came to be seen not as a capitulation to Al Capone and his ilk but as a means of putting both the bootleggers out of business and eliminating most of the costs associated with the Prohibition laws. . . . As was the case during Prohibition, the principal beneficiary of current drug policies is organized crime" (gangs).[5]

Trying to Stop Supply and Demand

There are immense problems in trying to prevent suppliers from providing drugs. Obviously, the financial rewards are a terrific lure, and even when people are caught, there is only minor disruption to the market (local and international). James Ostrowski notes that "creating a vacancy in the lucrative drug business has the same effect as hanging up a help-wanted sign saying 'drug dealer needed, $5000/wk. to start, exciting work.'"[6]

The biggest problem with implementing a "war on drugs" is that the sale and purchase of drugs are mutually beneficial—both parties perceive that they benefit. Most crimes involve one party harming another. In those cases, there is always an incentive for someone to provide evidence against the party causing harm. In drug transactions and other "crimes" of this sort (prostitution, gambling, and so on.), both parties believe they benefit. Why would they want to talk to the police? For this reason, drug laws are especially difficult to enforce.

In addition, high profits lead to corruption. Bribes are mutually beneficial as well. And they are especially tempting for those in the criminal justice system whose incomes are not especially high. Evidence of this is seen in the rampant drug use of our prison population and the occasional "bust" of police officers themselves. If drug use can't be stopped in prison, how can law enforcement stop drugs in the community? Moreover, because the illegal drug market is tax-free in both product and labor markets, it is mutually beneficial to remain outside the law, in black markets. Finally, even if the government is successful in reducing supply, it makes all of these problems worse.

Other Effects on Low-Income Inner-City Youth

As we have seen, Prohibition II causes high profits and wages. These opportunities are a great temptation to young unskilled laborers, especially given the low-quality education they often receive from the public schools. What are the available options? Welfare? Flipping burgers? Working like a dog, struggling to make a living? Or the excitement, responsibility, and big income of dealing drugs? Too often, our government's education and drug policies amount to providing kids with a ninth-grade education, luring them with high-paying drug jobs, catching them, and throwing them into prison.

Another perversity of our judicial system makes this even more likely. In the 1960s, there was a movement to give children a fresh start when they became adults—to erase or hide their juvenile criminal records. Although this policy may have some benefits, it also encourages teenagers to become involved in illegal activities and provides an incentive for older dealers to recruit younger kids who are less likely to be prosecuted.

In addition, the opportunity to earn a large income undermines traditional role models—parents, teachers, and other respectable members of the community. Which will kids want to be when they grow up—their mother or father, who works 60 hours a week to put bread on the table, or Joe Cool who drives a sports car and gives away money? Families in the inner city have enough trouble with the high proportion of one-parent heads of household. With prohibition and the incomes that accompany illegal activity, the job of inner-city parents becomes even more difficult.

Prohibition: Moral High Ground, Convenience, or an Appeasement of Guilt?

For years, I have discussed this issue with my friends. Occasionally, they argue that I shouldn't advocate legalization until I visit crack babies in a hospital and go to a drug rehabilitation center to see someone struggling with a heroin addiction. I respond that they shouldn't advocate prohibition until they visit the spouse of a cop who has died in the drug war or the mother of a three-year-old killed in the cross fire of a gang turf war. The moral high ground is not so easy to find. There are costs either way. Which ones should we choose?

The difference between morality and legality seems to be a stumbling block for many. Whereas they are related, they are not equivalent; there are illegal acts that are not immoral and vice versa. Eventually going through a stoplight that is stuck is not immoral, although it is illegal. Many would say that adultery and inappropriate anger are immoral, but we do not have laws against those things. Slavery has been legal and illegal in this country, but presumably its immorality has remained constant. Not wanting something to be illegal does not necessarily imply that people condone the behavior.

Further, how prohibition should work is not the issue. How prohibition works practically is the concern here. Ethan Nadelmann says that "ultimately the moral quality of laws must be judged not by how those laws are intended to work in principle but by how they function in practice. When laws intended to serve a moral end inflict great damage on innocent parties, we must rethink our moral positions."[7]

One could argue that Prohibition II benefits the middle class at the expense of those in the inner city. Drug dealing is primarily done by those who would otherwise be poor. Middle-class America is primarily concerned with limiting supply to its children instead of working with its own kids one-on-one to prevent demand. The easiest way to accomplish this is to punish drug dealers. Charles Murray admits, "Keeping drugs illegal makes it easier for me to keep my children off drugs. On the drug issue, I'm a Libertarian who has been willing to sell out."[8] For the middle class, prohibition may be, on net, a good deal. For the inner-city poor, it is a raw deal.

To a large extent, current drug laws may serve to appease guilt and provide a way to look good politically. Thomas Sowell has remarked that "policies are judged by their consequences, but crusades are judged by how good they make the crusaders feel."[9] On Prohibition I, Hodding Carter notes wryly that "drinkers had their liquor, preachers had their prohibition, sheriffs made their money."[10] With respect to our politicians, Lewis Lapham wrote that "the war on drugs thus becomes the perfect war ... a war in which the politicians who stand so fearlessly on the side of the good, the true and the beautiful need do nothing else but strike noble poses as protectors of the people and defenders of the public trust."[11]

But regardless of the intents and motivations, who is made better or worse off with Prohibition II? Organized crime and gangs that deal drugs clearly benefit. Also, those prevented by the law from taking drugs benefit in some sense. In contrast, those who continue to use drugs are made worse off through drug impurities, a greater threat from AIDS, criminal penalties, and higher prices.[12] And unfortunately, a number of innocents are victims as well.

Again, we are implicitly more concerned with intended beneficiaries of policy rather than unintended and innocent victims; we see the benefits but ignore or fail to see the costs. For this reason, Ostrowski argues that "the war on drugs is immoral as well as impractical. It imposes enormous costs, including the ultimate cost of death, on large numbers of non-drug-abusing citizens in a failed attempt to save a relatively small group of hard-core drug abusers from themselves. It is immoral and absurd to *force* some people to bear costs so that others may be prevented from *choosing* to do harm to themselves" (italics added).[13]

Policy Choices in the War on Drugs

There are three basic choices: pursuing the status quo, escalating the "war," or legalizing drugs. With the status quo, we get more of the same, which will obviously not solve the problem. Thus, the other two possibilities are more interesting. Criticism of the War on Drugs sometimes parallels the criticisms of our efforts during the war in Vietnam. As then, hawks count "bodies" (drugs confiscated, people arrested) and advocate escalation while doves encourage a different approach and are labeled as cowards.

(1) Escalation

Years ago, former mayor of New York Ed Koch prescribed that all people entering the United States from Southeast Asia and South America be strip-searched. Others have called for bringing the National Guard to Washington, D.C., to stop the flow of drugs and the violence associated with the drug trade. Some have advocated death penalties for drug deal-ers.[14] Proposals to escalate the war on drugs vary widely, but all have this in common: They point fingers at the area farthest from themselves.

In part, this is an attempt to avoid responsibility. But mostly, from their area of expertise, they have learned it is not possible to stop the drug trade where they are. Koch focuses on supply because he knows demand cannot be stopped. World leaders focus on demand because they know they cannot stop supply. Each is half right and half wrong. Neither demand nor supply will be stopped with current policy.

What about more aggressive deterrence? Charles Murray looks at the numbers to explore the possibilities.[15] In 1988, there were 28 million drug users, 839,000 arrests of users (for a less than 3% arrest rate), and 317,000 arrests of dealers. Murray asks how many we would need to incarcerate to provide adequate deterrence. Moving the arrest rate up to 10% (of drug users) would amount to 2 million more arrests. But our national prison population already exceeds 1 million and is considered overcrowded. We already imprison more per capita than all countries except Russia. (We exceeded South Africa's per capita rate in the past few years.) Murray's "thought experiment" shows us that a strategy of escala-tion against demand is not practical.[16]

(2) Legalization

Many Americans perceive that drug legalization will cause a large increase in the number of drug addicts. Perhaps, but this seems un-likely.[17] How many people are currently prevented from taking illegal drugs? Others are concerned about more people driving under the influ-ence of drugs. However, the problem here is not drugs per se but driving while unable to perform and causing harm. Such behavior should be rig-orously punished.

What would legalization look like? Many proponents would model it after current policy concerning the sale of alcohol and tobacco. There would be warning labels, prohibition of sale to minors, and restricted advertising. And one would hope we could learn from the past and avoid the equivalent of the alcohol and tobacco lobbies.[18]

What would happen? We would get the opposite of what occurs under prohibition. Prices would fall dramatically and quantity would rise some (depending on the number of people being stopped from using drugs now). The crime and corruption related to drug prohibition would dis-appear along with the extra-normal profits. With selling and taking drugs no longer considered crimes, money and law enforcement resources devoted to stopping drugs would be diverted to stop other types of crime. Government would no longer spend $12 billion per year (nearly

$200 for the average family of four) to fight a failed war. Scarce prison space would no longer be a problem; we would not have to make decisions any longer about which criminals to release because our prisons are overcrowded. In sum, our streets, especially those of the inner city, would be considerably safer and less expensive to police.[19]

A Difficult Issue

Ironically, Prohibition I's origins were not based on concerns about morality. The Harrison Act of 1914 was designed to allow pharmacists and physicians monopoly power in prescribing medication. What began as using government to restrict competition quickly evolved into a total restriction on the purchase and sale of currently illegal drugs.

I understand this is an extremely difficult issue. As an Evangelical Christian, I often receive incredulous looks whenever I say ending prohibition is the third most important issue facing the poor (behind education and welfare).[20] Prohibition might be best for middle-class America, but the costs to the inner-city poor are tremendous: gangs and gang violence, a seductive enticement for low-skilled inner-city young people, and the creation of improper role models. The suburbs may benefit, but the inner cities suffer greatly.

From Mayor Schmoke again: "It takes great maturity and willpower for a society to step back from a policy that on the surface seems noble and justified, but in reality has only compounded the problem it is attempting to solve."[21] Randy Barnett draws a humorous analogy to another type of addiction: "Each year Americans spend more and more to maintain a self-destructive habit. . . . The addiction is not to drugs. It is to drug laws."[22] Current policies have failed and will continue to fail. The costs of effective deterrence are probably too high. Support for ending Prohibition II will most likely continue to grow as the costs of current policy or escalating the war become more visible.

Legalization would be a solution only to drug-related problems, not to drug abuse itself. Again, from Nadelmann: "It is important to stress what legalization is not. It is not a capitulation to the drug dealers—but rather a means to put them out of business. It is not an endorsement of drug use—but rather a recognition of the rights of adult Americans to make their own choices free of the fear of criminal sanctions."[23] In the absence of a "war on tobacco," its use has decreased from 42% to 20% over the period 1956–1981.[24] Practically speaking, our best route to reduce drug use may be to treat drugs as a health problem rather than a crime problem. From the perspective of the poor, there can be no other choice. The costs of prohibition to those in the inner city are prohibitively high.

Notes

1. J. Ostrowski, "Thinking About Drug Legalization," CATO Policy Analysis no. 121, p. 1 (reprinted in *The Crisis in Drug Prohibition*, ed. D. Boaz [Washington, DC: Cato Institute, 1990], pp. 45–76).

2. K. Schmoke, "Drugs: A Problem of Health and Economics," in Boaz, *The Crisis in Drug Prohibition*, p. 10.

3. D. Boaz, "The Consequences of Prohibition," in Boaz, *The Crisis in Drug Prohibition*, p. 1.

4. Schmoke, "Drugs: A Problem of Health and Economics," p. 11.

5. E. Nadelmann, "The Case for Legalization," in Boaz, *The Crisis in Drug Prohibition*, p. 24. Government should also pursue some combination of greater law enforcement, less liberalized judicial decisions, and greater punishment. This would make crime "more expensive" and thus, less frequent.

6. Boaz, "The Consequences of Prohibition," p. 6.

7. Nadelmann, "The Case for Legalization," p. 34.

8. C. Murray, "How to Win the War on Drugs," in Boaz, *The Crisis in Drug Prohibition*, p. 78.

9. T. Sowell, *Compassion Versus Guilt and Other Essays* (New York: Morrow, 1987), p. 74.

10. H. Carter, "We're Losing the Drug War Because Prohibition Never Works," in Boaz, *The Crisis in Drug Prohibition*, p. 103.

11. L. Lapham, "A Political Opiate," in Boaz, *The Crisis in Drug Prohibition*, p. 126.

12. (1) Illegal drugs vary in their potency and purity. In a normally functioning market, people would have a much better idea of what they were buying. Most overdose deaths can be attributed to variance in drug quality and prohibition; (2) Prohibition II is somewhat responsible for spreading AIDS. Because needles are frequently illegal, addicts share them, which contributes to transmitting the AIDS virus. In 1986, 18% of AIDS cases were drug users. Given 50,000 deaths from AIDS in 1991, as many as 9,000 people may have died as an indirect result of Prohibition II (Ostrowski, "Thinking About Drug Legalization," p. 56); (3) Prohibition II keeps addicts or those who overdose from seeking health care. Len Bias, the number-one draft choice for the Boston Celtics a few years ago, died after repeated seizures from a drug overdose. If his friends had not had to worry about criminal sanction, they probably would have sought medical attention immediately.

13. Nadelmann, "The Case for Legalization," p. 40.

14. Boaz, "The Consequences of Prohibition," p. 5.

15. Murray, "How to Win the War on Drugs," pp. 79–82.

16. Also, one can imagine the consequences of a "war on tobacco" or a "war on alcohol."

17. The experience with decriminalization of marijuana in the 1970s in Alaska and the Netherlands did not result in dramatically increased drug use. (See C. Thies and C. Register, "The Criminalization of Marijuana and the Demand for Alcohol, Marijuana, and Cocaine," *Social Science Journal*, October 1993, pp. 385–399.) Although prohibition certainly prevents some people from ever start-

ing, it also creates a forbidden-fruit aspect that may encourage others to try drugs. Further, the immense profitability of the drug trade is a great enticement for dealers to get children to try drugs at an early age. In addition, note that Germany, Italy, and Colombia legalized marijuana and hashish in 1994. Britain has recently decriminalized drug use (de facto) by only issuing "cautions" to offenders (*USA Today,* May 12, 1994).

18. A comparison to our treatment of alcohol and tobacco use is instructive. For the most part, currently illegal drugs are not as addictive, dangerous, or deadly as alcohol and tobacco. First, war proponents have always *talked* about drugs causing violent behavior (first marijuana, then heroin, and now cocaine). Second, taking illegal drugs resulted in 3,562 deaths in 1985 (curiously, appendicitis killed more people than cocaine) compared to 300,000 from tobacco and 200,000 from alcohol abuse (Nadelmann, "The Case for Legalization," p. 36). In a perverse application of Hazlitt's lesson, people seem to see only the acute (short run) deaths from illegal drug use while they are seemingly blind to the chronic (long run) deaths from legal drug use. The only consistent positions on this issue are to make everything legal or illegal.

19. Proponents of drug legalization include former secretary of state George Shultz, a number of prominent economists including Milton Friedman and Thomas Sowell, and numerous federal judges. Many judges are advocates of legalization; for them, the costs of prohibition are easy to see. The outgoing Drug Enforcement Agency head, Richard Bonner, has said that the current drug war is not winnable. Former surgeon general Joycelyn Elders became infamous for merely saying we should "take a look at legalization." Although currently only a fringe support legalization, as the war drags on and continues to be ineffective, ending Prohibition II will become more and more attractive.

20. For Christians who are bothered by my stance, (1) the use of government to restrict the behavior of non-Christians is not mentioned or sanctioned in the New Testament, and (2) prohibition is not "Christ-like." Can you imagine Christ lobbying Congress to have certain drugs made illegal?

21. Schmoke, "Drugs: A Problem of Health and Economics," p. 12.

22. R. Barnett, "We Need a Legalization 'Fix,'" in Boaz, *The Crisis in Drug Prohibition,* pp. 95–96.

23. Nadelmann, "The Case for Legalization," p. 42.

24. A. Trebach, "Peace Without Surrender in the Perpetual Drug War," *Justice Quarterly,* 1984, p. 136.

11

Where They Live and Breathe: Government Policy in the Markets for Housing and Health

Part 2 concludes with a discussion of government intervention in the markets for housing and health. Government has pursued a variety of policies in housing markets to try to help the poor. Unfortunately, the best of intentions have been sidetracked by reality—how economic and political markets function. In the market for health services, government has inadvertently chosen policies that hurt the poor as well. As before, we will see how the poor have been harmed by a combination of well-intentioned but misguided policies and by the pursuit of self-interests in political markets.

Government in the Market for Housing

Rent Control

Rent controls are a price ceiling (maximum) on housing rent. The benefits of this policy are easy to see—tenants have lower rent payments—and thus are politically popular. In the short run, this amounts to a transfer of income from landlords to tenants and supposedly, an outcome with "economic justice." Unfortunately, the analysis of rent control usually ends prematurely; there are other significant costs to consider.

The main problem with price controls of any sort is that they cause shortages or surpluses. The rental housing market is no different; rent controls cause shortages of rental housing. To the extent that rent control affects only lower-quality rental housing, it specifically causes a shortage of the housing that lower-income people try to rent. Owners are likely to convert affected rental properties to other types of housing, and additional people are attracted to the rental market by below-market prices.[1] In 1984, every city with rent control had a vacancy rate of less than 3%; in every city without rent control (except Worchester, Massachusetts), the vacancy rate exceeded 4%.[2]

Since prices are not allowed to function properly, a variety of troubling "non-price" rationing mechanisms allocate the available rental units. First, the lack of available rental housing causes people to consider other housing markets, including "homelessness." As with most markets in centrally planned (socialist) economies, people in this centrally planned market wait in line to obtain rental housing.[3] Second, discrimination becomes costless in this context. If I turn down prospective renters because I do not like their "group," I can easily choose someone from the group standing in line. (Remember that discrimination is independent of concerns about productivity—in this context, how people will treat the rental property, ability to pay, and so on.)

Third, over time, quality will deteriorate. With a $400 apartment under a rent control of $300, imagine that a window breaks, lowering its value to $380. What incentive does the landlord have to repair the window? With the price ceiling in place, it is not in the owner's interest to fix anything until the market value falls below $300. Further, what incentive do renters have to leave this situation? None. They are still getting a good deal, and their only other option is to stand in line with those experiencing the shortage.

This decline in quality will occur gradually over time—largely from a reduction in maintenance and repair. Thus, rent control partially explains why urban housing has become so dilapidated. As the socialist economist Assar Lindbeck once said, "Next to bombing, rent control seems to be the most effective technique so far known for destroying cities."[4] The beauty of this policy from a politician's standpoint is that the costs are difficult to see and occur long after the law was passed. Because of this, people rarely understand the cause and effect behind rent controls.[5]

Urban Renewal

In the 1950s and 1960s, government undertook a policy called "urban renewal," which involved tearing down "substandard" housing and replacing it with better housing. In theory, the program would allow people who had lived in relative squalor to have a decent house. Unfortunately, public housing has not always been particularly pleasant. As before, results have deviated significantly from the intent of the policies.

When better housing was built, lower-income people were frequently priced out of the market. Like the minimum wage, the policy failed to address the key problem—incomes too low to afford better housing. The effect resembles that of mandatory occupational licensing in that poor consumers were forced to consume "adequate" housing or none at all—the "Cadillac effect" revisited. The policy often forced poor families to pay more for housing or merely displaced them from their homes. The good news was that better housing was built; the bad news was that the poor could no longer afford it.

This failed policy resulted largely in redistribution to the non-poor. Sometimes the non-poor lived in the housing that was built or subsidized. And as always, they benefited along with the people who were paid to plan and implement the program.

Exclusionary Zoning and Other Regulations

Zoning regulations are laws that govern and restrict the use of property. In instituting such laws, policymakers can be motivated by economic, racial, or other concerns.[6] But regardless of their intent, zoning laws restrict competition and are, therefore, always in the best interests of incumbents. For example, prohibiting lot sizes of less than two acres restricts entry into a particular housing market and increases the prices of existing homes in the area.

In addition, all levels of government impose a great variety of regulations and fees on new homes. These artificially increase the price of housing and also serve as a barrier to entry for new homes and homeowners. Even Habitat for Humanity (a charitable group that relies on volunteer labor to build low-cost homes for the needy) has had trouble with regulations. For example, after ten months of negotiations in San Diego, assorted regulations, licenses, and fees still added more than 20% to the cost of the homes it built.[7]

In recent years, environmental regulation has become the newest form of zoning. The effect is the same: The price of housing increases and some people are prevented from obtaining adequate housing. (This is an appropriate time to recall that one need not take a particular policy stance to acknowledge the redistributive element of these policies and the difficulty they cause for new homeowners and the poor.)

Tucker's *The Excluded Americans*

William Tucker argues that two-thirds of "homelessness" (among the non-substance abusers) has been caused by government interventions in the market for housing.[8] Why does he blame government? As we have seen, it has restricted the housing market with exclusionary zoning, torn down low-income housing with urban renewal, and created a shortage of low-income housing in many cities with rent controls. He argues further that one used to be able to move to the suburbs, but housing prices have become prohibitively expensive there unless one relocates far away from the center.

There are other problems as well. In the past, housing policy was fraught with inefficiency and fraud; every presidential administration has had a scandal in its Department of Housing and Urban Development (HUD). With money changing hands so often (among bureaucrats, builders, and landlords—everyone but the poor), it was easy for money to be embezzled. With the Davis-Bacon laws, public housing projects also served to redistribute money to union members. In addition, poor people were crowded into public housing, which often resulted in worse accommodations than what was previously available.

One reform that began to change this was the introduction of housing vouchers ("Section 8 certificates") for the poor in the mid-1980s. Vouchers are given directly to the poor to spend on housing as they choose (like food stamps). This empowers individuals and greatly lessens opportunities for fraud. Proponents of vouchers argue that the only role of government should be to enable individuals to obtain sufficient housing. The alternative is for government to be in the business of building, owning, and operating public housing. (As with education, why should government do that?) During and since their emergence, vouchers have been vociferously opposed by Congress because it would have less control over who gets the money. This reform gives it one less opportunity to transfer money to special interest groups.

It could easily be argued that the poor would be best served if the government would limit its interventions in the housing market to (at most) subsidizing consumption with vouchers. Without a plethora of policies that end up causing shortages or artificially increasing the price of homes, many of the poor would be able to afford better housing and many of the homeless would be able to afford some housing. If government wants to help, it can provide direct financial assistance to the needy and empower those individuals to find "decent housing."[9]

Government in the Market for Health Services

In this arena, the current conventional wisdom is that government can be the solution to the nation's health care problems. In fact, government involvement *is* the problem. To cover this premise in sufficient detail would require an entire book. And since John Goodman and Gerald Musgrave's *Patient Power* does a laudable job already, I will restrict my comments to the more important facets and then focus on the policies that impact the poor in particular.

Since 1965, government has dramatically increased the demand for medical services. As a result, costs have risen as well. First, with the genesis of Medicare (for the elderly) and Medicaid (for the poor), the cost of health services exploded well beyond the government's wildest expectations or projections. For instance, in 1966, the government projected that Medicare would cost $12 billion in 1990 (accounting for inflation); instead the cost was $107 billion.[10]

Second, because health insurance is subsidized through the tax code (as covered in Chapter 8), people are encouraged to obtain more health insurance than they would otherwise—through their employer as a non-taxable fringe benefit. This promotes the use of lower deductibles and co-payments, since the subsequently higher insurance rates can be paid for with *pre-tax* dollars. The alternative is to incur out-of-pocket expenses that are paid for with *after-tax* earnings.[11] Since they artificially decrease the cost to consumers, lower deductibles and co-payments greatly increase demand and also discourage monitoring for fraud and waste. With taxes increasing significantly since the mid-1960s, this trend has been exacerbated. Out-of-pocket spending on health care fell from 61.6% in 1965 to 18.7% in 1990.[12]

In addition to the general problems caused by government's meddling with the effective price of insurance through the tax code, many other government policies in this market harm the poor.

Price Controls in Health Care

Medicaid sets reimbursement rates for most procedures.[13] These "price-fixing schemes" establish prices that are sometimes too low to ensure high-quality care. And since for the most part, patients are not allowed to add money to the government's financial input from Medicaid, they are unable to influence the quality of care they receive. Further, doctors who provide care to Medicaid patients must deal with additional overhead costs and worry about penalties from violating a wide assortment of vague and changing rules. Having to deal with the immense paperwork and fluctuating regulations makes treating Medicaid patients less attractive.

Price-fixing and driving up the costs of providing care to Medicaid patients (through paperwork, regulations, and so on) causes either implicit or explicit non-price rationing of health care for the poor. The symptoms are reductions in quantity and quality and having to wait in line. Currently, more and more "good" doctors refuse to see Medicaid patients. Further, under price restrictions, doctors have an incentive to provide lower quality—to process rather than treat people. With the price held artificially low, where else are the patients going to go?

The solution here is to allow the price mechanism to ration health care, to end the subsidy to the non-poor, and to subsidize the consumption of health services by the poor but allow them to supplement the assistance with their own money. Only then will the poor be empowered to pursue appropriate care; only then will they receive the optimal quality and quantity of health care services.

The Medical Cartels

The American Medical Association (AMA) and the American Dental Association (ADA) are labor market cartels, examples of the labor unions detailed in Chapter 7. With control over the professional schools and state licensing boards, they restrict the number of entrants into each field. The incentives in these cartels, as in others, are to restrict competition and decrease quantity in order to charge higher rates. And as always, their "stories" are attempts to convince the public that the cartel is in the best interests of consumers. Contrary to this assertion, the cartel locks potential workers out of labor markets while increasing prices and restricting the choices of consumers. Although occupational licensing can provide information to consumers, it should be optional, not mandatory.

Consumers are hurt because their choices are restricted and they are forced to pay higher prices. Patients presumably get higher-quality service, but they are forced to consume that quality or nothing at all. This is the "Cadillac effect" again—one gets the quality mandated by law (at a higher price) or none at all.

Along the same lines, there are restrictions on the ability of doctors and hospitals to advertise on the basis of price.[14] This is another way to prevent price competition and allows suppliers to charge higher prices. Can you imagine other markets being allowed to operate with similar restrictions? Limiting information and making the market less competitive ties into the public choice themes and incentives developed throughout Part 2.

There are also laws that prevent potential competitors from entering this labor market. There are prohibitions on the activity of nurse practitioners and physicians' assistants—including those who gave medical care to our troops in the Vietnam and Persian Gulf Wars.[15] In many states, chiropractors and midwives are also severely regulated. These restrictions serve to protect the AMA's monopoly power in this market.

Finally, Terree Wasley has noted the adverse effect of the AMA's monopoly power on women and minority doctors. For each, the percentage of doctors had been rising until the AMA began to shut down nearly half of the medical schools in the early 1900s. Then their numbers stagnated or fell. Likewise, Jews in the 1930s faced personal discrimination here and went to study in Europe. Ninety percent of American medical students studying in Europe during that time were Jewish.[16] If one gives monopoly power to a group, explicit or implicit discrimination is more likely.

In sum, the medical community's cartels serve to transfer income from taxpayers and consumers of medical services to themselves—a fine example of redistribution to the upper class. Along the way, they also restrict labor-supply options for some workers.

Hospital Regulations

There are 111 rural (and often poor) counties in the United States with no physicians. There are about a half-million people who live in counties with no obstetric care. Rural hospitals are shutting down at twice the rate of urban hospitals.[17] These figures are disconcerting enough before we determine that government policies contribute to the state of affairs.

As we have seen, there are numerous restrictions on those who can practice medicine even if no doctors live in the area. These laws prevent rural communities from having easier access to medical services. Many other regulations also limit health services in rural communities. These include Medicare rules requiring hospitals to maintain a staff of numerous professionals, including a full-time director of food and dietary services. Some states require fully equipped operating rooms and a surgical staff even in hospitals where surgery is not performed.[18] The net result is that hospitals are prohibitively expensive to operate in rural communities.

The solution here is to give hospitals and localities the freedom to determine the best and most appropriate solutions. They have better knowledge of specific problems and potential solutions and can respond with more alacrity and flexibility. They can also be held to greater levels of accountability than a federal bureaucracy.

Mandated-Benefit Laws

States often require that certain health services be covered by insurance policies. In 1970, there were 48 such laws; today, there are over 1,000.[19] Again, not allowing choice makes health insurance too expensive by requiring coverage of less important types of treatment—including acupuncture, in vitro fertilization, marriage and pastoral counseling, sperm bank deposits, and hairpieces.[20] Why is this done? Public choice economics tells us that special interest groups have an incentive to pursue such mandates to enhance the demand for their specialty.

This hurts all consumers but especially the poor, who might otherwise be able to afford health insurance. A National Center for Policy Analysis study estimates that one-fourth of those not covered by health insurance are without insurance as a result of the added expense of these regulations.[21]

Other Issues

Medicaid is supposed to target poor people but fails to do so effectively. Although the elderly compose only one-eighth of the prospective beneficiaries, they receive about one-third of all Medicaid dollars (in addition to the Medicare assistance they receive). Given the relatively low poverty rate of the elderly, Goodman and Musgrave attribute this perverse outcome to "regulations and special-interest political pressures."[22]

Government-provided or -subsidized health care for the poor is a complicated issue because it is a form of welfare. Work disincentives are inevitable whenever any type of benefit is reduced as income increases. (I cover this in detail in Part 3.) In addition, restrictive immigration policy limits our possible supply of qualified medical personnel. Because numbers are limited and because decisions to allow immigration are not based on skill, we miss the opportunity to increase the supply of doctors. Even if doctors speak only broken English, this level of quality should also be available in our market for health.

As we have already seen, our tax code subsidizes those who receive health insurance from their firms. The working poor are often not included in this group. And they often cannot afford to take advantage of group rates that are offered if the employee pays—especially if the coverage is artificially extensive and unnecessarily expensive. Thus, only the working poor are left out of this subsidy. David Ellwood has argued that public policy does not treat the working poor very well.[23] Government interventions in the market for health care are an excellent example.

Some people believe government should require firms to provide health insurance for workers. There are two problems with this approach. First, it ignores the cause to try to treat the symptoms; the distortion in this market is caused by the current subsidy through the tax code. Second, as with a minimum wage, mandating any level of compensation is equivalent to mandating that the relatively unskilled become unemployed.

People often point to the uninsured burdening hospitals with bills they cannot pay. But Goodman and Musgrave illustrate that the higher taxes collected from the uninsured (since they do not take advantage of the subsidy) would be nearly equal to the unpaid hospital bills they generate. They conclude that "what is unfair about the current system is not that uninsured people are not paying their own way; it is that, unlike most people with health insurance, most people without it never get an opportunity to purchase it at a tax-subsidized price."[24]

Extending the subsidy to all, including those who obtain health insurance outside of their employment, would be equitable. This would also help with the "welfare dilemma"—in this context, that the working poor have a financial incentive to rely on government assistance because health care is provided for free if one's income is low enough. However, extending the subsidy to another group would further exacerbate the demand-driven cost problems in the market for health care. The current system directly subsidizes all except the working poor. Thus, the optimal solution is to end the subsidy for all except the poor (and lower income taxes by the amount of the increase in tax revenue from taxing these fringe benefits). From there, Goodman and Musgrave advocate the use of "medical savings accounts" (MSAs)—a concept similar to IRAs for retirement.

Government Versus the Poor

As with virtually every other problem discussed in Part 2, the answer has been to get government out of the way of poor people. If government did not intervene in the market for housing, the poor would be more likely to find housing and would avoid the incentive for landlords to allow quality to deteriorate in the long run. If government did not subsidize health care for workers, allow the medical cartels to have monopoly power, and impose burdensome regulations on hospitals and firms, the poor would clearly benefit.

If government did not constantly redistribute income to interest groups in product and labor markets, the poor would have improved standards of living. There may be a limited role for government, but our current system has gone well beyond the appropriate level. The results are beneficial for the interest groups that manipulate the system. But the same outcomes are detrimental to the economy as a whole and especially traumatic for the "unorganized" poor.

Notes

1. To avoid the consequences of rent controls, landlords often try to circumvent the intent of the law by charging large deposits or by imposing large fees on keys or furniture. ("To rent my $400 apartment for $300 per month, you have to rent this key for $100.") Usually legislators foresee this and add appropriate restrictions.

2. W. Tucker, "The Source of America's Housing Problem: Look in Your Own Back Yard," Cato Policy Report no. 127, p. 17.

3. Note also that the price ceiling and the subsequent shortage provide an incentive for mutually beneficial, but illegal, trade. With a rent control of $300 on an apartment worth $400, someone waiting in line would have an incentive to offer $350 for the apartment. Certainly the landlord would enjoy this arrangement as well.

4. A. Lindbeck, *The Political Economy of the New Left: An Outsider's View* 2nd ed. (New York: Harper and Row, 1977), p. 39.

5. This policy is like the minimum wage, since it tries to mask the true problem by manipulating prices. Instead of helping lower-skilled workers, mandating

a higher minimum wage ensures they will be unemployed. Likewise, rent controls hurt those the policy supposedly targets for assistance.

6. For this reason, it is difficult or impossible to know the "true" reasons behind particular zoning ordinances. In Houston (the only major U.S. city without zoning laws), the pro-zoning *Houston Post* reported that low-income blacks and whites were the strongest opponents of a recently defeated zoning law (R. Saltzmann, "Houston Says No to Zoning," *Freeman*, August 1994, pp. 431–435).

7. P. Mehta, "Zoning: Bad Habitat," *Reason*, October 1990, p. 14.

8. The term "homelessness" implies its own solution—providing homes. Unfortunately, fixing the problem is not so simple. In *The Homeless* (Cambridge, MA: Harvard University Press, 1994), C. Jencks argues that the elimination of skid rows through urban renewal and deinstitutionalization merely made homelessness more evident. Tucker and Jencks also debunk a number of myths about housing policy in the 1980s, including the idea that Reagan slashed spending for housing policy. Jencks notes that between 1979 and 1989, the number of tenants in subsidized housing increased from 2.9 to 4.2 million.

9. Frequently, government empowers foundations, charities, and government agencies to help the needy. This creates other perverse incentives that are covered in Chapter 17.

10. S. Hayward and E. Peterson, "Medicare Monster: A Cautionary Tale," *Reason*, January 1993, pp. 18–25.

11. If this concept is unclear, imagine the extremes. Without insurance, all expenses would be paid for out-of-pocket after paying income taxes. Without 100% coverage through a firm, the only cost is reduced wage income.

12. J. Goodman and G. Musgrave, *Patient Power: The Free-Enterprise Alternative to Clinton's Health Plan* (Washington, DC: Cato Institute, 1994), pp. 45.

13. Much of the following analysis holds for Medicare as well.

14. See J. Goodman and G. Musgrave, *Patient Power: Solving America's Health Care Crisis* (Washington, DC: Cato Institute, 1992), pp. 52–54.

15. Ibid., p. 65.

16. T. Wasley, *What Has Government Done to Our Health Care?* (Washington, DC: Cato Institute, 1992), pp. 43–44.

17. Goodman and Musgrave, *Patient Power*, 1992, p. 65.

18. Ibid., p. 66.

19. Ibid., p. 47.

20. Ibid.

21. National Center for Policy Analysis, *An Agenda for Solving America's Health Care Crisis: A Task Force Report* (Dallas, TX: NCPA, 1990), p. 15.

22. Goodman and Musgrave, *Patient Power*, 1992, p. 67. (Only the poverty rate of the 55–64 age group is lower.) As a lobbying group, the elderly are perhaps the strongest interest group in political markets.

23. D. Ellwood, *Poor Support: Poverty in the American Family* (New York: Basic Books, 1988). Ellwood is a Harvard economist who co-chairs President Clinton's welfare reform advisory board.

24. Goodman and Musgrave, *Patient Power*, 1992, p. 69.

Part 3

How Government Tries to Help the Poor

12

The Historical Role of Ideology in Efforts to Fight Poverty

Economists tend to avoid or downplay many important cultural factors such as ideology and tradition. One reason is that these issues are not in their realm of expertise; they are subjects studied by other disciplines in the social sciences. Furthermore, economists are uncomfortable with these topics because they cannot be quantified. For instance, sociologists analyze the stigmas associated with particular activities. Certainly a stigma can be a significant deterrent, but what do economists know about it and how would they measure it anyway? Despite their usual absence from economic models, such factors are important and sometimes even pivotal in public policy matters and economic decisions made by individuals. In this chapter, we will look at the historical role of political ideology and its impact on redistribution to the poor.[1]

The Original Ideology: Individual Responsibility

Before the 20th century, the prevailing ideology drew sharp distinctions between the "deserving" and "undeserving" poor. Being poor was considered bad, but being poor and dependent on others was worse. There was even a term for this latter state—"pauperism." It was to be avoided if at all possible. Summarizing this mind-set, Thomas Malthus said, "Hard as it may appear in individual instances, dependent poverty ought to be held disgraceful."

In *The Tragedy of American Compassion*, Marvin Olasky traces this difference in ideology to the long-standing theological and philosophical debate over "the nature of man."[2] The then-dominant view of human nature was that man did not naturally *want* to work; it assumed people were not inherently good. Today, policy implicitly articulates a belief that people want to work hard and are poor only because of the absence of opportunity. This ideological disagreement leads to the following question: When a person is down and out, is the individual primarily responsible or is it the system's fault? If most individuals bear responsibility for their situations, a distinction may be drawn between the deserving and the undeserving poor; if poverty is the system's fault, all are deserving.

Further, one's ideology determines his policy prescriptions—whether to focus on helping individuals or on changing the system. Because the pre-20th century focus was on individual responsibility, the prevailing ideology prescribed a very limited role for government intervention. The idea that government should not be particularly active is so alien today that a few examples are useful to illustrate its extent.

Olasky discusses President Franklin Pierce's 1854 veto of a bill to pay for the construction and maintenance of mental hospitals. Although "he wished to help the mentally ill ... even worthwhile appropriations would push the federal government down a slippery slope" of government activism.[3] In *Crisis and Leviathan,* Robert Higgs explains why President Grover Cleveland refused to bail out farmers devastated by the drought of 1887. He vetoed the bill (which called for spending only $10,000) because he could "find no warrant for such an appropriation in the Constitution." His philosophy was that "the people should support the government, the government should not support the people."[4]

Olasky provides further historical context for the changes that led to the War on Poverty. "Outdoor relief," an earlier version of indiscriminate giving, blossomed in the 1850s but was beaten back in the 1870s and 1880s. When the weaknesses of outdoor relief (such as long-term dependence and fraud) became evident, the opposition was able to abolish it. Thus, until late in the 19th century, private charities dominated the poverty scene. For reasons I discuss in Chapter 15, local and private charitable efforts were probably more effective in helping the people they reached. But policymakers and "poverty warriors" began to grow impatient with the perceived lack of progress in the fight. So they relinquished control to government. It was thought that government could simply extend the successful private efforts with more money and the war would be won.

Into the 20th century, the ideological changes among charity leaders led to legislative efforts that allowed welfare to get in the door for good in 1921 with the Maternity and Infancy Act. Given the public's unchanged animosity toward welfare, it is noteworthy that government assistance (then and with the New Deal) targeted only the "most vulnerable." In addition, the programs had small appropriations, stressed work programs, and were sold as a temporary response to the "economic emergency" of the Great Depression. Nevertheless, welfare programs were able to put down roots that would blossom during the War on Poverty.

Growth in Government Activism:
The New Deal

Franklin D. Roosevelt's New Deal began the evident growth in government activism and the noticeable erosion of belief in individual responsibility. The onslaught of government programs during the Great Depression moved us into an era increasingly dominated by the public sector's paternalism and bureaucracy. The programs of the New Deal targeted the "needy" and for the first time, the "able." But because the general public remained mostly unconvinced, activism with respect to the able had to proceed at a cautious pace.

The idea of providing direct assistance to the needy had been popular for some time. For these recipients, the only change with the advent of the New Deal was the continued evolution toward the public sector and away from private charity. For those deemed needy—orphans and widows for example—the established programs transferred cash for an indefinite period of time. Further, policymakers were mostly unconcerned with incentives, since these were people who would probably not work anyway.

For the able, temporary programs were established that mostly provided jobs instead of a handout. Without the understanding that government was inadvertently extending the Great Depression, those normally considered able were redefined as "needy" and "unable to find work." Thus, helping the able became politically feasible.[5]

After World War II, the distinction between the deserving and undeserving poor remained strong. For the public to agree to allow income transfers, the redistributive cause had to be just—assisting the needy. The public also continued to focus on the fact that welfare programs are detrimental to work incentives. And from the perspective of potential recipients, the stigma associated with accepting assistance from anyone (especially the government) still existed.

As we entered the 1960s, the consensus on welfare policy had begun to fray from both sides. Some were concerned that the system did not provide equal opportunity; others were troubled by examples of the permanency of welfare and the diminished incentive to work. As in other arenas, John F. Kennedy was able to get the public to respond to calls for activism. He believed that if we devoted the appropriate energy and resources, progress against poverty could be achieved. The focus was to provide a "hand, not a handout"—to allow people to escape dependency on the government. Again, given the general optimism, especially toward the abilities of government, this seemed like an attainable goal.

A Change in the Public's Perspective: The War on Poverty

In the opening section of *Losing Ground,* Charles Murray provides a fascinating discussion of how the public's view of the poor changed dramatically in the second half of the 20th century. Even though there was far more poverty than today, the 1950s were marked by a lack of concern about poverty issues. With 45 million people living in poverty (almost 30% of the population if one uses the poverty line from the 1960s), government spending on the poor averaged $3 billion per year (less than $450 per poor person in 1993 dollars)—hardly a significant effort. Amazingly, Murray notes that people found the "lack of poverty" to be a "challenge to philanthropy."[6]

In contrast, 1968 featured a smoothly running economy (economic growth for nine consecutive years, inflation of 1.6%, unemployment of 3.6%). The civil rights movement was well under way and the number of people living in poverty continued to fall quickly and consistently. Surprisingly, people were concerned about a "lack of reform" and "the need for job creation"; thus, there was "reason for satisfaction, but very little of it."[7]

So why did the public's perception change? Why did the War on Poverty occur at this particular point in history? First, the American public "discovered" poverty in the early 1960s. Thanks to a pivotal book by Michael Harrington called *The Other America,* the media's subsequent awakening, and the growing prominence of television, the issue vaulted toward the top of public concerns.[8] A prerequisite for action was the public's awareness of the problem and a desire for change.

Second, the War on Poverty began during a time of prosperity. For the first time, Americans felt wealthy enough to have government redistribute money to the poor on a large-scale basis. The Great Depression, World War II, and the Korean War were becoming distant memories. The idea was that Franklin Roosevelt had been hampered by the Great Depression, but Lyndon Johnson would be able to start the War on Poverty from a position of economic strength.

Third, the American public had confidence that government could win this "war." In economic matters, the Keynesian idea that the economy could be controlled by activist fiscal policy was still dominant; it appeared that we had entered an era of perpetual economic growth.

Further, we had not yet seen Vietnam, Watergate, and assorted other governmental failures. In other words, our faith in government's ability to perform was very high. The belief entering this "war" was that it could be won if we devoted sufficient resources to the battle.

Blaming the System

The concept of structural poverty became popular in the early 1960s with Harrington's *The Other America* and other contemporary writing. If poverty was structural in nature, then the poor did not bear responsibility for their circumstances. There was little if any need to look at the circumstances of each person or to require changes in individual behavior that might be contributing to poverty. This was a monumental shift in attitude because it involved not only how the non-poor viewed the poor but how the poor viewed themselves, and it completely altered policy prescriptions. Because the system was blamed, reform centered on fixing it—by expanding the dole.[9]

This mind-set also encourages blanket solutions for the problems of the poor; the ideological shift promoted a move toward federal activism over local efforts. Again, the key is that individual circumstances are assumed to be unimportant. If so, the federal government is better equipped to formulate general solutions to improve the system. Finally, the emergence of "white guilt," along with the idea that the system was wrong, led to prescriptions that assumed whites should be willing to provide money to help blacks. Again, groups were emphasized over individuals.

The debate over the individual versus the system is interesting as well. It is noteworthy that there was so little public discussion concerning such a dramatic change. In 1964, Hubert Humphrey referred to "equality of opportunity"; in 1965, Lyndon Johnson talked about "equality of results." As in the early days of the "political correctness" movement, dialogue was greatly diminished. It was not fashionable to disagree, and if some did, their motives were impugned. Proposing alternative means to the same end was deemed inappropriate.

The speed of change is also noteworthy because it illustrates the dictum that ideas have consequences. The intelligentsia actively promoted the idea and a willing public followed. As a result, in a short period of time, a radically different set of policy prescriptions emerged. Before LBJ, most benefits went to the jobless because workers "didn't deserve welfare"; such an attitude assumed personal responsibility. With the Great Society and the War on Poverty, those who worked began to receive assistance as a result of the focus on the system's responsibility.

Implementing the New Ideology

The change in ideology caused a variety of policy changes. Obviously, there were direct changes—the implementation of new programs and the expansion of current programs, among others. Although the programs of the Great Society originated and were legitimized by Lyndon Johnson, most of the money came later. In fact, Richard Nixon is most responsible for the vast increase in social spending on the poor. Murray notes that the food stamp program began with 424,000 participants in 1965. When Johnson left office, it had risen to 2.2 million. Four years later, it had quintupled again. By 1980, 21.1 million people were covered (50 times the number of people covered 15 years earlier).[10]

In addition, there were many indirect changes. Enforcement of standards became more lax and the stigma of accepting assistance was alleviated somewhat because more people—specifically, workers—were receiving help. Murray notes that although disability program standards tightened slightly, rolls expanded from 687,000 in 1960 to 4.35 million in 1975.[11] Olasky cites increased litigation for welfare rights and concludes that subsequently, the goal of social welfare programs "became not challenge but lubrication."[12] Further, a number of restrictions were rescinded and the ability of officials to monitor was compromised by weakened rules that increased the rights of welfare recipients.[13]

Murray provides insight into how the poverty warriors felt as the "war" began. Since they were now fighting the battle in earnest, they would be able to succeed; the "political will" and necessary effort had simply been lacking before. Murray also notes that they suffered from a "fallacy of composition"—that the poor would behave the same way as the "warriors" would if they were offered assistance. "If I were in their shoes, I would use the government assistance to support myself while I looked for another job." However, it was a mistaken notion to think that a blanket system would affect different people in similar ways. Some viewed assistance as a safety net, but others used it as a hammock.

Finally, Higgs notes that whenever government extends its involvement, the rhetoric commonly associated with war is used as often as possible.[14] This approach gets taxpayers in the mood to give control of their financial resources and freedom to the government. The same was true with the War on Poverty.

Ideology and the Potential for Reform

Ideology is a crucial component in determining policy. It follows that without a change in ideology, substantive reform is unlikely. With respect to welfare reform, there are reasons for both optimism and pessimism. With people losing faith in government's ability to solve poverty and other problems, the perpetual concern about work disincentives for those on welfare, and growing distress over budget deficits, it would seem that significant welfare reform is likely in the near future.

However, the 1980s provide a sobering dose of reality. Despite a change in ideology, Ronald Reagan was vilified for "slashing spending for social programs." As we saw earlier, this accusation is false. Although he cut the appropriations desired by Congress, social spending and spending on the poor continued to grow under his administration.[15] If there is so much opposition to cutting the rate of growth of spending, it is, of course, unlikely that actual spending can be reduced—whether the goal would be to lessen assistance or move toward private charitable efforts. Only a complete change in our faith in government will allow substantial reform.

Notes

1. We will look at stigmata more closely in Chapter 14. Tradition and its impact on policy and potential reform appear throughout Part 3.

2. See also T. Sowell's *Conflict of Visions: Ideological Origins of Political Struggle* (New York: Morrow, 1987) and his distinction between "constrained" and "unconstrained man." R. Nelson distinguishes the two schools of thought as the Roman and the Protestant in *Reaching for Heaven on Earth* (Lanham, MD: Rowman and Littlefield, 1991).

3. M. Olasky, *The Tragedy of American Compassion* (Washington, DC: Regnery Gateway, 1992), p. 49.

4. R. Higgs, *Crisis and Leviathan: Critical Episodes in the Growth of American Government* (New York: Oxford University Press, 1987), pp. 83–84. On the occasion of funding an orphanage during an economic crisis, L. Burkett also quotes Cleveland: "I will not be a party to stealing money from one group of citizens to give to another group of citizens—no matter what the need or apparent justification. Once the coffers of the federal government are open to the public, there will be no shutting them again. (*The Coming Economic Earthquake* [Chicago: Moody Press, 1991], p. 33.)

5. Between 1929 and 1940, the United States had endured the high-wage policies of Hoover, protectionist trade policies, a restrictive money supply, other poor monetary policy decisions, and four tax increases. Unemployment was still 19% six years into FDR's administration. (For a fascinating discussion of Hoover's use of moral suasion to keep wages artificially high, see R. Vedder and L. Galloway, *Out of Work: Unemployment and Government in Twentieth-Century America* [New York: Holmes and Meier, 1993], chapter 5.)

6. C. Murray, *Losing Ground: American Social Policy 1950–1980* (New York: Basic Books, 1984), p. 4.

7. Ibid., p. 6.

8. M. Harrington, *The Other America: Poverty in the United States* (New York: Macmillan, 1962).

9. This is related to my argument in Part 2—that government hurts the poor through various policies. My subsequent prescription was to *limit* government. However, in this context, "fixing the system" meant expanding the role of government.

10. Murray, *Losing Ground*, p. 48 (with statistics from *Social Security Bulletin*, November 1982, Table 24). Similar increases occurred in AFDC roles. See also Olasky, *The Tragedy of American Compassion*, pp. 182–183. Somehow S. Reed and C. Sautter attribute "cutbacks in Great Society programs" to the Nixon administration (*Kappan Special Report* [Bloomington, IN: Phi Delta Kappa, June 1990]).

11. Murray, *Losing Ground*, p. 47.

12. Olasky, *The Tragedy of American Compassion*, p. 181.

13. Ibid. He also cites the Office of Economic Opportunity, which actively taught that welfare was a right, making the "war on shame a success."

14. Higgs, *Crisis and Leviathan*.

15. See D. Frum's *Dead Right* (New York: Basic Books, 1994) for a cogent analysis of the Republicans being unwilling or unable to reduce spending in the 1980s.

13

Equity Versus Efficiency:
The Costs of Pursuing
Income Equality

In Part 2, I argued that the use of political markets to redistribute income to the non-poor is often unjust and impractical given the facility with which interest groups engage in political market transactions. Now we face more difficult issues. If redistribution could be done "appropriately," is it helpful to transfer income to the poor? If so, who should be eligible? How much assistance should we provide? Should welfare benefits be temporary or available indefinitely?

Because of the value judgments inherent in the pursuit of income equality, people will disagree on prospective welfare policies simply because their tastes and preferences for equality differ. Concerning redistribution to the poor, people usually invoke a version of equity or "fairness" by arguing that current outcomes are unjust and should be altered by the government.[1] Others question why we redistribute income to the poor at all, especially those who are capable of working. They invoke a very different equity argument, saying it is unfair to take money from people through (coercive) taxation to give to anyone else. (Because the former version of equity dominates the latter in popular use, it will be used throughout this chapter.)

Another factor to consider is the costs of transferring income to the poor—costs borne by taxpayers and potentially the poor. Some say that government cannot solve the poverty (or any other) problem; the raw poverty rate numbers certainly support this contention. Most often however, one hears "efficiency" concerns about reduced work incentives for recipients.[2]

In this chapter, I focus on the main arguments from each camp—equity (defined as equality) and efficiency (defined as disincentives).

Equity and Equality

Economists tend to focus on efficiency and incentive arguments because they are considered objective, or "value-free." Incentive effects can often be quantified. (For example, a given welfare program may reduce average hours worked by X%.) In contrast, one's concept of equity is completely subjective and is based on value judgments—what an individual considers fair. But despite its subjectivity, as with ideology in Chapter 12, equity should not be ignored.[3]

Equity is usually synonymous with "equality." Thus, the question becomes, Equality of what? Some view the proper goal to be equality of opportunity. This means that all individuals have the right, generally established and guaranteed by government, to be treated equally.[4] Although somewhat vague and impossible to measure directly, this ideal is consistent with liberty; it does not require an imposition on others.

The other possibility is equality of outcomes. Proponents of this view often argue that equal opportunities are not truly equal unless outcomes are equal as well. (Of course, equal outcomes at every point in time are impossible—at least random chance prevents this.[5]) The definition of equality as equal outcomes, although vague, has the advantage that outcomes can be measured—if sometimes improperly. However, unlike equal opportunity, this ideal requires force to achieve; it reduces liberty. Even when the rules of the game are enforced equally, supporters of this view would force winners to give some of the winnings to the losers.

In addition, there are a number of other practical problems with using this definition of equality. First, how does one know the proper population to survey in order to measure outcomes as a proxy for opportunity? If the number of black professors at a university is "too low," is that in comparison to the national population, the local population, the number of black PhDs, or the number of black PhDs in that field? In addition, the frequent choice of income comparisons is merely a proxy for opportunity. Would it be "fair" to equalize incomes if opportunities were already equal but hours worked were different?

Second, reaching equal outcomes often compromises equal opportunity. Affirmative action programs are a frequently cited example. But sometimes, the results are more perverse. For example, in recent years in Louisville, Kentucky, the percentage of whites living in public housing has decreased. In the early 1980s, the Housing Authority "tried to maintain racial balance by placing whites in vacancies."[6] Also in Louisville, ten black students were forced to leave Central High School Magnet Center Academy a month into the academic year because of desegregation guidelines. In the pursuit of racial quotas (ironically, "equal outcomes" designed to help minorities), minorities were prevented from having equal opportunities to obtain housing and education. In addition, many schools now use racial quotas for admittance. The result is that higher test scores are frequently required of orientals than whites and of whites than blacks. This falls short of equal opportunity and is a perverse form of personal discrimination; striving for equal outcomes usually results in compromises in equality of opportunity.

Third, who decides what is fair? People involved in political markets. As before, we should be aware of the chasm between the theory of government intervention and its practice. In every country, there is substantial inequality of political and economic power between rulers and those they rule. And nowhere is the gap greater than in feudal societies and centrally planned economies (where governments are most active). Further, as we have seen, the non-poor are rather adept at wielding power in political markets—using government to increase their incomes. Once the redistributive game is legitimized, the poor are likely to lose. It could easily be that the poor would benefit most with limited government.

Finally, there is often little actual direct support for income equality from its proponents. Often, the same people advocate lotteries that make the income gap wider. And frequently, proponents fail to bolster their words with individual action. On an episode of CNN's *Crossfire*, economist Walter Williams noted that in 1988, 40 million people (presumably compassionate people) voted for Michael Dukakis when there were (an estimated) 400,000 homeless people. He reasoned that if only 1% of Dukakis's supporters had been willing to shelter a homeless person, the problem would have been solved. Williams then asked co-host Michael Kinsley if he had a spare room. Kinsley had no response.

Arthur Okun has observed that society accepts more inequality in economic assets (income and wealth) than in social and political assets (freedoms of speech and religion, voting rights, and so on).[7] Why is this? Because the costs of equalizing the former are greater. The cost of giving someone the freedom to vote is negligible. But the costs of equalizing incomes are that some individuals will lose money from the income transfer and society as a whole will lose income if work incentives are affected at all. Since income equality is costly, Okun argues it is noteworthy that society redistributes income at all. It must be that we value income equality to some extent—otherwise, we would be unwilling to bear those costs.[8]

Existing redistribution to the poor through the political process reveals a preference for equality, constrained by the costs to individuals and society. What are those costs?

Efficiency and the Cost of Equality

Independent of preferences for income equality, one should recognize that redistribution is costly for many reasons. Income transfers cause incentive problems for recipients, probably lead to disincentives for taxpayers, and impose other costs on society as well. The combination may make the poor worse off and certainly lowers the standard of living for the nation as a whole.

Incentive Problems for Recipients

By definition, any welfare program (food stamps, earned income tax credits, Medicaid, and the so on) involves three variables: (1) the maximum benefit level (with no earned income); (2) the benefit-reduction rate (or marginal tax rate) as earned income increases; and (3) the minimum income level at which benefits equal zero—the cutoff point.[9] There are other variables—work requirements, multiple benefit-reduction rates, time restrictions, and so on—but the fundamentals are the same.

The benefit-reduction rate is the rate at which government decreases its assistance as the recipient's income rises. The idea is that recipients need less assistance as their earned income grows. The problem is that reducing benefits lowers the rate of return for working, thus reducing work incentives.

For instance, before 1967, AFDC had a 100% benefit-reduction rate; for every dollar earned, benefits were reduced by a dollar. In that case, an hour of additional work yielded no additional total income; the effective wage for that hour was reduced to zero. Clearly, this provided no incentive to work; one would give up leisure and receive no net increase in total income. But remember that before Lyndon Johnson's Great Society, welfare programs targeted the "truly needy"—people for whom incentives were not an issue because of their inability to work.

After 1967, the target population expanded to include people who worked but still had "inadequate" incomes. Given concerns about incentives for this group, officials decided on a 67% benefit-reduction rate; for every additional $3 earned, benefits were reduced by $2.[10] Thus, the effective wage rate for recipients was one-third of their market wage. Incentives were better than under the old system, but they were still greatly diminished.

Today, recipients get benefits from a variety of government programs that are tied to income levels—Medicaid, housing vouchers, food stamps, AFDC, and others. The relevant benefit reduction rate—the rate that would affect behavior—is the sum of the rates for all of the programs for which a recipient is eligible. For instance, if the benefit-reduction rate is 20% for each of the four programs in which a person is participating, the effective benefit-reduction rate is 80%.[11] (This does not include income and Social Security taxes or any child care costs.)

It should be intuitively clear why work incentives are diminished with welfare programs.[12] Economists break this disincentive to work (an incentive to consume leisure) into two parts. First, with more income from the benefits, recipients will consume more of most goods, including leisure. In other words, recipients can "afford" to consume more leisure. Second, because the benefit-reduction rate necessarily reduces the rewards for working, work becomes relatively less attractive and one is likely to consume more leisure.[13] (Note that "leisure" encompasses all "non-market activity," including labor supplied in illegal/underground markets.)

Beyond intuition and theory, we are fortunate to have experimental evidence of the disincentive effects of welfare programs.[14] In the late 1960s and early 1970s, social scientists ran a series of experiments using a negative income tax (NIT)—a type of welfare program. They established an experimental group that received welfare benefits and compared their behavior to a control group.[15] For the longest and best-run experiments, the results were stunning.

The "income maintenance" experiments in Seattle and Denver revealed that husbands reduced their hours worked by an average of 9%. This decrease was caused by lower labor force participation rates; that is, those who kept their jobs continued working the same number of hours, but some left their jobs and no longer participated in the labor force by looking for other work. Wives reduced their hours worked by 20%. Most important, the behavior of "young" males changed dramatically: Those who were married reduced their hours worked by 33%; singles decreased theirs by 43%. (An increase in school attendance was only a minor factor in reduced labor force participation.) The experimental group also experienced longer periods of unemployment and more marriage dissolutions (40% higher than the control group).[16]

Obviously, these results support the concerns about the disincentives of welfare programs. The numbers for young males are extremely troublesome. When they are young is precisely the time when they need to be in the labor force developing work habits and job skills. Aside from anecdotal evidence, one can imagine why people point to welfare programs as the cause of higher illegitimacy rates and long-term dependence on government.

Moreover, these numbers understate the effects of welfare programs. First, those in the experimental group knew the benefits were only temporary. They were less likely to engage in behavior that would be detrimental in the long term, since they knew the experimental benefits would not be extended. Second, the control group was not "pure"— members of this group received a minimal level of benefits as well. Thus, a comparison to the "experimental group" would understate the total effect of welfare programs on hours worked and on marriage dissolution.

The Welfare Dilemma

Why not lower the benefit-reduction rate to provide better incentives? The answer is called the "welfare dilemma." The first problem is that the levels of the three policy variables mentioned earlier are not independent of each other. Once you choose levels for any two variables, the level of the third is already determined.

For instance, Table 13.1 shows an arbitrary maximum benefit level of $12,000 (with zero earned income) and a benefit-reduction rate of 40%. As earned income rises by some amount, benefits fall by 40%, causing *total* income to rise by only 60% of the additional earned income. Under such a program, welfare benefits would cease when earned income reached $30,000—a level above the median household income for the United States.[17]

The other problem is the impossibility of reaching all three goals at the same time. Policymakers need to (1) provide a benefit level high enough for the truly needy to survive, (2) determine a benefit-reduction rate low enough to limit work disincentives, and (3) establish a cutoff point for benefits that is low enough to avoid extending the program and its directives well into the middle class (which would be prohibitively costly).

I encourage you to try your own numerical example. You will find there is no way to reach all three goals simultaneously.[18] This is the welfare dilemma. Unfortunately, with the status quo, there are no satisfactory answers to this part of the puzzle.

The Good Samaritan's Dilemma

Short-run financial assistance can also promote long-term dependence on aid.[19] Even Franklin D. Roosevelt was wary of this aspect of providing assistance: "Continued dependence upon relief induces a spiritual and moral disintegration fundamentally destructive to the national fiber. To

TABLE 13.1   Hypothetical Negative Income Tax Example (in dollars)

Earned Income	Benefit Level	Total Income
0	12,000	12,000
1,000	11,600	12,600
5,000	10,000	15,000
15,000	6,000	21,000
30,000	0	30,000

dole out relief in this way is to administer a narcotic, a subtle destroyer of the human spirit."[20]

It is not that all people will become addicted to aid, but it becomes more likely as income transfers increase (amount of money or length of time). Similarly, many parents are careful about giving their children candy in a store because they know the gift may have long-term implications. Rules against feeding bears in national parks are based on the same principle. Remember that the goals of the War on Poverty were to increase standards of living for the poor (short run) and to end their dependence on the dole (long run). It is difficult to do both.

The possible long-term implications of welfare also point to the "non-money" issues associated with welfare and poverty. The ultimate goal of providing assistance is not merely to provide an adequate standard of living. Given a subsistence level of income, happiness is not closely related to more income; there are more important components to happiness—self-esteem, "self-actualization," independence and so on—that are not measured by dollars.[21] We need to be careful to recognize that money alone cannot ultimately solve the issue of poverty.

The Good Samaritan's dilemma is especially problematic given the movement toward blanket and federally imposed solutions. If aid is distributed in a uniform manner or from a long distance, bureaucrats will be unable to discern those who are likely to fall into long-term dependence, those who will use welfare as a hammock rather than a safety net. A local program with considerable flexibility would be more likely to avoid this problem.

Note that it is possible for behavior to change so much that recipients are actually worse off in the long run. If education, training, and work experience are neglected, one's earning potential may be irrevocably damaged.

Other Costs to Society

The incentive to work is probably lowered as well for workers who are not on welfare. Some lower-income working families are lured onto welfare roles and then face the previously discussed disincentives. In addition, the higher taxes needed to pay for the transfers lower the after-tax incomes of workers. This probably decreases their incentive to work.[22]

Taken to an extreme, these disincentives may discourage people from pursuing education and job training. For instance, Sweden has extremely high marginal tax rates. Such high taxation provides a disincentive to pursue training. Why train to be a surgeon if the after-tax income represents only a marginal gain over a nurse's income? It follows that high taxation contributes to "brain drain," that is, talented people emigrate to avoid high taxation.[23]

Finally, income redistribution is not as simple as transferring money from A to B. Some money is "lost" along the way. A portion is paid to the bureaucrats who make the income transfer, some is lost through work disincentives, and some is lost through fraud and other criminal activities. Okun calls this "the leaky bucket"—a portion of the money leaks out as it is transferred.[24]

Thus, when we attempt to equalize incomes, taxpayers must be willing to bear considerable costs and to impose other costs on the poor. If the costs are large enough, we need to ask ourselves if it is "fair" to impose those costs on taxpayers. If these policies are ultimately detrimental to the poor, we should ask ourselves if the purpose of transferring income is simply to relieve our guilt about the poor.

Economic Growth and the Poor

The inefficiency associated with redistribution and taxation is also significant because it hampers economic performance, and economic growth is perhaps the best weapon in any battle against poverty. (Similarly, recessions are one of the poor's worst enemies; the relatively unskilled tend to be laid off first because firms have invested least in those employees.) But since the late 1960s, although the growth of government has exploded, income growth has slowed considerably. With incomes rising in general, the incomes of the poor usually increase as well. Since income growth has slowed, it should come as little surprise that our success in fighting poverty has been so limited. One clear emphasis should be to encourage policies that stimulate our economy and provide opportunity for individuals.

As we extend the concept of income transfers and equality, we increase the degree of socialism in our country. With respect to the relationship between the size of government and economic growth, we know from the successes of relatively free-market economies and the failures of socialist economies that low taxation, individual property rights, and personal freedom are the best ways to ensure economic prosperity. The pursuit of activist government runs counter to those goals.

A short story by Kurt Vonnegut illustrates these principles. In "Harrison Bergeron," Vonnegut describes a world in the year 2081 where the Handicapper General enforces a constitution with 213 amendments.[25] Her job is to fit people with handicaps that make them equal to everyone else—masks for the physically attractive, weights for the strong to wear, and ear implants that emit loud noises to disrupt the thoughts of the intelligent. Vonnegut begins his story with "Everybody was finally equal." But as is illustrated throughout, total equality was achieved at the cost of economic efficiency and growth. In a fitting conclusion, a rebellion is quelled with a shotgun—hardly the technological advance one would expect to see so far into the future.[26]

In Vonnegut's world, people are equal but equally poor. This is not the goal. The optimal outcome is for all people to have the opportunity to achieve a reasonable standard of living. The best way to achieve this is to pursue policies that promote economic growth.

Framing the Debate

It is also interesting to watch the debate over redistribution to the poor. As we have seen, people's tastes for income equality differ, and there is considerable ignorance about the inefficiency associated with redistribution. As in any debate, each side is likely to stress points that make its prescription seem optimal. In this context, equality-minded people generally ignore or overlook inefficiency, and efficiency-minded people tend to downplay equality considerations. Often, the equality-minded merely assert that we must do something, assuming it will help. William Ryan supposed that "we have so much, and it would cost so little to end poverty."[27]

For proponents of income transfers, a prominent theme is the assumption that incentives are not a major factor—that behavior is not changed significantly in the face of higher benefits or taxation. In *Who Gets What from Government?* Benjamin Page initially assumes a "*fixed* amount of income to (re)distribute" and argues that disincentives "may not be so serious as they seem at first. . . . *If* material incentives are needed to encourage work, the prospect of redistribution *may* affect how much is produced" (italics added).[28] Lester Thurow claims that "*substantial* equalization could occur before growth would be adversely affected. . . . The distribution of economic *prizes* could be substantially equalized before conflicts would emerge, *if at all*" (italics added).[29]

Those who favor greater income equalization also tend to denigrate the NIT experimental results. Sometimes they cite the poorly done and shorter New Jersey effort. Sometimes they merely label the size of the behavioral changes "not significant." In addition, they typically ignore the role of income dynamics. They tend to view the world as a static one where people do not change their behavior in response to changes in prices, benefit levels, or taxes. To them, "incentives don't matter."[30]

Further, they do not acknowledge that the government's efforts to this point have mostly failed to help the poor, aside from increasing their standards of living; and long-term dependence has become a more severe problem. They generally do not see the public choice aspects of redistribution. In sum, proponents of income transfers ignore or downplay government's inability to help the poor in terms of long-term dependence.

Finally, their policy prescriptions often appear to be based on envy of the rich and are more punitive than practical. They seem mostly unconcerned with those living in poverty per se; their focus is largely that income is distributed unequally.[31] It would seem they would prefer everyone to be equally poor. This is evidenced by their preference for taxing the rich at higher rates despite the fact that subsequent tax revenues from the wealthy are often lower.[32] Is the goal to have higher tax *rates* for the rich or greater tax *revenue* from the rich?

Public Choice Considerations

As with virtually any other established government policy, the growth of programs for the poor is inevitable. Political support for these programs comes from the bureaucrats who administer them, "compassionate" politicians, and the poor themselves. Government is generally driven by the desire to maximize budgets, so bureaucrats always have an incentive to look for new constituents. In the context of welfare programs, this translates into generating greater "need" for income transfers.

In addition, political support has manifested itself in a number of policy outcomes. For instance, remember that benefits are largely given in the form of in-kind (non-cash) transfers. One reason is paternalism concerning the poor's supposed inability to spend money properly. Another factor is that politicians can target special interest groups with an increased demand for their products. Farm support for food stamps and the AMA's advocacy of Medicare and Medicaid are good examples.

As we have seen throughout this book, redistribution is not limited to the poor. Once the income-transfer game is legitimized, once it is deemed moral to coerce money from one person to give to another, the poor get a few programs but lose overall. They get visible help in the form of welfare payments but are invisibly harmed by product and labor market restrictions. The poor simply do not have or exercise much political power relative to other interest groups.

Reform: The Negative Income Tax

I will cover other welfare reforms later. Given disagreements about the appropriate balance of equality and efficiency, the negative income tax (NIT) is an initial approach to at least make the current system run more effectively and avoid some of the efficiency costs developed in this chapter.[33]

The NIT would take the place of the "dog's breakfast" of current welfare programs (food stamps, AFDC, EITC, and so on). It would result in a guaranteed annual income through transfers of cash to households depending on their earned income and family size. The NIT would allow families to earn "income credits" for the unused portion of their allowable tax deductions. These credits would be paid to recipients throughout the year in the same way as other income transfers (such as Social Security). As with current welfare programs, the NIT would implicitly have minimum benefit levels and a benefit-reduction rate. It would be similar to current policy in many ways, but it would be far less complex because it would replace many programs with one program.

It would also involve a move from in-kind transfers to cash.[34] Recipients would benefit from the flexibility to spend the income as they decide (assuming away paternalistic arguments). For better or worse, it would remove any remaining stigma associated with receiving welfare payments, since transfers would be in cash and would be implemented through the tax code. Clearly, bureaucratic and administrative costs would be much lower. With one program taking the place of many, "welfare" would run more smoothly and efficiently.

With the NIT, policymakers and the poor would find it much easier to understand the system. For many people, marginal tax rates (benefit-reduction rates) exceed 100% when all of the programs are added together—particularly with the provision of Medicaid for low income households. In 1970, the House passed a bill with marginal tax rates above 100% for millions of poor people.[35] With an NIT, lawmakers would avoid passing such legislation. Finally, it would be much easier to target dollars to the poor and to avoid fraud.

Despite the advantages, people might balk at this proposal. Some people would not be willing to relinquish their paternalism concerning the poor. Some bureaucrats would protest the loss of control over recipients and especially the lost jobs in the government's poverty industry. And certainly, some politicians would not be eager to lose the ability to funnel money to special interest groups.

An NIT would clearly be an improvement over the current system. In the next two chapters I look in more detail at current welfare programs and at the possible alternatives.

Notes

1. One way to formally express this taste and preference is "utilitarianism"—striving to maximize the utility (well-being) of society. Given "diminished marginal utility"—the fact that individuals receive less and less satisfaction from each additional unit of the goods they consume—the way to reach this goal is to redistribute from those who have much to those who have little. In other words, since $5,000 will be valued more highly by a poor person than a wealthy person, income should be redistributed from the rich to the poor to maximize society's

utility. Virtually everyone is a utilitarian to some extent. For example, if the government was going to award a grant of $5,000, would you prefer that it was given away randomly or that it targeted a relatively poor person instead of a wealthy person?

Extending the logic of pure utilitarianism yields the result that income should be redistributed until society reaches complete (income) equality. However, utilitarianism implicitly ignores that behavior (amount of labor supplied, compliance with tax laws, and so on) changes—either for recipients or for those who pay for the income transfers—and that the other costs of effecting the transfer are not zero.

2. Others point to the "public good" aspects of charitable giving—that I enjoy seeing the poor made better off whether the contribution comes from me or someone else. Since I may "free ride" off another person's contribution, the marketplace will produce too little voluntary redistribution. Others argue there are substantial positive externalities from redistribution that are not considered by charitable individuals (reduced crime, for example). Again, the market would fail to provide the "socially optimal level" of income transfers. These arguments are valid, although their quantitative impact is debatable.

3. Efficiency is not a purely objective matter either. In *Generating Inequality: Mechanisms of Distribution in the U.S. Economy* (New York: Basic Books, 1975), L. Thurow notes that with efficiency, we implicitly assume that (1) individuals make rational decisions, (2) more is better, and (3) the individual should be valued over the collective. The last two are subjective, and rationality is compromised regularly by a variety of paternalistic governmental policies. (For instance, Social Security implicitly assumes people are incapable of saving for retirement.) Thurow's points do have merit, but efficiency concerns are still far more objective than equity considerations.

4. Of course, this ideal is never reached. One can stretch the definition of opportunity to include how one is born and raised—whether one is treated equally by nature and nurture; most take equality in those areas as given. And of course, government often fails to treat individuals equally. Jim Crow laws and the policies from Part 2 such as education and labor laws represent some of government's failures in this area.

5. H. Schlossberg notes that "equality of opportunity guarantees inequality of results because people are unequal in motivation, ability, and will." (*Idols for Destruction: The Conflict of Christian Faith and American Culture* [Wheaton, IL: Crossway Books, 1990], p. 55).

6. N. Walfoort, "White Flight from Louisville's Public Housing Worries Many," *Louisville Courier Journal*, October 13, 1993.

7. A. Okun, *Equality and Efficiency: The Big Tradeoff* (Washington, DC: Brookings Institution, 1975), p. 4.

8. A cynic might respond that transferring income to the poor serves merely as a distraction to the main function of government—redistribution to the nonpoor. In other words, welfare programs are an elaborate ruse to trick people into thinking government cares about the poor. As we have seen, Uncle Sam uses one hand to give assistance to the poor and the other to increase their prices, lock them out of labor markets, and force them to consume a low-quality education.

9. When policymakers discuss the negative income tax (NIT), the cutoff point is also described as the break-even point. When they discuss wage subsidies, the benefit-reduction rate is assumed to be negative. As opposed to the NIT, which reduces benefits as earned income rises, a wage subsidy gives money to workers above their earned income.

10. Recipients were allowed to keep the first $30 in earned income before benefits were reduced.

11. G. Burtless estimates that the actual benefit-reduction rate "may easily exceed 80–90%." ("The Economist's Lament: Public Assistance in America," *Journal of Economic Perspectives*, Winter 1990, pp. 57–78.)

12. C. Murray calls this the "Law of Unintended Rewards" (*Losing Ground: American Social Policy 1950–1980* [New York: Basic Books, 1984], p. 212). By definition, if you increase the rewards, you decrease the penalties for the behavior in question. Welfare serves as the opposite of an excise tax (a tax on a particular activity); it is in effect an excise *subsidy,* lowering the cost of the "activity" of avoiding work. The exception is for those who are unable to change their behavior. But for those who have control over their circumstances, such policies must act as an enticement.

13. These are called the income and substitution effects, respectively. An alternative explanation of the latter is that the benefit reduction reduces the effective wage rate. Thus, the cost of enjoying an hour of leisure decreases because one gives up less income to enjoy an hour of leisure. Because leisure is less expensive, recipients will consume more of it.

14. Evidence is also available on "welfare magnets"—states that draw immigrants because of their high benefits. For example, poor people from Chicago often cross the border to nearby Wisconsin to take advantage of the latter's more liberal welfare benefits. Similarly, Latin American immigrants tend to remain unemployed longer and use welfare benefits longer in high-benefit California than in low-benefit Texas.

15. This was a compromise on a policy originally posed by George Stigler ("The Economics of Minimum Wage Legislation," *American Economic Review,* June 1946, pp. 358–365) and promoted especially by conservative economists—notably Milton Friedman. The immense technological advance in computers made such an experiment feasible, allowing measurement of the effect of welfare programs on incentives.

16. Murray, *Losing Ground*, pp. 151–152.

17. The earned income tax credit (EITC) provides the equivalent of a 40% wage-rate subsidy up to $8,425 in earned income and a lump-sum transfer up to $11,000 and then imposes a 21% benefit-reduction rate for additional income above $11,000. The subsequent cutoff point is $27,000, well into the middle class. (E. Browning, "Effects of the Earned Income Tax Credit on Income and Welfare," working paper, Texas A&M University, College Station, Texas, 1994.) Note also that EITC transfers are not included when the Census Bureau calculates the poverty rate.

18. To illustrate this principle, Murray uses a thought experiment involving the hypothetical implementation of a government anti-smoking policy. The problem is the impossibility of inducing smokers to quit without enticing non-

smokers to start. His analogy allows one to see other incentive problems as well (*Losing Ground,* pp. 205–211).

19. In *The Cider House Rules* John Irving discusses the Good Samaritan's dilemma in the context of orphans ([New York: Bantam Books, 1985], pp. 22–23).

20. R. Maynard, *World,* "Rhetoric and Reality," April 23, 1994, p. 14.

21. See C. Murray, *In Pursuit of Happiness and Good Government* (New York: Simon and Schuster, 1988).

22. It is conceivable that the need to earn more income by working harder would offset the tendency to work less in response to lower after-tax wages. In economic terms, the income effect might outweigh the substitution effect.

23. Economists have identified another cost of taxation. When resources move in response to the imposition of a tax, they go to lower-valued uses in other sectors of the economy. The subsequent decrease in economic wealth is called a "welfare cost" or "deadweight loss." Because of this additional cost, taxation and redistribution are less attractive. Concerning deadweight losses, E. Browning and W. Johnson estimate that taxpayers "sacrifice $350 for every $100 that the poor gained." ("The Tradeoff Between Equality and Efficiency," *Journal of Political Economy,* April 1984, pp. 175–203.)

24. Okun, *Equality and Efficiency,* pp. 91–95.

25. K. Vonnegut, *Welcome to the Monkey House* (New York: Dell, 1961), pp. 7–13.

26. The writings of Ayn Rand are far more prolific and explicit about these principles. *Atlas Shrugged* (New York: Bantam Books, 1957) describes a world between today and Vonnegut's tale. In *Anthem* (New York: Bantam Books, 1946), she takes equality to a far greater extreme by describing a world where the collective is valued exclusively over the Individual. (She uses a narrative form without any singular pronouns—"we" instead of "I" and "they" instead of "he" or "she".) Although complete equality is truly achieved in Rand's world (outside of the rulers), the price is too high: no freedom and a standard of living out of the Middle Ages.

27. W. Ryan, *Blaming the Victim* (New York: Random House, 1971), p. 274.

28. B. Page, *Who Gets What from Government?* (Berkeley: University of California Press, 1983), pp. 6–8. Page remarks later that "societies like China, which have tried to build a new socialist person, undoubtedly have some lessons (positive and negative) to teach us" (p. 220).

29. Thurow, *Generating Inequality,* pp. 49–50. M. Kaus (*The End of Equality* [New York: Basic Books; 1992], p. 12) identifies Page, Thurow, and their ilk as "Money Liberals" who fail to understand the tradeoff between income equality and efficiency. Kaus argues for a more pragmatic "Civic Liberalism."

30. Using an analogy to a chessboard, Adam Smith noted that such people do "not consider that the pieces upon the chessboard have another principle of motion besides that which the hand impresses upon them. . . . Every single piece has a principle of motion of its own, although different from that which the legislature might choose to impress upon it." (*The Theory of Moral Sentiments* [Oxford, England: Clarendon Press, 1976.])

31. Page admits that "indeed, the poor of the United States are already rich by the standards of much of the rest of the world. But the problem is that poverty is

not only absolute; it is also relative" (*Who Gets What from Government?* p. 16). Equality proponents also tend to merely assert that incomes are distributed very unequally. Often there are no comparisons drawn to other countries. Page does note, however, that Sweden's income distribution is very similar to ours (p. 216). See M. Kimenyi, *The Economics of Poverty, Discrimination and Public Policy* (Cincinnati: South-Western, 1995, pp. 397–405) for specific numbers.

32. Refer to the numbers in Chapter 2 as necessary concerning higher tax rates and subsequently lower tax revenues.

33. M. Friedman, *Capitalism and Freedom* (Chicago: University of Chicago Press, 1962), pp. 190–195.

34. Currently, four states and San Diego are allowing food stamp programs to be "cashed out." Two other states have been approved for this experiment; three other applications are pending. (J. Dixon, "Replacing Food Stamps with Cash Challenged," *Louisville Courier Journal,* March 18, 1994.)

35. E. Browning and J. Browning, *Public Finance and the Price System,* 3rd ed. (New York: Harper-Collins, 1987), p. 290.

14

Still Losing Ground

Charles Murray's *Losing Ground* was probably the most important book on welfare policy from the 1980s. Because of its importance and lasting relevance, it is worthwhile to summarize its contribution to the policy dialogue concerning welfare.[1] Murray sets out to explain the "poverty/spending paradox"—why did progress against measured poverty slow down or stop just as the War on Poverty began?

Murray's Thesis

Murray's explanation is that welfare programs changed the rules of the game, but only for the poor: "A government's social policy helps set the rules of the game—the stakes, the risks, the payoffs, the tradeoffs, and the strategies for making a living. . . . The most compelling explanation for the marked shift in the fortunes of the poor is that they continued to respond, as they always had, to the world as they found it, but that we—meaning the not-poor and un-disadvantaged—had changed the rules of their world. Not of our world, just of theirs.... We tried to provide more for the poor and produced more poor instead. We tried to remove the barriers to escape from poverty, and inadvertently built a trap."[2]

Murray contends that only the behavior of those with low incomes is directly affected by welfare programs. We see a similar effect with the minimum wage. When it is increased, unskilled (often poor) workers are the only ones directly affected. Murray's story is a well-developed version of the standard concerns about efficiency and work disincentives for the poor.

Murray's thesis concerns the impact of welfare on incentives for the poor. But because of limitations in the available data, he uses statistics on blacks (or non-whites) and whites as a proxy for the poor and non-poor. Obviously this is an imperfect proxy, since many blacks are non-poor and many whites are poor. Fortunately, the overlap between the groups serves to strengthen the ramifications of these numbers for reaching conclusions about the poor. To the extent that blacks are non-poor, blacks (as a proxy for the poor) will make the statistics concerning the poor "look better" than they should.[3]

Although Murray is more concerned with the impact on the poor, a disproportionate burden borne by minorities would also be troubling. As we saw throughout Part 2, a number of policies inadvertently hammer the poor and thus harm minorities in particular. Incentive problems as a result of welfare programs are a matter of income class, but they have ramifications for race as well.

After providing some historical background and perspective, Murray discusses the goals of the War on Poverty. The idea was to provide people with a reasonable standard of living and to enable them to escape dependence on the government (the long-term goal). To a great extent, the first goal has been met. Sar Levitan observes that "if poverty is defined as a lack of basic needs, it's almost been eliminated."[4] Unfortunately, the second goal has been far more elusive. As we saw earlier, there are problems with the government's measurement of poverty. But regardless, advances against long-term poverty have apparently been limited since money for the Great Society programs began to flow. This is the paradox Murray tries to explain.[5]

The Evidence

From there, Murray looks at how the state of the poor (proxied by blacks) has changed over time in a number of areas. In particular, he compares the pre–Great Society period to the time since the programs of the Great Society took effect. In general, the former time period featured improvement (sometimes quite substantial); the latter period has often been marked by stagnancy or even regress. We will look at the statistics he emphasizes most: employment and family structure.

It is easy to see why these are crucial categories. One would expect there to be a strong link between poverty and unemployment. (This also explains why government has often tried to provide jobs and job training.) And family structure impacts virtually all aspects of the lives of parents and their children. As Greg Duncan and Saul Hoffman note, "National data still support the claim that schooling and delayed childbearing are sufficient for most women, black and white, to avoid poverty."[6] Ironically, one of JFK's stated goals for welfare policy was to promote the "integrity and preservation of the family unit."[7] In stark contrast, the rapid increase in single heads of household since the mid-1960s is extremely troubling.

Unemployment

Murray looks at unemployment for black males and notes that until the mid-1950s, it was nearly the same as white unemployment. Murray points to the loss of Southern agricultural jobs and an increase in the real minimum wage to explain the increases in black unemployment into the 1960s. After stabilizing, there was another increase in the late 1960s and into the 1970s. This increase coincides with the rapid increase in funding for the Great Society programs.

In Table 14.1, Murray narrows it down further: Young black males behaved much differently than older black males. The difference between the 16- to 24-year-olds and those older than 25 is amazing. The older age group was not only immune to the ill effects of the Great Society programs, its numbers actually improved. This also illustrates why discrimination cannot be a primary explanation for poor economic outcomes in the United States. If so, older and younger blacks would have struggled in a similar manner. In addition, young whites (as a proxy for the non-poor) did not have the same trouble with unemployment as their black counterparts. Apparently, something changed for those who were young and poor.

Labor Force Participation

Murray also describes the decrease in black labor force participation rates after the late 1960s as the "first-ever large-scale voluntary withdrawal from the labor market by able-bodied males."[8] This is alarming for many reasons. First, these numbers are more troubling than the unemployment statistics, since these people were not even actively looking for work. Second, it runs counter to one of the goals of welfare policy: to promote long-term independence. Third, if young people fail to work at an early age, they will fail to acquire the job training and other

TABLE 14.1   Change in Mean Unemployment for Black Males by Age, 1951–1965 Versus 1966–1980

Age Group	Change in Mean Unemployment 1951–1965 vs. 1966–1980
55–64	-38.0%
45–54	-32.9%
35–44	-31.5%
25–34	-15.9%
20–24	+18.6%
18–19	+39.7%
16–17	+72.4%

SOURCE: C. Murray, *Losing Ground: American Social Policy 1950–1980* (New York: Basic Books, 1984), p. 73.

work-related experience they will need later in life to earn reasonable incomes.

When unemployment is high, low labor force participation is easier to understand—workers are said to be "discouraged." But this decrease came in a tight labor market, when unemployment was not a serious problem. Did the decrease occur because more black males went to school? School enrollments did increase somewhat, but not by nearly as much as labor force participation decreased. Further, school enroll-ments *and* labor force participation increased for whites.

In sum, Murray observes that poor (proxied by black) males who came of age in the late 1960s behaved differently in labor markets. Why? Murray argues that it was because the rules of the game were changed for the poor. Certainly, the results correlate with the work disincentives that accompanied the expanded welfare programs of the Great Society.

Female Heads of Household

To measure the state of the family, Murray discusses the increase in teenage pregnancies before focusing primarily on the staggering trends in female-headed households. William Raspberry notes that "the per-centage of black households headed by a husband and wife remained around 80% in every census from 1890 to 1960."[9] Murray notes that for blacks, the percentage of children born into two-parent households fell from 78% in 1950 to 72% in 1968 and 59% in 1980. Although the per-centage was diminishing before the Great Society, the rate of decrease accelerated afterward. From 1950 to 1968, the rate fell by .33 percentage points per year; from 1968 to 1980, the rate fell by 1.08 per year. The pro-portion of white children born into two-parent households also declined, but not as significantly as for blacks.[10]

Since then, black illegitimacy rates have skyrocketed. By 1991, only 32% of births to black women were within two-parent households; between 1980 and 1991, the rate had fallen by 2.45 percentage points per year. Meanwhile, white rates had fallen from 85% in 1985 to 78% in 1991, only four percentage points more than the rate that motivated Daniel Moynihan to write about the "breakdown of the black family."[11]

Is this a race or a class issue? Murray argues it is a class issue first—that the rules of the game changed for the poor, who happen to be dispropor-tionately minority. In 1991, women with a high school education or less were responsible for 82% of illegitimate births in the United States; women with family incomes under $20,000 were responsible for 69%. Further, Murray cites a Labor Department study that found that 44% of births to white women living below the poverty line were illegitimate; for those above the poverty line, the rate of illegitimacy was only 6%.[12] Illegit-imacy is mostly an issue of poverty and the policies that affect the poor.[13]

Summary

Murray devotes the second section of his book to the evidence concerning the state of the world for blacks (as a proxy for the poor). He finds that behavior in many arenas changed dramatically, but only for certain groups of people. He determines that young black (poor) males exhibited detrimental labor market behavior—both higher unemployment and lower labor force participation rates. In addition, the state of black families grew significantly worse as measured by teen pregnancies and illegitimacy rates. Finally, these trends either began or became worse just as the programs of the Great Society began to be substantially funded.

Murray illustrates that ironically, the general outcomes are just the opposite of what one would have expected upon entering the War on Poverty. Given the progress through the mid-1960s, the view from 1966 would have been that great gains against poverty were on the horizon. The idea was that "since government was now serious about ending poverty," certainly it would be able to defeat it. In addition, the civil rights movement had won great victories, economic growth seemed secure, and job-training programs were well established. With past progress against poverty and then-current reforms in civil rights, victory in the war against poverty seemed to be only a matter of time.

In fact, the results that followed were ludicrous compared to any reasonable expectations in the mid-1960s. Although progress has been made in some areas, many other areas have worsened dramatically. Once into the mid-1970s, policymakers began to realize that the situation was not getting much better, resembling a domestic version of Vietnam. In addition, the negative income tax (NIT) experimental results pointed to serious work disincentives. What went wrong? Why did behavior change and why didn't policymakers have the foresight to anticipate such changes?

Developing Murray's Explanation

Murray argues that after the fact, the results were not particularly surprising. The poor simply responded in a rational manner to the changed institutions and rules they faced. One crucial error underlying the lack of foresight was the assumption that the poor and the non-poor would behave the same given the same financial inducements.

As we saw in Chapter 13, it is easy to imagine that $10,000 in welfare benefits would be viewed as a safety net by someone from the middle class and as a hammock by someone who is poor. The key is that the inducement is the same in absolute dollars but is quite different relative to what each can earn in the labor market. Welfare benefits are not a long-term temptation for someone who can earn $30,000 per year; for someone who can earn only $12,000, it is a different story.

This also explains why the young have been more severely affected by welfare policies. As we have seen, young black males' employment experiences differed greatly from those of older black males. Since they had fewer skills and less experience, the ability of the young to earn income was less at the time the rules were changed. In addition, they probably had not earned income or developed a work ethic. Thus, welfare was a greater long-term temptation for young and relatively unskilled workers. As with the minimum wage, the rules of the game were changed for the poor and unskilled.

In Chapter 13, I developed the concept that by definition, welfare programs have disincentives. Murray develops this theme in the context of work and marriage, using a hypothetical average newly formed poor family. He compares the options for the couple under the 1960 and 1970 welfare plans and their subsequent incentives. Often, under the new rules, a couple could do better financially by not marrying but still living together.

Under AFDC, the government support given to a single woman with a child is often more steady than a husband's income; welfare makes bearing illegitimate children less of an economic risk.[14] In addition, the presence of unemployment insurance encourages people to leave the labor force. In other words, the economic incentives encourage intermittent labor force participation and single-parent heads of households. Murray concludes that the programs of the Great Society transformed traditional working-class families into welfare recipients.

Some "Non-Economic" Considerations

Since Murray is a sociologist, he also focuses on factors that cannot be measured but are nonetheless important—status, virtue, and stigmata. With the ideological changes behind the War on Poverty, responsibility moved away from the individual and toward the system. Workers and non-workers would now receive government assistance. At the same time, the distinction between the deserving and undeserving was blurred. Independent of what one thinks about the appropriate level of stigma to be associated with receiving welfare, removing it lowered the cost of behaviors that are usually considered inappropriate, including intermittent labor force participation and setting up single-parent households.

This trend continues today. Christopher Jencks says, "Now that the mass media, the schools, and even the churches have begun to treat single parenthood as a regrettable but inescapable part of modern life, we can hardly expect the respectable poor to carry on their struggle against illegitimacy and desertion with their old fervor. They will still deplore the behavior, but they cannot make it morally taboo."[15]

In addition, Murray argues that removing the blame from individuals requires removing credit as well. If the system gets the blame for failure, the system must get at least some of the credit for success. Finally, welfare compromised and discouraged standard beliefs about marriage and a work ethic. In many cases, the economic incentives were such that getting married instead of living together was considered stupid and working hard instead of collecting a government check was ridiculed. This may also explain some of the differences in behavior between the young and the old. Older workers are more likely to have ingrained traditional values and thus are less likely to succumb to the incentives associated with welfare programs.

Finally, Murray adds that one's willingness to bear risk differs with respect to income. The closer one is to "the edge," the less likely one is to take a chance and forgo a secure, although probably lower, income. He uses the illustration of a rice farmer who is told by a government agency that growing jute would be more profitable.[16] Even though this may be true, a farmer of few resources cannot afford to take the risk of having a bad crop—especially one he cannot eat. Given its riskiness, the farmer is likely to decline the proposition regardless of the advertised rate of return.

The same aversion to risk is evident among those living in dependence on the dole; welfare provides a steady, albeit small, stream of income. Imagine the difficulty in turning away from a consistent source of income to the labor market, especially if one hasn't held a job in a while. If the welfare recipient loses the job, getting back on welfare will be problematic and may involve substantial delays. Can quality child care be obtained at a reasonable rate? What about transportation—is the bus system quick, convenient, and easy to figure out? Although welfare may be unpleasant and degrading, for many, it may be easier and safer to simply remain on the dole.

Murray's Conclusions and Policy Recommendations

Murray questions whether government is able to effectively target those who are needy, and he voices the standard concerns about incentives and efficiency. In fact, the primary objective of his book is to develop the welfare and Good Samaritan dilemmas with intuitive stories and the relevant data.

Given the work disincentives and the subsidization of undesirable behaviors, Murray concludes that despite their intentions, the reforms of the Great Society were "a blunder on purely pragmatic grounds" and "wrong on moral grounds."[17] The rules of the game were changed for the poor in a way that hurt them, especially in the long run. Further, the ones imposing the rules were mostly unaffected by the change in regime.

In response, Murray proposes the complete abolition of public welfare. Although Murray admits this may seem harsh, he believes private charity would step forward (as it did in the 19th century) to take care of the truly needy. Murray also realizes this is currently not a particularly realistic proposal. As we saw earlier, President Reagan was pummeled for supposedly cutting social welfare programs. In the early 1980s, with ideology swinging in favor of less government, Reagan was unable to affect substantive change in this policy arena.

A primary factor standing in the way of such reform is a widespread ideology that at least implicitly espouses tremendous faith in government over economic markets and private charity. Robert Nozick has observed that the arguments surrounding public welfare are always about its size, not its existence. But in Murray's words, the question should not be "how much good we can afford to do, but how to do good at all."[18] We assume government will be more effective than the private sector in reaching the desired goals; the public has a vague sense that government-sponsored welfare is the "right thing to do."

This faith is still strong but has been diminishing since the 1960s. The tenets of public choice economics (self-interested behavior in political markets) tarnished the idea that our elected officials always serve the best interests of the country. Watergate and numerous other scandals have sullied the image we have of our elected representatives. Government's failures have been notable since the 1960s as well: the (Keynesian) failure to manipulate the macroeconomy and end recessions, the war in Vietnam, the War on Poverty, the War on Drugs, and so on. But until this faith diminishes further, a return to private charitable efforts is unlikely.

Murray describes the current debate as the "angels" (equality-minded) versus the "accountants" (efficiency-minded). Although their goals and motives are usually the same, angels frequently question the intentions of the accountants. Murray responds by questioning the "compassion" of the angels and the current system. He concludes that "it is time to reconsider a social policy that salves our consciences ('Look how compassionate I am.') at the expense of those whom we wished to help. . . . When reforms finally do occur, they will happen not because stingy people have won, but because generous people have stopped kidding themselves."[19]

Notes

1. *Losing Ground* was reprinted in 1994.
2. C. Murray, *Losing Ground: American Social Policy 1950–1980* (New York: Basic Books, 1984), p. 9.

3. This would be like surveying those who go to bowling alleys and ballet performances as a proxy for poor and rich people. Whereas there is a high degree of correlation between those activities and income, the relationship is far from perfect. As in this example, differences in the collected data would tend to understate the differences between poor and rich people.

4. Quoted in M. Arnold, "We're Winning the War on Poverty," *National Observer*, February 19, 1977, p. 1 (cited in M. Olasky, *The Tragedy of American Compassion* [Washington, DC: Regnery Gateway, 1992], p. 184).

5. Murray rejects two other explanations: (1) A slow economy and Vietnam derailed the War on Poverty. Vietnam can be only a short-term factor at best and the United States experienced economic growth throughout much of the 1970s and 1980s. (*Income* growth was not as strong; higher labor force participation, a shift toward fringe benefits as opposed to cash, and a shift toward smaller household size account for the difference.) (2) There were more elderly and thus more people dependent on government. But progress against poverty for those under the age of 65 stopped sooner than for those older than 65 (*Losing Ground*, pp. 58–61).

6. G. Duncan and S. Hoffman, "Teenage Behavior and Subsequent Poverty," in *The Urban Underclass*, ed. C. Jencks and P. Peterson (Washington, DC: Brookings Institution, 1991), p. 172.

7. Murray, *Losing Ground*, p. 124.

8. Ibid., p. 77.

9. W. Raspberry, "Hollowed Communities," *Washington Post*, November 19, 1993.

10. Murray, *Losing Ground*, chapter 9.

11. C. Murray, "The Coming White Underclass," *Wall Street Journal*, October 29, 1993.

12. Ibid.

13. Demographic changes are also influential: Higher divorce rates and marrieds having fewer children have also contributed to higher illegitimacy (percentage) rates.

14. D. Ellwood cites survey results that over half of all Americans believe that poor women often have babies so they can collect welfare, and an even larger number of poor Americans believe the same thing. (*Poor Support: Poverty in the American Family* [New York: Basic Books, 1988], p. 22, citing I. Lewis and W. Schneider, "Hard Times: The Public on Poverty," *Public Opinion*, June/July 1985, pp. 2–7.)

15. C. Jencks, "Deadly Neighborhoods," *New Republic*, June 13, 1988.

16. Murray, *Losing Ground*, pp. 155–156.

17. Ibid., p. 219.

18. Ibid., p. 204.

19. Ibid., pp. 204, 236.

15

Local and Voluntary
Versus Federal and Bureaucratic

In *The Tragedy of American Compassion,* Marvin Olasky digs through the Library of Congress and even poses as one of the homeless, looking for solutions to the seemingly intractable problems associated with welfare programs.[1] He concentrates on pre–20th century attempts—mostly voluntary and local—to help the poor. Using those, he focuses on the strengths of past charitable efforts, the weaknesses of contemporary programs, and the path we have taken to reach the current quagmire.

The Local Option

Throughout the book, Olasky emphasizes the role of ideology in determining the optimal prescriptions for dealing with the poor—whether to focus on helping individuals or on changing the system. When people are down-and-out, are they responsible or is it the system's fault?

If individuals are responsible for their situation, local or individual solutions have a number of potential strengths. Personal involvement can more easily lead to categorization and discernment, which are crucial in allowing a giver to distinguish between different types of poverty and to prescribe the appropriate remedy: Should assistance be in the form of a hand or a push? Olasky notes that pre–20th century charitable organizations frequently used "work tests" to separate the truly needy from the shiftless. For example, men were asked to chop wood and women were asked to sew to earn their keep.[2] These tests allowed discernment and taught good work habits. Further, since the fruits of their labor were donated to the truly needy, it helped to draw a distinction between the able and the helpless.

Personal involvement and a belief in individual responsibility also promote confrontation in areas where the recipient's behavior is not socially acceptable. Taken together, work tests and confrontation serve to minimize the Good Samaritan's dilemma—that short-run assistance encourages long-run dependence. Olasky notes that this "tough love" was often counter to the first instinct of givers to provide unconditional assistance. Leaders in the charitable movement had to encourage their new volunteers to stifle the impulse to provide immediate aid. Without discernment, well-intentioned aid could actually harm a recipient.

Volunteers Versus Bureaucrats

Olasky also discusses the differences between the volunteers of pre-20th century efforts and the bureaucrats who currently run governmental social welfare programs. Clearly, volunteers are apt to be more careful when distributing their own time and money than bureaucrat A, who is paid to use money taken from B to give to C. Further, pre-20th century efforts were often centered in the church, where members responded to Biblical imperatives to help the poor. Volunteers, because they work without pay, may have a greater dedication to helping the poor than a bureaucrat, who may tend toward finding new clientele and being relatively unconcerned with lifting people out of dependence on the dole.

Politicians also benefit from the ability to redistribute concentrated benefits to an interest group—the poor—while seeming simultaneously to embrace "compassion." Olasky quotes Nathaniel Ware, who in 1845 predicted an American governmental welfare system because "officeholders like to appeal to poor voters who would give them power to distribute large amounts of money and the patronage that accompanies expenditure."[3]

The Federal Solution

The roots of current policy lie in the ideological changes around the beginning of the 20th century. Olasky blames well-intentioned church leaders who were seduced by the opportunity to effect systemic change and politicians who pursued an extension of their power. He provides turn-of-the-century accounts that now look hopelessly naive and optimistic about their ability to end poverty using government. Poverty had been beaten back throughout the 19th century, and these new warriors were confident they would soon finish the job. After seeing what private-sector charitable efforts had been able to achieve, they thought government could simply extend those successful methods to eliminate poverty.

Why did the proposed solutions fail? Moving away from personal involvement and changing the view that individuals were mostly responsible for their plight led to indiscriminate giving by increasingly impersonal entities. What were the results? Existing charities that believed in the old-time religion were driven out by a variation of Gresham's law: Bad charity drives out good charity. In other words, the poor began to choose aid that did not require a work test. And those who tried to categorize and discern were labeled as Scrooges. "Work-tested" private charity was crowded out. For some, crowding out private charity was an unfortunate by-product. But for others, it was an explicit goal—bureaucrats wanted to restrict their competition. Others even argued that private efforts "let government off the hook."[4]

Further, government was not as effective. Without intimate knowledge of those who were to be helped, it was impossible to provide effective solutions. A universal approach to widely disparate problems resulted in people slipping through the cracks: fraud became much easier and the "welfare trap" so eloquently described in Charles Murray's *Losing Ground* was born.[5]

Defining Compassion

Olasky's final chapters provide explicit policy prescriptions and examples of contemporary charity success stories. But perhaps his most important contribution is that he reclaims the moral high ground in welfare policy by properly defining "compassion." In modern times, compassion has become a euphemism for "more funding," whether in education, welfare, or economic assistance to foreign countries. The idea that more money will help is simply taken as axiomatic.[6]

Those who disagree are often branded as bean counters who don't care. But in fact, money frequently harms recipients in the short or the long run. Olasky turns the usual compassion argument on its head by noting that those who give money are often the stingy ones; they fail to give what is truly needed—time and personal involvement. Too often, writing a check serves only as "miscalled charity which soothes its conscience with indiscriminate giving."[7]

Many argue that such "miscalled charity" is too widely available and should not be given without conditions. In the *Washington Post,* a Minneapolis homeless man wrote that "if 'help' alone were the solution, the Twin Cities homeless would have no problems. Or rather, the Twin Cities would have no homeless. Here, you see, help isn't just available, it's abundant. You can't swing a dead cat without hitting a church or a charity that gives away food or clothing seven days a week. . . . The homeless in Minneapolis, America's social service nirvana, are for the most part blithely disinterested in solving their problems."[8]

Is this approach compassionate? In the words of Walter Williams, giving money to people in this fashion is "to do to them what we would never do to someone we loved ... (give) money without responsibility."[9]

Olasky's Recommendations

Although Olasky is harsh toward government efforts, he repeatedly cautions that the key ingredient is personal involvement; a private charity dispensing aid indiscriminately is little improvement. In sum, to help poor people, the focus must turn to (1) local and voluntary efforts; (2) individuals giving time rather than just money; and (3) categorization and discernment instead of indiscriminate giving. In his words, "Change in poverty fighting is needed, but Americans need to be clear about the reasons for change. Governmental welfare programs need to be fought not because they are too expensive—although clearly much money is wasted—but because they are inevitably too stingy in what is really important. . . . At the same time, the crisis of the modern welfare state is not just a crisis of government. Too many private charities dispense aid indiscriminately and thus provide, instead of points of light, alternative shades of darkness. . . . It's time to learn from the warm hearts and hard heads of earlier times."[10]

In *With Justice for All,* John Perkins describes his efforts with Voice of Calvary Ministries to help the poor in Jackson, Mississippi. Perkins calls individuals and churchgoers to voluntary frugal living and advocates investing money and time in others. "When I mention redistribution, people think I'm talking about taking all the money from the rich and giving it to the poor. That wouldn't help a bit! . . . our redistribution must involve us—our time, our energy, our gifts and our skills."[11]

There are a number of potential criticisms of this approach. Public choice considerations dictate that bureaucrats will vigorously oppose any attempts to move from current welfare programs toward local and voluntary efforts. They will argue that only trained specialists can help the poor. However, their arguments are far from objective; they have an economic incentive to maintain the status quo. Other people believe the system is to blame; they view categorization and discernment as paternalistic and moralistic, or as an excuse not to help the needy. They are correct to an extent, but the goal of categorization and discernment is not to avoid helping people but to require self-confrontation and change that would benefit them.[12] (This is the method used by Alcoholics Anonymous.) There are others who cannot see significant long-run benefits to this approach.

Finally (and I believe most important), many opponents lack the courage to allow people to suffer in the short run to encourage progress in the long run. William Bennett notes that "virtue by itself is no guarantee of right action, which requires more than good intentions. We need in addition both the wisdom to know what the right thing to do is, and the will to do it."[13] Too often, aid givers are not strong enough to provide the tough love that is truly compassionate.

Olasky is careful to say his book should not be used as an excuse to avoid helping the poor. The problem is not giving too much but giving in the wrong way. Olasky provides compelling evidence that the right way is to return to the personal involvement that was the hallmark of charitable efforts to help the poor in the pre–20th century "war on poverty."

Is Relying on Voluntary Efforts Practical?

With all the people who claim to be compassionate—tens of millions of liberals and followers of any religion, we certainly have the capacity to assist the poor on a voluntary basis. With disposable incomes five times higher than before 1900 (when voluntary efforts were quite effective), we certainly have the financial resources.[14] In addition, if government relinquished control over welfare, taxes would fall and disposable incomes would rise, enabling individuals to help others even more.[15] Finally, as disposable incomes increase, the *percentage* of charitable giving should increase as well. But although we undoubtedly have the capacity, do we have the desire? Pre–20th century Americans supported the poor without assistance from the government, but has our current ability to be compassionate atrophied too much? Has the government controlled poverty relief for so long that the private sector would be unable to respond adequately?

One can only speculate, but we have historical basis for believing people are capable of supporting the poor through private means. As Olasky illustrates, voluntary charitable efforts were quite effective until they were superseded by government efforts in the 20th century. For example, in 1891, more than 2,000 volunteers in Baltimore made 8,227 visits to 4,025 families.[16] They provided housing and other material needs and dealt with substance abuse.

More important, we have recent evidence that the desire to help voluntarily is far from dead. First, whether the disaster is floods in Iowa, hurricanes in Florida, or earthquakes in California, people overwhelmingly respond to others in need. Second, charitable giving by individuals has been increasing more rapidly than income since at least the 1950s. From 1955 to 1979, donations increased by an average of 3.1% (after inflation). And contrary to its label "the decade of greed," the 1980s witnessed more rapidly increasing levels of charitable giving by individuals; the growth rate rose to 5.1%.[17]

Perhaps the 1980s are an accurate test case of what would happen if government shut down its poverty industry. With (1) the perception of decreased governmental assistance and the subsequent guilt or desire to help the poor, (2) growing real incomes,[18] and (3) lower marginal tax rates, charitable giving increased dramatically. In the past, people have responded appropriately; it seems likely that people would respond again to the opportunity to help the poor.

Additional evidence can be garnered by analyzing charitable contributions as a percentage of personal income. From 1950 to 1964, charity steadily increased from 2.05% of income to 2.65%. From 1964 to 1980 (the beginning of the Great Society programs to the Reagan administration), government became more actively involved and private efforts fell consistently from 2.65% to 2.1%. In the 1980s with the perception that government was pulling back in its efforts to help the poor, charity again increased steadily from 2.1% to 2.7%.[19]

In addition, it seems that people are willing (if not eager) to help those whose circumstances are beyond their control and those who want to help themselves. Think of how you feel when you assist people who are likely to embrace the opportunity to get back on their feet again. For the truly needy, one would imagine that government intervention in providing financial relief would be replaced more than adequately by private efforts. For the not so needy, receiving assistance might become more difficult or might have work tests attached. In Olasky's world, that's not such a bad thing.

Reform: Moving to Private and Local Efforts

It seems likely that the private sector would respond appropriately, but this is speculation. Although some may perceive such a leap of faith as too risky, we should certainly move toward private-sector involvement. At the very least, for the advantages enumerated, we should choose local government involvement over state or federal efforts while encouraging private charitable efforts over public welfare programs.

For example, Mississippi governor Kirk Fordice has begun to implement the Faith and Families Project. The goal is to be a catalyst in motivating churches to provide requisite skills to those currently on welfare by using true compassion. Obviously, individual attention given by volunteers to address disparate needs is bound to be more effective than most government efforts.[20]

In addition, the private sector should be used in other areas such as job training and helping people move from welfare to the workforce. For example, America Works, a private training agency, contracts to provide these services with state welfare agencies in Connecticut and New York.[21] It has an 85%–90% success rate—measured in terms of workers who stay with the same firm for at least a year. Its average client gets a private-sector job starting at $15,000 (with fringe benefits) after having been on welfare rolls for five years. America Works is paid as much as $5,300 per client, but only after the client completes four months with a firm. Instead of providing lengthy periods of training, the company focuses on helping its clients to quickly obtain and then keep a job. To this end, it provides one week of general training (teaching "strict standards" as well as relevant job-seeking and job-holding skills). After clients complete the initial training and are successful at finding a job, counselors continue to monitor their progress and provide other services to ease the transition to the labor market.

As a small private firm, America Works is better equipped than public agencies to match prospective employees with firms. As a company driven by profits instead of a bureaucracy driven by maximizing its budget, it has better incentives to perform. What is the best role for government? Should it pay for such services or provide them directly? As before, the private sector operating under the profit motive has better incentives to provide efficient, high-quality service.

And if government is to be directly involved, it should be as local as possible. Local efforts provide more flexible solutions for widely varying circumstances. How does a federal bureaucrat know what is best for every city or for every poor person in that city?[22] Local government can be held more accountable by voters; local welfare is more capable of dealing with widely disparate problems and different standards of living; local efforts can reduce fraud and "milking the system."[23]

Reform: Returning to Categorization and Discernment

Moving toward local and private efforts would clearly be an improvement. Independent of the level of assistance, local and private efforts will be the most efficient and flexible. Yet two key questions remain: What is the best way to help the needy? And is there one best way to help the needy? The answers are dependent on ideology. If people are mostly responsible for their own plight, the solution involves individuals changing their behavior. This requires categorization and discernment from those who dispense aid. In this case, there is no one best method for helping all poor people. Some need a helping hand, others need a push; some use the current system as a safety net, others use it as a hammock. Only a system that categorizes and discerns can hope to differentiate between the two and provide effective solutions.[24]

As such, shelters and job-training programs should embrace the idea of individual responsibility. In Louisville, Kentucky, the Morgan Center enforces rules of conduct to categorize and discern: Drinking is not allowed and residents have certain duties such as mopping down their area every morning.[25] Center director Jay Davidson says, "We didn't want to be just another warehouse for the homeless. . . . We wanted to go from a bowl-of-soup-and-place-to-sleep shelter to a place for homeless men who want to make something of themselves." For his decision, the center has received complaints from some of the homeless, homeless advocates, other shelters, and the ACLU. In response, Davidson asks, "Why shouldn't the sober homeless have a place where they don't have to deal with a drunk carrying on a conversation at 3:00 in the morning?"

In 1983, Sisters Connie Driscoll and Therese O'Sullivan began a ministry to help Chicago's homeless women and children. They also focus on accountability and personal responsibility. They enforce strict rules about wake-up, curfew, neatness, and cleanliness. They require education (at least through a GED) and substance abuse programs when necessary. And all participants take classes in parenting, comparative shopping, and "life skills." Despite all of the rules, Driscoll says they are regarded as "tough but fair" with the result that "women beat our doors down." Driscoll concludes that "discipline and responsibility are what these women need, and this 'tough love' works."[26]

In Durham, North Carolina, the Durham Service Corps teaches job skills and work habits to the most at-risk members of the local community—dropouts who have had trouble with drugs or the law.[27] The rules are stringent. To enter the program, one must pass a work test: three days of "orientation," including two days of "hard, dirty work." After that, prospective corps members may be accepted into the program after a month's probation period. Members are required to be on time every day (7:45 AM), participate in calisthenics, and work 25 hours per week (earning at least the minimum wage). In addition, they attend nine hours of classes per week to earn a high school diploma, to prepare them for college, or to learn specific job skills. Further, they are not allowed to use profanity, alcohol, or other drugs. Half of those who begin the program drop out or are expelled. But those who remain take firm steps toward a better life in the future.[28]

Categorization and discernment exclude some but allow a way up for others. Such an approach removes distractions from reaching goals, provides self-control mechanisms for those who want to end their dependence on the dole, and teaches people that they can help those who can't help themselves. Finally, it gives more hope to those who are trying to help.

Advocacy of tough love is not equivalent to inactivity. Elie Wiesel once commented that "the opposite of love is not hate but indifference." Edgar Nye has said that "kind words will never die—neither will they buy groceries."[29] Helping the poor in a compassionate way involves time and effort. The optimal solution to the problem of poverty is working with people one-on-one, requiring changed behaviors, and practicing tough love. "Let no close-fisted brother hide behind our words, and find in them an excuse not to give at all. What is censured is not giving too much, but giving in the wrong way."[30]

Notes

1. The early parts of this chapter borrow from my book review of Olasky's work that appeared in *Public Choice,* November 1993.

2. M. Olasky, *The Tragedy of American Compassion* (Washington, DC. Regnery Gateway, 1992), p. 105.

3. Ibid., p. 48.

4. Ibid., p. 137. In *Abortion Rites: A Social History of Abortion in America* (Wheaton, IL: Crossway Books, 1992), p. 248, Olasky quotes a prominent contemporary social worker who complained about "untrained" people "taking positions for which they were not fitted."

5. C. Brace labeled fraud "the science of alms." (*The Dangerous Classes of New York and Twenty Years' Work Among Them,* 3rd ed. [New York: Wynkoop and Hallenbeck, 1880], p. 384.)

6. D. Lee remarks that "the notion that compassion toward the poor requires favoring expansion of government transfer programs has achieved the status of revealed truth" ("The Tradeoff Between Equality and Efficiency: Short Run Politics and Long Run Realities," *Public Choice* 53, no. 2, 1987, pp. 149–165).

7. Olasky, *The Tragedy of American Compassion,* p. 108. C. Murray comments that "the barrier to radical reform of social policy is not the pain it would cause the intended beneficiaries of the present system, but the pain it would cause the donors" (*Losing Ground: American Social Policy 1950–1980* [New York: Basic Books, 1984], p. 236).

8. D. Hobbes, "Down, Out and Overindulged," *Washington Post,* February 14, 1993.

9. W. Williams, *Christian Science Monitor,* September 23, 1991.

10. Olasky, *The Tragedy of American Compassion,* p. 233. In Murray's words, "When reforms finally do occur, they will happen not because stingy people have won, but because generous people have stopped kidding themselves" (*Losing Ground,* p. 236).

11. J. Perkins, *With Justice for All* (Ventura, CA: Regal Books, 1982), p. 154. Perkins also mentions Mendenhall Ministries, a similar effort led by Dolphus Weary in Mendenhall, Mississippi.

12. This is different than earlier discussions of paternalism. In this case, money is withheld (deciding not to intervene) as opposed to a law being imposed on one's behavior (intervention).

13. W. Bennett, *The Book of Virtues: A Treasury of Great Moral Stories* (New York: Simon and Schuster, 1994), p. 665.

14. U.S. Bureau of the Census, *Statistical Abstract of the United States* (Washington, DC: U.S. Department of the Treasury, 1994), Table 691.

15. It is also possible that contributions would decrease, since the desire to shelter income from taxation would diminish.

16. Olasky, *The Tragedy of American Compassion*, p. 80.

17. R. McKenzie, "Was It a Decade of Greed?" *Public Interest*, Winter 1992, pp. 91–96. McKenzie also found that in the 1980s, donations increased more quickly (58%) than spending on jewelry (41%) and eating out (22%).

18. During the 1990–1992 "recession," average household contributions fell by 7.1%. (D. Cross, "No Brother, I Can't Spare a Dime," *Washington Post National Weekly Edition*, April 25–May 1, 1994.)

19. See McKenzie, "Was It a Decade of Greed?" and C. Murray, *In Pursuit of Happiness and Good Government* (New York: Simon and Schuster, 1988), p. 276. D. Lee and R. McKenzie note that after the New Deal, charity began to shift from helping the poor to supporting religious organizations and the arts. (*Failure and Progress: The Bright Side of the Dismal Science* [Washington, DC: Cato Institute, 1993], p. 116.)

20. J. Maxwell, "Real Welfare Reform: Will the Church Be the Church?" *World*, November 5, 1994.

21. See S. Stern, "Back to Work," *Wall Street Journal*, September 7, 1993, and Indianapolis mayor Stephen Goldsmith's "End the Welfare Delivery Monopoly," *Wall Street Journal*, August 23, 1994.

22. In *Urban Illusions: New Approaches to Inner-City Unemployment*, poverty warrior Michael Bernick quickly returned from Washington, D.C., after learning that policymakers had "no understanding of how welfare operates at a local level: the dependency, the child care difficulties, the lack of skills and motivation. . . " ([New York: Praeger, 1987], p. 150).

23. In the old days, local provision of assistance in tightly knit communities and the inability to move easily from town to town because of poor transportation technology limited opportunities for fraud. Although fraud would be easier today, it would diminish compared to current federal programs.

24. In *The Cider House Rules* John Irving discusses tough love in the context of orphans ([New York: Bantam Books, 1985], pp. 22–23).

25. M. Quinlan, "Shelter's Rules Drive Some Away," *Louisville Courier Journal*, October 23, 1992.

26. Sister Connie Driscoll, "Chicago's House of Hope," *Policy Review*, Summer 1993, pp. 50–54.

27. J. Boyce, "Depression-Era Corps Inspires Test Program for 'At-Risk' Youths," *Wall Street Journal*, November 25, 1992. The Durham Service Corps is affiliated with Public/Private Ventures, a not-for-profit social research group in Philadelphia and the National Association of Service and Conservation Corps. The latter operates about 75 similar programs across the country.

28. The program costs $10,000 per corps member, less than half the cost of similar government programs. Part of their revenue is generated from contracting services to private firms and public works projects.

29. E. Nye, quoted in *Prism*, January 1994, p. 6.

30. Olasky, *The Tragedy of American Compassion*, p. 90 (paraphrasing Deuteronomy 15:7–8).

16

Religion and Poverty

There are many reasons for this chapter. First, religious organizations have been active in recommending policy on issues involving "social justice." To a large extent, their prescriptions have been ill-advised.[1] For instance, late-19th-century Christians supported the movement from private to public schools and giving government control of welfare efforts. In the past, Catholic leaders and the National Council of Churches were among the strongest advocates of socialism.[2] All three policies have had brutal consequences. Without a better understanding of economics, religious leaders should stick to religion.[3]

Second, as an Evangelical Christian (and an economist), I am eager to identify policies that help and harm the poor independent of what the church teaches about issues concerning the poor.[4] As should be evident by my advocacy of drug legalization and abolishing the minimum wage, my views do not always align with conventional Christian "wisdom" about what is best for the poor or others.

Third, although my religious beliefs are at the core of my interest in this area, I certainly do not claim a corner on morality, interpreting the Bible, or concern for the poor. Hindus, "cultural Christians," atheists, and others often have the same concerns. In fact, there seems to be a nearly universal desire to help the poor that stems from either religious beliefs or an arbitrary rule-of-thumb morality. Remember, Okun observed that given the costs of equalizing incomes, it is noteworthy that we see any equalization efforts at all; current welfare programs and charitable efforts reveal widespread concern for the poor.

Fourth, in debates over public policy, there are nearly incessant attempts to seize the moral high ground. We have seen this tension throughout the book—referring to the minimum wage as a "living wage," discussing the potential costs of drug legalization while ignoring the costs of prohibition, Murray's describing the debate between the angels and the accountants, Olasky's redefining how one usually thinks of compassion, and so on. Discussions about policy are often cast in terms of morality.

Finally, a faith in either markets or government underlies any informed debate about the optimal solutions to the country's problems, including poverty. Such a faith is implicit in discussions throughout the book; this chapter closes with an explicit discussion of free markets and government intervention as alternative "religions."

Angels Versus Accountants

Faith in government or markets also explains much of the rhetoric that surrounds public policy. If one believes government is best able to accomplish a given task, then objections to proposals for government activism are naturally met with the conclusion that the opponents must not care about the poor. In this case, those who disagree with the means to the end are accused of lacking compassion.

However, if one believes government is not able to accomplish the task more effectively than markets, then proposals for government activism are naturally met with concerns about costs, incentives, and government control. In this case, those who propose government solutions are accused of lacking understanding.

In sum, angels question the motives of the accountants and accountants question the understanding of the angels. But both sides need to recognize that although the means are different, the goals are often the same and each group is usually well intentioned. Most accountants have compassion despite the fact they do not advocate an activist solution. Angels are either relatively unconcerned with the costs of activism or do not see its relatively subtle costs.

Economic Laws

Sometimes, however, the means and ends are not reconcilable. For instance, if I insist with the greatest of intentions that I will flap my arms and fly from San Francisco to Los Angeles, my desires will be grounded by my inability to overcome the law of gravity. Similarly, many economic prescriptions implicitly ignore the laws of economics. Despite the good intentions underlying those "solutions," such proposals will be equally frustrated by reality.

Religious leaders and policymakers need to work within economic laws whether these laws are fair or not. Likewise, whether the law of gravity is fair is irrelevant. To be kind, one should note that the laws of economics are less obvious than the other laws of nature.[5] But we cannot believe in economic dictates as we want them to be or as we think they should be; we must accept them as they are.

Paul Heyne notes that often, "moral analysis is misguided because economic systems cannot operate in the way (people) suppose they do."[6] In those cases, "vision" is placed above facts, and ends are elevated above the means to those ends. In some sense, the concern is admirable and the desired goals are laudable, but the subsequent policy recommendations are often incompatible with reaching those goals. It is often said that the road to hell is paved with good intentions. This is certainly true for many proposals advocating government activism.

The point is not to tell religious leaders or others to be silent on economic questions. Blaise Pascal argued that "working hard to think clearly is the beginning of moral conduct." Concern for the poor must be supplemented with the reality of economic laws. Louis Brandeis warned about "men of zeal, well-meaning, but who lack understanding." Having zeal and compassion is great, but understanding is equally important— it needs to be a prerequisite, not an option, for policy prescriptions.[7]

A Call to Socialism?

In the past, the omission of "understanding," substantial zeal for the poor, and an avid faith in government have led many religious leaders to embrace socialism as the most desirable economic system. Although less prominent since the collapse of the Soviet bloc, the notion of the efficacy of government activism is still prevalent. (I am defining "socialism" as large degrees of government activism—generally involving redistributive policies whose spoken rationale is to promote more nearly equal incomes and other "fair" outcomes.)

This advocacy is based on four ideas. First, there is a general perception that socialism is less harsh than capitalism (or that government intervention is needed to smooth the rough edges of free markets). Market outcomes are far from pristine—factories shut down, workers are displaced, and so on. But as we have seen throughout the book, it is doubtful that political markets and government intervention are more friendly than economic markets, especially toward the poor. Second, some believe that the two economic systems are equally capable of providing material well-being. On anything but a small scale, this notion is historically unfounded. But because the economy of a church is "socialistic," its success may lead church leaders to commit a fallacy of composition. Third, some believe that material pursuits should be discouraged.[8] Although this may be true, it is a matter of opinion and thus should be a matter of individual choice, not coercion. In addition, restrictions on social, religious, and political freedoms usually accompany government control over economic freedoms.

Most important, many religious leaders infer from Scripture that socialism is the optimal system to pursue. On the surface, this might appear to be correct; "the people of Israel" (Old Testament) and "the early church" (New Testament) lived under a self-imposed socialistic system. From the Old Testament: "If there is a poor man among your brothers . . . be openhanded and freely lend him whatever he needs. Be careful not to harbor this wicked thought: 'the seventh year, the year for canceling debts, is near,' so that you do not show ill will toward your brother and give him nothing. . . . Give generously to him and do so without a grudging heart."[9]

This passage speaks primarily of lending, but it also implies outright gifts given the command to retire unpaid debts every seven years. Leviticus 19:10 is even more explicit: "Do not go over your vineyard a second time or pick up the grapes that have fallen. Leave them for the poor and the alien."[10]

From the New Testament's description of the early Christian church, Acts 2:44–45 reports that "all the believers were together and had everything in common. Selling their possessions and goods, they gave to anyone as he had need." This sounds similar to Karl Marx's dictum "From each according to his ability, to each according to his need." Further, Acts 2:47 reports that "the Lord added to their number daily those who were being saved." Clearly, God was happy with this behavior. Acts 4:32–35 continues: "All the believers were one in heart and mind. No one claimed that any of his possessions was his own, but they shared everything they had. . . . There were no needy persons among them. For from time to time those who owned lands or houses sold them, brought the money from the sales and put it at the apostles' feet, and it was distributed to anyone as he had need."

The early Christian church lived out socialism—all income and wealth went into a common pool to be distributed by the leaders as necessary.[11] It is easy to understand why some religious leaders have interpreted these verses as a call to pursue socialism as a national economic system and government intervention in general.

Government as the Good Samaritan

The parable of the Good Samaritan (Luke 10:30–37) is probably the most famous Biblical story about helping those in need. Christ describes a man who was robbed, stripped, beaten, and left for dead. Two religious leaders passed by, but a Samaritan stopped and rendered aid. After that, he brought the victim to a nearby town and paid for two months of lodging. He told the innkeeper he would return and pay for any other necessary expenses. Christ closes the parable by encouraging his audience to follow the example of the Samaritan.

With the examples of the way the early church lived and this parable, one could infer that government should be a good Samaritan for those in need.[12] However, there are a number of crucial distinctions between these biblical examples and the call for government intervention or the establishment of socialism as the national economic system. The history of the early church and Christ's parable do not imply greater *government* involvement.

First, the early church and the parable of the Good Samaritan are examples of voluntary behavior.[13] In stark contrast, government activity is coercive by definition. It is sad that even the founder of the American Economic Association, Richard Ely, failed to understand this crucial distinction. He believed that government should be engaged in "coercive philanthropy."[14] In contrast, the early church fully preserved personal property rights and used voluntary efforts to redistribute to those in need; socialism compromises or eliminates property rights by redistributing income using force.

Second, both stories were at a local level and on a relatively small scale, where socialism is more likely to be effective. Government activity is often non-local and is almost universally conducted on a large scale. Thus, there are important differences between the biblical call for individual Christians and what the Bible has to say about the optimal role of government.

Incentive Problems Revisited

With any form of wealth redistribution based on need, there are incentive problems for recipients—those in need. These problems are extended when one moves from voluntary to coercive, from local to non-local, and from small to large scale.

For instance, it is easier to discern true need and monitor the behavior of recipients in a smaller and local setting; fraud and long-term dependency are less likely. Further, to the extent that guilt is a factor, people are more likely to abuse a system that involves an impersonal government donor instead of an individual. This is not to say all people will reduce their work efforts but that at the margin, shirking becomes more likely for each individual. Certainly, there are those who will work despite receiving little directly from the fruits of their labor. The early church, some communes, and the kibbutzes in Israel are groups based on "voluntary socialism" that have avoided shirking by individuals. But those people are driven by something in addition to economic incentives—a devotion to religious teachings or some type of work ethic.[15]

Even in these special cases, incentive problems are still present. Again, the example of the early Christian church is instructive. Acts 5 relates the story of Ananias and Sapphira, a couple who voluntarily sold a piece of property and claimed to give the entire proceeds to the church. Instead, they kept part of the money for themselves. By lying to the leaders, the couple responded to the economic disincentives at the expense of their supposed moral beliefs.

The same tension is evident throughout Paul's letters to the early churches. Paul encourages work, condemns laziness, and discourages financial dependency on others.[16] Paul was trying to teach against the incentive problems inherent in any socialistic system. Implicitly, he was encouraging an increase in monitoring and punishment to stem the tendency to free ride off the efforts of others.

Wealth redistribution also carries long-run incentive problems—the Good Samaritan's dilemma revisited.[17] For instance, giving a child candy today is likely to increase the child's demands for candy in the future. Why was the Good Samaritan's dilemma less relevant in Christ's parable? The Samaritan was confident that the circumstances were beyond the recipient's control. The key was the local involvement, categorization, and discernment promoted by Olasky. The Samaritan knew incentives were not much of a problem in this case; fraud and abuse were unlikely.

Further, assuming that bureaucrats will be as effective as volunteers is troublesome because bureaucrats in a government system have different incentives from those who help the poor voluntarily. Bureaucrats are often more interested in expanding their budgets than in helping people per se—"when in doubt, give it out." In the public sector, spending money is often independent of concerns about efficiency in helping the targeted population. It is also less likely that bureaucrats will care as much in a more centralized and large-scale program, since the efforts are more impersonal. In contrast, voluntary efforts are likely to be efficient because people are spending their own resources to help the poor. When bureaucrats use our money to help others, it is unlikely they will spend it as well as we would. Or as Diane Sawyer says, "The welfare bureaucracy is not as angry as the taxpayer is—on making sure cheating doesn't go on."[18]

Because volunteer efforts are usually smaller-scale and local, volunteers are more capable of providing true assistance and compassion. They are closer to the action and can more easily identify those who would use aid as a hammock instead of as a safety net. In contrast, as a government program becomes more centralized, it is less likely that a bureaucrat will be able to categorize and discern.

Since government has become involved with what individuals should do voluntarily, we are left with the current welfare system: "the ultimate in bureaucracy—an anonymous public supporting anonymous machinery supporting anonymous clients."[19] Once again, we have returned to whether one has faith in government or in the market to be more efficient and in public employees or private individuals to be more concerned about helping the poor.

Finally, even though helping the poor is a biblical principle, this does not ensure that efforts to help will be either practical or moral. Indiscriminate giving can harm recipients. In addition, public choice considerations cause government to be involved in hurting the poor on a regular basis. And to redistribute money through the tax code is coercive by definition—it is legalized theft. Do moral ends justify immoral means?[20] In sum, there is a biblical call to help the poor, but the use of government is not sanctioned as a means to that end.

Doug Bandow concludes that socialism is inconsistent with Christianity because "it exacerbates the worst of man's flaws. By divorcing effort from reward, stirring up covetousness and envy and destroying the freedom that is a necessary precondition for virtue, it tears at the just social fabric that Christians should seek to establish."[21] Some leaders in the Christian church have been in keen pursuit of social justice and substantial income equality in both the domestic and international arenas. However, their prescriptions for politically organized redistribution misinterpret the biblical call to Christians.

If Not Government. . . ?

If the Bible does not encourage Christians to pursue government and coercive redistributive policies as a vehicle for helping the poor, what is the proposed solution? Instead of relying on government, Christians are called to live in a radically new way. In Matthew 5, Christ contrasts the Old Testament teaching of an eye for an eye by directing his believers to respond instead by turning the other cheek and going the extra mile. He continues by telling Christians to "love [their] enemies and pray for those who persecute [them]."

One of the crucial tenets of Christianity is that it provides more than a moral code to which its believers should adhere; God provides the means as well, through the Holy Spirit dwelling in the heart of his believers.[22] Christ told his disciples: "I will ask the Father, and he will give you . . . the Spirit of truth. The world cannot accept him, because it neither sees him nor knows him. But you know him, for he lives with you and will be in you."[23] For believers, because "God sent the Spirit of his Son into our hearts," "Christ lives in us" and "it is God who works in you to will and to act according to his good purpose."[24] (Of course, this requires a Christian's participation as well as God's provision.)

Without this enabling power, Christians would be akin to players taking tennis lessons from Jimmy Connors for a few months and then competing against John McEnroe. Despite the lessons, Mr. McEnroe would defeat his opponents quickly. But if Jimmy Connors could play from within the students, the result would be different. Instead of merely receiving instructions through "the Law," Christians can be empowered to live this radically new life with a "new heart," empowered by Christ through the Holy Spirit.[25]

The bottom line is that there is no relation between the biblical call to Christians and the use of government to help the poor. In fact, they are diametrically opposed. The use of government to reach certain ends is based on coercion. The change in behavior designed to accompany the Christian's Spirit-filled life is completely voluntary.[26]

The Christian's Call
to Avoid Government Solutions

Christ's teachings on the subject of dependence on government can be best summarized by "give to Caesar what is Caesar's, and to God what is God's" (Matthew 22:21). Paul Heyne remarks that "the first step in the wrong direction is the very idea that the Gospel presents any agenda at all for government."[27]

Despite this, many Christians advocate an active role for government in social arenas and economic markets. One problem with this approach is that the means to the desired ends are often not practical. Moreover, any government policy necessarily restricts freedom; Christians should support policies that promote individual liberty. However, the most significant problem is that the Bible gives no examples of believers using government to reach social or economic objectives for non-believers.[28]

Instead, the teachings of the Bible emphasize ministering to people individually. Thus, Christians should focus their energies on working with people directly (in this context, the poor). Theologian Francis Schaefer says we should avoid giving more power to the "monolithic monster of a bloated state" and instead emphasize the "compassionate use of accumulated wealth."[29] The focus should be on individual action, not on invoking the powers of the state.

The Government Advantage

Although using government is not supported by Scripture, it is still a tempting option. Because government is powerful, it can enforce great change. It can certainly get things done; the question is whether those are the right things. With the preferred (biblical) method of voluntary efforts, one gets only slow progress. Unfortunately for religious leaders, the pursuit of government solutions amounts to abandoning biblical principles regarding secular power. Heyne says that "the determination to have as little to do with [government] as possible is far closer to the spirit of the Gospel than are the persistent efforts of church officials since Constantinople to gain control of government for their own ends."[30]

Olasky documents an example of this idea: the 20th-century fight against poverty. Proponents of government intervention (including religious leaders) saw the successes of late–19th-century private charitable efforts. They thought the effort could be extended using the resources of government and the war could be won—poverty would be abolished forever. But as discussed, the incentives for bureaucrats are not often conducive to effective charity.

Around the turn of the century, worship of the state by Christian leaders was at an appalling level. Olasky quotes the canon of Canterbury, William Fremantle, concerning government: "[It] calls forth a worship more complete than any other," and only government "can embrace all the wants of its members and afford them the universal instruction and elevation which they need." As Olasky continues, he notes that "the worship of power had rarely been stated so explicitly by a church leader" before quoting Fremantle a final time: "When we think of the Nation as becoming, as it must do more and more, the object of mental regard, of admiration, of love, even of worship (for in it God preeminently dwells), we shall recognize to the fullest extent its religious character and functions."[31]

With respect to the Catholic bishops' past policy prescriptions for socialism and greater welfare programs, Paul Heyne comments that "the bishops want to transform institutions; they are therefore wise to focus on gaining control of governmental policies. However, honesty requires they give up the authority of the New Testament as support for what they are doing."[32] Although pursuing government solutions in order to change undesirable behavior and to quickly reach desirable outcomes is seductive, it is not biblical.

Faith in Government: Belief Without Basis

With few exceptions, it is clear that economic markets and capitalism are the most effective way to "deliver the goods."[33] But explaining how markets accomplish those results is quite difficult; the "invisible hand" is just that—invisible. Thus, belief in markets requires little faith concerning the historical evidence but requires immense faith in the market process itself.

In contrast, socialism and government intervention are known failures; there is little evidence that government can do much of anything efficiently (compared to the private sector). But to the limited extent that government is able to achieve results, it is easy to see the "visible hand" of government at work. This is a very different kind of faith. No faith is required in the process itself; the limited results are easy to see and explain. But tremendous faith is required to believe in the (as yet) unseen ability of government to deliver the goods. When people propose government intervention as the solution to a problem, they implicitly believe government is the most effective way to achieve the desired goals.

Mrs. G. Harris Robertson, one of the leading proponents of welfare in the early 20th century, exhibited tremendous faith in government: "The state is a parent, and, as a wise and gentle and kind and loving parent, should beam down on each child alike." And describing the supposed merits of socialism, she claimed that "every step we make toward establishing these lines (socialism) means an advance toward the Kingdom of Peace."[34] Pope Paul VI said of government that it "always intervenes with careful justice and with devotion to the common good for which it holds final responsibility." His policy recommendations followed his faith: "It pertains to the public authorities to choose, even to lay down, the ends to be achieved, and the means of attaining them, and it is for them to stimulate all the forces engaged in this common activity."[35] To advocate government as a solution places more faith in government than in markets.

Faith in government is the most important topic when discussing the possibilities for reform in any realm of public policy. Although this faith has been shaken by the failures and corruption of our leaders and their policies, it is still strong enough that we still turn to government first for a solution to our problems. As Bandow says, "The United States is a remarkably religious nation. Our god is not the God of traditional faiths, however. It is the modern state."[36] Until this faith fades, we will continue to grasp for government solutions that are doomed to be less effective, if not outright failures. Gary North puts it well when he says:

> Every culture rests on moral presuppositions. The culture of state spending rests on a false one: the belief that the state is a morally legitimate instrument of coercive wealth redistribution. Until this moral presupposition is abandoned by most voters—a moral conversion which may have to be stimulated by the attention-getting occurrence of national bankruptcy—there are no believable technical solutions to the culture of spending. . . . It is not enough to show enraged, envy-driven voters that the welfare state has failed to deliver the goods. Voters must be led into a crisis; that repentance—a change of mind—is necessary for social healing. The culture of spending must be shown to be the moral low ground, not just an inefficient solution to the problem of scarcity.[37]

Christ said, "The poor you will always have with you."[38] Today, absolute poverty is certainly prevalent—around the world if not in the United States. This does not mean individuals should do nothing to help the poor. Personal involvement with categorization and discernment can improve people's lives. And as we have seen throughout the book, those inclined to change government policy have a wide menu of options from which to choose. But all too often, government has been used to further impoverish the poor instead of helping them. Political markets are complicated and should be embraced with care. When using government to intervene, compassion and idealism are nice, but understanding and pragmatism are crucial.

Notes

1. In 1986, the National (U.S.) Conference of Catholic Bishops advocated redistribution to the non-poor (farmers in paragraphs 242–245), a higher minimum wage (197), stronger labor unions (104, 108), mandated employee benefits (103), the public education monopoly (205), and government jobs programs (154). The notion that these policies promote "justice" or benefit the poor has been refuted throughout this book. (See also Psalms 94:20 and Isaiah 5:20.) Further, the bishops argued that discrimination is rampant and a primary explanation for income differentials (182 and 199). See Chapter 3 for a discussion of this improbability. (*Economic Justice for All: Pastoral Letter on Catholic Social Teaching and the U.S. Economy* [Washington, DC: U.S. Catholic Conference, 1986].)

2. Although they no longer openly promote socialism, many of their policy prescriptions still advocate government activism. However, the Catholic bishops reaffirmed the major themes of their 1986 Pastoral Letter at their 1995 annual conference. (P. Steinfels, "Catholic Bishops Urge Rejection of Accords on Curbing Welfare and Cutting Tax Credit," *New York Times*, November 15, 1995.) Michael Novak, Templeton Prize–winner in 1994, expresses it this way: "While Catholic thinkers have been adversarial to socialism, many have been too optimistic about the state as a tool of social policy." ("The Free Market and Public Morality," *Religion and Liberty*, May/June 1994.) Their general argument is that "the market alone" cannot produce the optimal result. "Therefore, the government must act to ensure that this is achieved by coordinating general economic policies" (National Conference of Catholic Bishops, *Economic Justice for All*, paragraph 154).

3. In this chapter I discuss mostly Christian views on poverty because (1) Christianity is the religion I know the most about; (2) in this country, Christian (particularly Catholic) leaders have been very involved in this arena; and (3) Christianity is the dominant cultural and religious institution in the United States.

4. See Proverbs 31:8–9, Isaiah 58:9–11.

5. This stems from the complexity of human behavior. Nonetheless, if the price of a good or the cost of a behavior decreases (holding all else constant), more of it will be "consumed."

6. P. Heyne, *The Catholic Bishops and the Pursuit of Justice* (Washington, DC: Cato Institute, 1986), p. 2. M. Kaus (*The End of Equality* [New York: Basic Books, 1992], pp. 9–12) provides a similar critique of what he calls "Money Liberalism."

7. From Pascal again: "Percepts [perceptions] without concepts are blind; concepts without percepts are empty." We must have both in order to find effective policy.

8. Note that this contradicts the last reason by implicitly confessing that capitalism is a surer way to achieve material success.

9. Deuteronomy 15:7–10. All quotes are taken from the New International Version (NIV) of the Bible.

10. Leviticus 25 describes the "year of Jubilee," when property was released to its original owner (equitably determined by God when the land was first apportioned) and indentured servants were released from their obligations. See Ruth 2:7, 15–17, for Boaz's "wage subsidy" to supplement hard-working Ruth's income.

11. See also Luke 8:3, Acts 11:29, and II Corinthians 8:1–7. In II Corinthians 8:14, Paul writes, "At the present time your plenty will supply what they need, so that in turn their plenty will supply what you need. Then there will be equality."

12. For an example, see R. Sider's *Rich Christians in an Age of Hunger* (Dallas: Word, 1990), p. 58, and his theses about the role of government in chapters 6 and 9. Elsewhere, Sider argues that charitable efforts by individuals are inferior to government redistribution because the former can lead to pride. (H. Schlossberg, *Idols for Destruction: The Conflict of Christian Faith and American Culture* [Wheaton, IL: Crossway Books, 1990], p. 244.)

13. See also Acts 5:4, II Corinthians 9:5.

14. M. Olasky, *The Tragedy of American Compassion* (Washington, DC: Regnery Gateway, 1992), p. 121. He also provides a quote from a speech by Ely that has the "ominous sound of potential totalitarianism": "Everything must be devoted to the service of humanity. The old Mosaic ten-percent rule was given for the hardness of men's hearts. We now live under a hundred-percent rule" (p. 261, footnote 22).

15. These special cases are equivalent to high benefit-reduction rates in the context of welfare programs. Some people continue to work while hamstrung by benefit-reduction rates above 100%, making them worse off financially for working. Again, something in addition to short-run economic considerations drives their behavior.

16. Ephesians 4:28; I Thessalonians 4:11–12; II Thessalonians 3:10–12; and I Timothy 5:3, 8–10, 13, 16.

17. The possibility that short-run assistance can promote long-run need was developed in Chapter 13.

18. ABC's *Primetime Live*, transcript from September 17, 1992.

19. Olasky, *The Tragedy of American Compassion*, p. 150.

20. P. T. Bauer notes that these "solutions" have other spiritual and moral implications as well. Political markets and redistribution encourage people to "focus on man" and to be preoccupied with others' wealth. He argues that these policy prescriptions "legitimize envy and resentment." (*Reality and Rhetoric: Studies and Debates in Development Economics* [Cambridge, MA: Harvard University Press, 1984], p. 84.)

21. D. Bandow, *The Politics of Envy: Statism as Theology* (New Brunswick, NJ: Transaction Press, 1994), p. 17.

22. Another important distinction with Christianity is that for believers, God provides mercy (they can avoid judgment they deserve) and grace (they can receive something they do not deserve or earn—eternal life and the indwelling of the Holy Spirit). See John 3:16 and Ephesians 2:8–9. Many religions have mercy; only Christianity has grace.

23. John 14:6–7. Christ seemed to be almost in a hurry to leave when he said, "It is for your own good that I am going away. Unless I go away, the Counselor [Holy Spirit] will not come to you; but if I go, I will send him to you" (John 16:7). Ezekiel 36:26 prophesied that God would give believers a new heart and a new spirit.

24. Galatians 4:6, 2:20; Philippians 2:13.

25. W. Nee draws an analogy to grafting a branch from a good tree onto a bad tree in order to grow good fruit. "If a man can graft a branch of one tree into another, cannot God take of the life of his Son and, so to speak, graft it into us?" (*The Normal Christian Life* [Wheaton, IL: Tyndale House, 1957], p. 97.) Without this provision, Christ's standards would be truly unreasonable. (For more on these standards see Matthew 5:38–48, Romans 12:9–21, I Thessalonians 5:16–18, and Ephesians 5:25 for instructions to husbands.)

26. In *Our Enemy, the State* (San Francisco: Fox and Wilkes, 1992), Albert Nock illustrates that moral decisions require freedom.

27. Heyne, *The Catholic Bishops and the Pursuit of Justice*, p. 21. See also I Corinthians 6:1–6, where Paul chastises the Christians in Corinth for relying on non-believers in the secular judicial system to resolve their disputes.

28. The Old Testament is replete with examples when human government— led by God—was used to reach objectives for believers.

29. Olasky, *The Tragedy of American Compassion*, p. 180.

30. Heyne, *The Catholic Bishops and the Pursuit of Justice*, p. 21.

31. Olasky, *The Tragedy of American Compassion*, p. 122.

32. Heyne, *The Catholic Bishops and the Pursuit of Justice*, p. 23.

33. There are a few exceptions. For instance, government is likely to provide (economic) public goods such as national defense more effectively than economic markets.

34. V. Postrel, "The Character Issue," *Reason*, p. 4.

35. Pope Paul VI, "Octogesima Adveniens," no. 46, Vatican City, 1971; "Populorum Progressio," no. 33, Vatican City, 1967.

36. Bandow, *The Politics of Envy*, p. ix. Of course, the biblical term for this is "idolatry." See Schlossberg's *Idols for Destruction* for an excellent discussion of the state as one of many idols. Schlossberg also argues that redistribution results from an "idolatry to mammon" with its "insistence that it is more blessed to receive than to give" (p. 137).

37. G. North, "The Politics of the 'Fair Share,'" *Freeman*, November 1993.

38. Matthew 26:11; see also Deuteronomy 15:11.

17

Fixing Welfare: Take It Behind the Barn . . .

Prescriptions for welfare reform are subject to much disagreement. When we take money from the working poor to give to the non-poor, disdain for such policies is nearly universal. But when we take money from the average taxpayer to give to poor people, widely different value judgments concerning equality and efficiency yield different preferences for policy.

In addition, given the trade-offs inherent in the welfare and Good Samaritan's dilemmas, the solution is more difficult or even impossible to determine. David Ellwood expresses the problem this way: "We want to help those who are not making it, but in so doing, we seem to cheapen the efforts of those who are struggling just to get by [and] we reduce the pressure on them and their incentive to work. We recognize the insecurity of single-parent families, but in helping them, we appear to be promoting or supporting their formation. We want to target our money to the most needy, but in doing so, we often isolate and stigmatize them."[1]

In the preceding chapters, I have recommended significant proposals for improving the system. Some take offense at the use of "categorization and discernment," but objective opposition would be difficult for the following prescriptions: (1) choosing a negative income tax (NIT) over the current smorgasbord of welfare programs, (2) using local involvement as opposed to federal efforts, and (3) moving toward voluntary charitable efforts as opposed to coercive and inefficient governmental programs.

Public Support for Current Programs

In my reading of many books on welfare and potential reforms, I find that regardless of ideology, most authors believe welfare should be dismantled (although they disagree on what should replace it). The consensus is that our current welfare policies should be taken behind the barn and shot.

The current welfare system is ineffective and has little popular support. It has been ineffective in reaching its long-term goal: to promote independence among "capable" welfare recipients. It is disliked by liberals for treating welfare recipients like children or numbers and by conservatives because it is viewed as a trap and because "it makes a mockery of the efforts of working people."[2] It is despised by a public that sees many of the recipients as lazy, and that focuses on "welfare queens" and other examples of fraud and misuse.

The only supporters of the status quo (or minor variations of current policy) are the bureaucrats who administer the programs. As before, they have a vested interest in fighting substantial reform. This makes reform difficult, since the "rationally ignorant" public has little at stake.

Further, it is nearly impossible to please everyone with minor changes. People are labeled as callous if they recommend lower benefits and as spendthrifts if they prefer greater benefits. As with education, marginal reforms are likely to be impotent; because of the welfare and Good Samaritan's dilemmas, minor changes to the status quo would be largely ineffective. Something more dramatic must be done. Requiring work ("workfare") is currently popular, but how does government implement the idea? Eliminating benefits after some period of time has many proponents, but is this always fair?

Why Welfare Policy Must Change

The war on poverty has been successful in the short run in raising standards of living for the poor, but it has failed miserably in its second goal: reducing long-run dependence on government handouts. Unfortunately, many groups have been harmed by the government's inability to win this second battle.

For most workers in the poverty industry, the excitement and satisfaction of helping people improve their lives has been replaced by the paper-shuffling and faceless casework of a bureaucracy. A former reporter who realized a "long-standing dream" to be a caseworker writes: "I lasted two months. . . . I got more forms and documents on my first day than I had seen in seven years at *The [New York] Times*. . . . Nothing was allowed to interfere with [the] lunch break."[3] The incentives of a bureaucracy are not conducive to productivity. And for those who truly want to help, the paperwork and hoop jumping are frustrating. Welfare policy must change for the morale of people who want to work with the poor.

Concerning the poor themselves, the idea that welfare may harm them in the long run is a sobering thought. As discussed in Chapter 13, welfare programs encourage leisure and the formation of single heads of household by definition. It is difficult enough to emerge from poverty after receiving a pathetic education, and it is difficult enough raising children with *two* parents—without the disincentives that accompany a government check. Welfare often makes these problems worse. Giving assistance (indefinitely and without conditions) can make it more difficult for people to escape long-term dependency. This has limited their social and economic mobility. Welfare policy must change for the sake of the young poor who are enticed into a life of poverty and dependence.

With the abandonment of categorization and discernment and with the enticement of a small but steady income, tremendous self-control is necessary for the poor to escape dependence on the dole. Further, the current approach combines those who want to advance with people who are quite content to live off the system. In addition, they often encounter ridicule in their communities if they go against the financial inducements inherent to welfare. Seemingly, it should be particularly important to preserve the morale of those who are trying to climb the ladder of responsibility and financial independence. Welfare policy must change for the sake of those who want to improve their lives.

Perhaps the working poor are hurt most by welfare policies. According to Ellwood, "Even though these families start out less poor than those in other categories, they get so little aid that they are actually the poorest group after transfers."[4] Remember, the only ones who are not subsidized for health care are the working poor. The working poor must deal with the temptation of welfare and Medicaid. Welfare policy must change for the working poor, whose efforts are mocked by a system that makes less industrious people better off financially.

The Voluntary Option

As developed earlier, voluntary assistance to the poor is superior to welfare in every way with one possible exception: providing enough support. Whether private efforts would be sufficient is subject to argument because there are differences in opinion about what defines "sufficient" and because we can only speculate about how the public would respond in a world without welfare.

Aside from this, there can be little doubt that voluntary solutions are optimal. As opposed to the coercion necessary to pay for government programs, private efforts would be mutually beneficial transactions based on voluntary exchange; when A gives time or resources to B, both parties benefit. Voluntary efforts are less likely to be inefficient or fraudulent, since people spending their own time and resources are more likely to be careful about how those are allocated; nobody spends A's money more effectively than A. Finally, compared to policy dictated by Washington, D.C., and the state capitals, solutions from the private sector are more likely to be appropriate and truly compassionate, since assistance can be more individualized.

Clearly we should move in this direction. And *at least* eventually, a system based completely on voluntary charity would be best. But until then, what other policies can government undertake to help the poor?

What Else Can Government Do?

Earlier Prescriptions

Because the problems of the poor are widely varied, reform must occur in areas other than merely welfare. Christopher Jencks argues that "if we cannot manage piecemeal reforms, looking for metasolutions is almost certain to be time wasted so far as the American underclass is concerned. If we want to reduce their poverty, joblessness, illiteracy, violence or despair, we will surely need to change our institutions and attitudes in hundreds of small ways, not one big way."[5] The policy prescriptions in Part 2 would be extremely helpful in alleviating the plight of the poor. To summarize:

1. Government should pursue policies that foster a growing economy, since increasing everybody's income seems to be the most effective way to increase the incomes of the poor. This can be achieved by promoting freedom, property rights, and individual opportunity through limited government intervention and taxation.

2. Government should end its monopoly provision of public schooling to enable the poor to obtain a better education. If higher incomes allow choice for the wealthy, government should promote choice for the poor as well.

3. Government should legalize drugs to curtail the gangs and violence that surround the drug war, to limit illegal labor-supply options, and to allow proper role models to reassert their influence on inner-city communities. Government should also pursue some combination of greater law enforcement, less liberalized judicial decisions, and greater punishment. This would make crime "more expensive" and thus, less frequent.

4. Government should greatly limit its interventions in labor markets. It should desist in pursuing policies that lock the unskilled out of

labor markets, for example, minimum wages, Davis-Bacon laws, and mandatory licensing.

5. Government should increase the real income (purchasing power) of the poor by ending subsidies and price supports for domestic producers and protectionist policies against foreign products. These programs inadvertently increase prices and taxes for the poor with the goal of increasing the incomes of the non-poor.

6. Government should limit its various distortions in the markets for housing and health.

If these government interventions are eliminated, the need for income transfers to the poor will be greatly reduced. To the extent that assistance to the poor would still be desirable, the following apply:

7. With respect to welfare, government should pursue local as opposed to federal efforts and voluntary as opposed to bureaucratic efforts. Further, in its attempts to help the poor, it should reintroduce categorization and discernment as well as emphasize individual responsibility.

8. If eliminating welfare altogether is not politically feasible, welfare policy should still be drastically altered within its current framework. In lieu of current policy, government should use one (or at most, two) of the following: wage subsidies, (reduced) earned income tax credits, child care tax credits, and an NIT instead of the current smorgasbord of programs. Unlike the minimum wage, these proposals would increase the incomes of the poor without preventing them from obtaining jobs. And they limit the welfare dilemma by keeping benefit-reduction rates lower and easier for policymakers to understand.

Additional Prescriptions

First, if governmental welfare assistance continues, there should be a time limit on one's ability to receive benefits from governmental welfare. Current discussion seems to focus on providing assistance for a limited time; proposals range from six months to two years. Although the length of time is somewhat arbitrary, this general approach has obvious advantages for dealing with the most dependent in our society: (1) it limits the ability to use welfare as a hammock instead of a safety net; (2) it allows us an opportunity to see private charitable efforts in action (beyond the time limit); (3) the subsequent individual approaches would be especially effective in dealing with this population, which is presumably the most helpless (and the most challenging to help); and (4) as a result, people previously receiving assistance would be moved out of the welfare culture into an environment where categorization and discernment could better determine what a given individual needed. Except for the truly needy, welfare benefits should be provided only for a short time.

Second, government should pursue private instead of public child support. This could include everything from tougher enforcement of current child-support laws to identifying the fathers of illegitimate children and encouraging mothers to pursue alternative sources of financial assistance. "Deadbeat dads" owe $34 billion per year in uncollected child-support payments.[6] Our child-support laws should be enforced and prosecuted in the same manner as bad loans and delinquent tax payments. Further, child-support collection could be privatized or financial incentives could be offered for local government's success in collecting. In sum, fathers, families, and voluntary organizations should be the first to assist poor single mothers—not taxpayers and government bureaucrats.

In addition, government should liberalize its adoption and foster care policies. Too often, optimal arrangements are prevented by arcane rules or quibbles over an agency's jurisdiction. When the bureaucracy does not allow willing and capable adults access to children in need of homes, all are made worse off except perhaps the bureaucrats who administer the foster care and adoption programs.

Third, to the extent government remains involved in trying to help the poor, it should improve the efficiency of its efforts. Often, this will entail privatization of government activities. Government should empower individuals to obtain goods and services in the private sector. As such, it should provide, not produce—provide food stamps instead of operating farms and grocery stores, housing vouchers instead of building and maintaining public housing, and private-sector instead of public-sector job training and placement. After all, it is no great achievement for government to do efficiently what it shouldn't do in the first place.

Technological advances can be harnessed as well. Maryland leads the way with its electronic benefit-transfer cards. Funds are deposited into two accounts—one to buy food, the other for cash—that can be accessed at 3,200 participating stores and automatic teller machines. This program reduces the costs of fraud and bureaucracy. And for better or worse, it removes the stigma associated with using food stamps.

A Proposal for More Equitable and Efficient Taxation

We should change our current tax system to a flat tax on personal (wage and pension) income and corporate profits. Under a plan most recently proposed by U.S. House majority leader Dick Armey (R–Tex.), all income would be taxed at a single (lower) rate.[7] There would be large personal deductions for taxpayers and their dependents. But most or all other deductions (loopholes) would be eliminated.

Table 17.1 illustrates the subsequent tax burdens for two-parent, two-children families with different income levels. (I am using a 20% tax rate with $4,000 deductions for each child and $12,000 for the personal exemption for a married couple.[8]) Such a tax system would have many advantages, especially for the working poor.

First, the flat-tax plan would be much more equitable (as "equity" is commonly defined). Foremost, it would be better for many of the working poor, since they would be removed from the tax rolls. In Table 17.1, those with incomes below $20,000 would be exempt from taxation.[9] The plan would be more equitable, since all people would be treated "the same"—taxed at the same marginal rate. Note also, as discussed in Chapter 2, that the same marginal tax rate can yield different average tax rates. In this context, the wealthy would pay more in taxes than the poor. And they would be much less willing or able to escape taxation by changing their behavior. In Chapter 2, we saw that the rich have responded in the past to lower tax rates in such a way that tax revenues from the rich were actually higher. The same would probably be true here as well. And the flat tax would limit redistribution to the non-poor through the government's use of subsidies and other loopholes in the tax code.

Second, it would be far more efficient. Filing taxes would be much simpler, saving time and money. With only a ten-line tax form, we would eliminate most of the 5.4 billion hours Americans currently use to complete their tax forms.[10] Moreover, this would end the indirect redistribution to accountants and lawyers resulting from our unnecessarily complex tax policy. A truly simple tax code would also shrink bureaucracy, inefficiency, and waste in many government agencies, especially the IRS. Another important feature of increased efficiency is that it would

TABLE 17.1 Hypothetical Flat Tax Example (in dollars)

Income	Taxable Income	Taxes Paid	Average Tax Rate (%)
< 20,000	0	0	0
30,000	10,000	2,000	6.7
40,000	20,000	4,000	10.0
50,000	30,000	6,000	12.0
60,000	40,000	8,000	13.3
80,000	60,000	12,000	15.0
100,000	80,000	16,000	16.0
200,000	180,000	36,000	18.0

Note: This example uses a marginal tax rate of 20%, $4,000 deductions for each child (total: $8,000) and a $12,000 deduction for a married couple. Thus, the total income exempted from taxation is $20,000.

encourage economic growth. (Remember that economic growth is a prime weapon in increasing the incomes of the poor.) Most important, such a tax system would end federal income tax on the working poor; thus, the welfare dilemma would be less of a concern. With government no longer reducing the rewards for working through taxation, fewer of the working poor would find welfare as tempting.

Finally, ending the current double taxation of capital gains would spur investment, creating jobs and wealth. This would directly benefit anyone with investments of any type (houses and retirement, for example) and indirectly benefit everyone through a stronger economy. South Korea, Taiwan, Hong Kong, Germany, and, until recently, Japan have had no taxation on capital gains; this is one of the reasons for their strong economic growth.[11]

Other Popular but Ineffective Proposals

Government Job-Training Programs

Many efforts to battle poverty have concentrated on unemployment or earnings capacity.[12] Clearly these are important factors: without a job that pays adequately, a life of dependence or poverty is inevitable. Often, policymakers have perceived it as government's role to provide jobs and training opportunities. But has government been successful in creating jobs for the unskilled? How well have its training programs functioned?

Unfortunately, the record is mostly abysmal. Since the Great Society, government has tried a variety of programs but with only limited achievement.[13] In general, there are high dropout rates and completion of the training does not translate into significantly higher earnings. There are some success stories, but the vast majority of training and job programs have been riddled with low success rates and plagued by high costs.

Given that they have been nearly universal failures, how have government agencies promoted them? Sometimes proponents cite improvements in lifetime earnings, thus making the gains seem larger. Most often, they rely on anecdotal evidence—variations on the Horatio Alger story of overcoming adversity with assistance from a benevolent government. With (1) a "rationally ignorant" public, (2) degrees of guilt and the desire to "do something," and (3) the fact that everyone enjoys compelling stories, such hopeful tales are often enough to distract us from the overall failure and expense of such programs.

The 1983 jobs-creation bill provides a typical example. It approved $4.6 billion for public-sector jobs. But in fact, few jobs were actually created for those who were targeted. And the creation of those jobs was very expensive (estimates begin at $40,000 per job).[14] In fact, one could argue that the primary beneficiaries were the elected officials who were afforded the opportunity to distribute funds; unions who received some of the work; and the lawyers, accountants, and consultants needed to establish the projects.

Workfare

Currently, proposals requiring work from welfare recipients are popular. This trend in conventional wisdom came to legislative fruition in 1990 when a work requirement was added for recipients whose children are more than three years old. The law requires 16 hours per week for at least six months per year. However, the law was written so that it will take several years for the program to take full effect. And recipients may choose job training instead of work if they cannot find work. As a result, Mickey Kaus estimates that by 1997, only 6% of welfare families will be required to work.[15] The Clinton administration has proposed work requirements that it estimates would mandate work for 2.3 million people.[16]

Although workfare is a good idea in principle, it has both efficiency and equity problems. It is difficult to determine whether someone is adequately seeking work. And if people do not find work, government must provide opportunities to obtain training or jobs. As just detailed, government training programs are costly and mostly ineffective. And such publicly provided jobs usually amount to make-work. These results make the workfare proposal subject to Hazlitt's critique that government cannot create net jobs: While government spends money to create jobs for welfare recipients, it destroys jobs by lowering consumers' disposable incomes through higher taxation. In addition, workfare creates the need for greater bureaucracy. Finally, with single heads of household, the desirability of having parents working in the labor market (as opposed to staying home with their children) is not clear.

Government "Compassion": *The Tyranny of Kindness*

Among the diverse group of people who feel welfare should be eliminated, Theresa Funiciello is a former welfare mother whose critique of welfare policy is far from conservative; she does not question the right to income transfers but nonetheless despises the current system.[17]

On the system's kindness and compassion, she asks her readers to "think of the worst experience you've ever had with a clerk in some government service job and add the life-threatening condition of impending starvation or homelessness . . . and you have some idea of what it's like in a welfare center."[18] She also notes that New York City spends $18,000 per year to shelter a single homeless person. Each such person gets three meals per day and a cot in a grim armory—surrounded by drug addicts and the mentally ill.[19] Is it any wonder that Olasky questions the contemporary definition of "compassion"?

Public Choice Economics and the "Sacrifices" of Bureaucrats

Funiciello's cynicism toward the welfare system peaks when she notes that "while poor people have become poorer in the past twenty years, social work has become a growth industry [and has] prospered beyond anyone's wildest dreams. . . . Welfare mothers wanted an adequate guaranteed income, which would have rendered many activities of social welfare professionals meaningless. The agencies wanted a guaranteed income, too; for themselves."[20] To support her contention, she cites the salaries of heads of various foundations and charities that range as high as $500,000.[21]

This is simply a variation on the public choice considerations we have seen throughout the book—people wielding power in political markets to benefit themselves, regardless of the stories they tell. Because there are relatively few "chronic poor"—and presumably they are the least capable of functioning well in economic or political markets—bureaucrats and others are the dominant interest groups benefiting from policies that directly affect the poor. Often, their interests run counter to those of the poor. Funiciello says the true beneficiaries of welfare policy need to be exposed. Quoting an African proverb, she notes that "until the lions have their historians, tales of hunting will always glorify the hunter."[22] She is a historian for the lions.

Political markets also determine who receives government contracts to help the poor. Not-for-profit agencies with multimillion-dollar endowments receive most of the tax-deductible charitable dollars and human service government contracts.[23] As before, bureaucrats and politicians are better off; whether taxpayers or the poor benefit is debatable. Funiciello notes that "incompetence is a heavy contender with greed as the prime motivator of the bureaucracy. . . . Any time there is money to be had, every manner of opportunist crawls out for a piece."[24]

Using Political Markets and the Poor: "Discard Markets"

Funiciello devotes a section of her book to looking at "discard markets"—where companies donate food to be given to the poor. Discard markets assist companies by taking products that cannot be sold because they are past their "pull date," poorly packaged, short-weighted, over-produced, or damaged. Unfortunately, "the corporations get a tax break [and good will] for much of what is actually garbage."[25] Adding to the problem, donations are not audited for quantity or quality. And

Good Samaritan laws usually prevent companies from being liable for trouble caused by donations.[26] As a result, tax-deducted corporate donations quadrupled from 1975 to 1985.[27]

If the donated products were high quality or practical, this arrangement might be more palatable. But many of the donated items are not useful or appropriate for poor people. Second Harvest's 1986 annual report documents that by weight, 24.2% of donations were desserts, snack foods, crackers, and cookies; 8.3% were spices and condiments; 13.3% were "non-food items." Microwave browning spray, meat marinade, and tenderizer are among the more popular donations.[28]

Funiciello concludes that "at each level of the discard market, the players calculate and pursue their interests, using economic and political power to achieve their ends. Poor people are the shills, otherwise irrelevant to the process and exempted from the real dividends."[29]

The Problem with Government Revisited

Government is effective at engineering redistribution of income and providing funding for its programs. But overall, it is not particularly adept at helping the poor. The non-poor use political markets to make themselves better off at the expense of all others, including the poor. The use of political markets to transfer income to the poor is fraught with incentive problems and public choice considerations that may make the poor worse off in the long run. John Perkins concludes that government "has a serious responsibility to the poor. But given its poor record of ineffectiveness, it is foolish to expect our government to lead the way in providing creative, constructive and nurturing social services."[30] The federal government is ill equipped to help poor individuals—it does not use categorization and discernment, it is too far away from the problem to pose effective solutions, and it lacks the incentives that accompany private and voluntary efforts.

In a section entitled "Turning a Head of Lettuce into an Ounce of Gold," Funiciello argues that giving poor people cash to buy their own food would be a lot easier than moving funds through the food-bank system.[31] Thus, she concludes: "Do we need to increase government spending? Not really. Truth is, billions are being pissed away in soup kitchens and the like. Shut them down."[32]

But as we have seen before, the status quo will fight substantial reform because it will be made worse off; entrenched charity bureaucracies will be among the biggest impediments to reform. With compassion currently defined as "more spending," with a still-strong faith in government's ability to fix social and economic problems, with bureaucrats who will defend their turf, with a mostly apathetic public, reforming the policies that affect the poor will not occur.

Funiciello summarizes by asking the question, "Who do you want to put your trust in: an agency replete with champagne fund-raisers, political deal making, and its own bulging belly to fill, or a mother who is directly responsible for feeding, clothing, sheltering . . . her children?"[33] Or as Bret Schundler wryly notes, parents "love their children more than the politicians . . . and they do it for free."[34] The optimal prescription is to take control out of the hands of bureaucrats administering the current welfare system. The answer is to move toward local and private solutions.

Notes

1. D. Ellwood, *Poor Support: Poverty in the American Family* (New York: Basic Books, 1988), p. 6. (Ellwood is one of the leaders of President Clinton's welfare reform task force.) He disaggregates his analysis by family type and the special problems that concern each. In addition to offering a number of proposals that might help the poor, Ellwood for some reason advocates a higher minimum wage.

2. Ibid., p. 4. Some join me in arguing both points. In *With Justice for All*, John Perkins says, "Society gives them dehumanizing welfare programs that stifle their motivation, rob them of their dignity. . . . Well-intentioned government programs designed to relieve the poor actually turn the poor into crippled dependents. They treat symptoms without touching causes" (Ventura, CA: Regal Books, 1982), pp. 149, 159.

3. M. Olasky, *The Tragedy of American Compassion* (Washington, DC: Regnery Gateway, 1992), p. 189.

4. Ellwood, *Poor Support*, p. 100.

5. C. Jencks, "Is the American Underclass Growing?" in *The Urban Underclass*, ed. C. Jencks and P. Peterson (Washington, DC: Brookings Institution, 1991), p. 98.

6. W. Wilson and T. Skocpol, "Welfare As We Need It," *New York Times*, February 9, 1994.

7. See R. Hall and A. Rabushka, *The Flat Tax*, 2nd ed. (Stanford, CA: Hoover Press, 1995) for a concise and readable exposition on the merits of the flat tax.

8. Armey originally proposed spending cuts and a 17% tax rate with $5,000 deductions for children and $12,350 for a personal deduction. In 1993, deductions were $2,350 for dependents, $3,700 for single taxpayers, and $6,200 for married couples. The numbers chosen here allow us to avoid both computational complexity and the issue of spending cuts.

9. One could append a "negative income tax" to this as well—allowing those who earn less than $20,000 to receive a credit for their personal deductions.

10. R. Armey, "Review Merits of Flat Tax," *Wall Street Journal*, June 16, 1994.

11. Once explained, this policy prescription is relatively easy to sell despite the rhetoric of its opponents. If a more politically feasible solution is desired, one could choose to limit the amount of capital gains to be exempted from taxation and at least to index capital gains for inflation.

12. M. Bernick's *Urban Illusions: New Approaches to Inner-City Unemployment* (New York: Praeger, 1987) is the story of how he and some colleagues tried to cre-

ate jobs for the poor in San Francisco in the 1980s. Bernick is a lawyer with an education from Harvard, Oxford, and the University of California at Berkeley. A similar story by a typical social worker would be impressive, Bernick is one who has sacrificed immensely for something he believes in passionately.

13. There are currently 150 different education and training programs, costing $24 billion ("Job Programs Flunk," K. Salven and P. Thomas, *Wall Street Journal,* December 16, 1993). The article also notes that "the Agriculture Department's Official report on the program for the year, 67 pages long, spins out column after column of statistics, except the one that actually counts: how many people actually got jobs through it."

14. Bernick, *Urban Illusions,* p. 131.

15. M. Kaus proposes to "replace AFDC and all other cash-like welfare programs with a . . . jobs program." (*The End of Equality* [New York: Basic Books, 1992], cited by C. Krauthammer, "Subsidized Illegitimacy," *Washington Post,* November 19, 1993).

16. R. Nathan, "Welfare, Work and the Real World," *New York Times,* January 31, 1994, p. A17.

17. T. Funiciello, *Tyranny of Kindness: Dismantling the Welfare System to End Poverty in America* (New York: Atlantic Monthly Press, 1993). Funiciello reaches some unfortunate policy conclusions but also provides grim and vivid detail about the workings of the poverty industry. She assumes the right to a guaranteed income; for illustrating the NIT, she starts with $14,000 in post-tax income for a three-person family and a 50% benefit-reduction rate (thus, $28,000 for the cutoff point). Although an excellent documentation of welfare machinations, the book is laced with personal attacks. For example, she refers to one welfare policy leader as a "dull tool . . . a budding mandarin . . . with delusions of adequacy" (p. 181).

18. Ibid., p. 24.

19. S. Stern, "Review of *Tyranny of Kindness,*" *Wall Street Journal,* July 29, 1993. Funiciello also questions the compassion of a paternalistic and self-interested system that promotes in-kind assistance instead of cash. The shift to commodities in the late 1970s included surplus cheese that carried warnings about its high sodium content (ibid., pp. 124, 129).

20. Ibid., Funiciello, *Tyranny of Kindness,* pp. 213, xvii.

21. S. Greene, "How Much Should Charities Pay?" *Chronicle of Philanthropy,* March 24, 1992, p. 32, quoted by Funiciello, *Tyranny of Kindness,* p. 248). In *Urban Illusions,* Bernick ridiculed former U.S. Housing and Urban Development director Jim Califano's description of himself as a "humanitarian who sacrifices" by noting the salary and perquisites that accompanied his job.

22. Funiciello, *Tyranny of Kindness,* p. 162. Funiciello also laments the disparate treatment for a woman whose husband leaves her as opposed to a woman whose husband dies. If the former, she is decried as a "welfare mother"; if the latter, she is a "social security widow" who receives good benefits without stigmata. In addition, the latter's benefit-reduction rates are lower and start later than for those on welfare. Funiciello asks sarcastically if the widow "suffers from dependency" (ibid., pp. 8–9).

23. She notes the irony that charities "not only beg on the streets but follow people right into their homes to ask for money via the mail, television . . . " (ibid., p. 213).

24. Ibid., p. xvi.

25. Ibid., p. 131. The details in her section on discard markets are lengthy and grim; this is only a summary.

26. Ibid., p. 141. "In 1991, Beech-Nut donated a half-million jars of baby food to Food for Survival. The subsequent press release failed to mention that the jars were past their pull dates" (p. 135).

27. U.S. Department of the Treasury, Internal Revenue Service, *Statistics of Income Bulletin,* Spring 1991, p. 118 (quoted by Funiciello, *Tyranny of Kindness,* p. 140).

28. Funiciello, *Tyranny of Kindness,* p. 134.

29. Ibid., p. 145.

30. Perkins, *With Justice for All,* p. 164.

31. Funiciello, *Tyranny of Kindness,* p. 138.

32. Ibid., p. 161.

33. Ibid., p. 255.

34. Speech at National Taxpayers Conference, Washington, D.C., November 18, 1994.

Part 4

Myths and Causes of Poverty Around the World

A Brief Introduction to Part 4

There are two reasons for the inclusion of an international section. First, the issues I will analyze are important to people in less developed countries (LDCs). Although we are generally not as concerned about people in other countries, their quality of life is probably of some consequence to us. All things being equal, we would prefer that other individuals have higher standards of living than they do currently. To that end, readers of this book will have varying levels of interest about the causes of poverty in LDCs.

Second, the "poor policies" of LDCs either parallel or provide a stark contrast to our government's efforts. Thus, we can use LDC experiences to provide further evidence about the efficacy of specific government programs or government intervention in general. Often, our policies differ not in kind but only in degree. Because the pursuit of government activism has prevented LDCs from emerging out of abject poverty, we should hesitate before we embrace similar measures.

We will find there is no "vicious circle of poverty" for LDCs—at least in the way it is commonly defined: that countries have "fallen and can't get up" without government intervention. Similarly, there is no "benign circle of growth." Economic prosperity does not happen by itself; it is not random. It is largely the result of certain institutions—secure property rights and political and economic freedom, for example. Therefore, we should be careful not to take those institutions for granted. They are vital to our current standard of living and crucial to perpetuating economic growth into the future.

Finally, an aside on terminology: Throughout Part 4, I will avoid using "the third world" and "the South" to describe less developed countries. Unfortunately, these popular terms imply that LDCs are a single homogeneous entity. This provides a view of the world that is too simple. Some LDCs are relatively wealthy; others struggle in abject poverty. Some experience economic growth; others are stagnant. Some have democratic governments; others are ruled by dictators. Of course, the term I have chosen can be misused in a similar fashion. But by using a more open ended and less familiar term, I hope I will be less likely to make this mistake. (Merely omitting the word "the" from the terminology implies greater openness.)

Although generalizations can be helpful, one should use them judiciously. For instance, when I visited Honduras a few years ago, I expected to see something out of a televised plea on behalf of starving children. Although not wealthy by American standards, the country was far from the level of malnutrition, starvation, and disease disproportionately portrayed by charitable groups and the media. As we saw in the case of welfare, the perception that all problems are the same leads to the impression that blanket solutions by the government will be effective. As with welfare, nothing could be further from the truth.

18

The Cause and Effect of
Population, Resources, and Food

When discussing less developed countries (LDCs), people often cite perceived problems with population, natural resources, and food. Some are concerned about the impact of population on LDCs. They argue that rapid population growth in LDCs is a primary cause of their poverty and starvation.[1] Others are worried about the effect of the LDC population on the rest of the world—specifically, the long-term availability of natural resources.[2] For them, population growth is anathema because it exacerbates the condition of our supposedly diminishing natural resources.

These arguments are intuitively appealing on the surface, but the issues are more complicated and less problematic than might be imagined. After examining these issues—and foreign aid in the next chapter—I turn to the results of "poor policy" by the governments of LDCs.

Population

As with virtually all environmental issues, there are elements of fad and fashion in current concerns about population. In the mid-1970s, scientists were worried about falling temperatures and speculated about the consequences of global cooling.[3] By the 1990s, the focus had turned to global warming. Likewise, the 1930s and 1940s featured gnashing of teeth about a "birth dearth," the opposite of contemporary concerns about a population explosion.[4] Grossly inaccurate predictions in the past would seemingly make people less likely to form policy conclusions on the basis of such forecasts; perhaps we forget the past too easily. To put the population "problem" into perspective, if the entire world's population were placed in Texas, each individual would have 1,400 square feet (5,600 for a family of four).

Population continues to grow at a rapid pace, but birth rates for the world have been declining for some time. The birth rate fell from 5.0 children per woman in 1950–1955 to 3.6 in 1980–1985; 2.0 is required for zero population growth.[5]

However, there are notable differences between specific regions. Over the same period, where fertility rates used to be high, there have been dramatic decreases everywhere except Africa (6.5 versus 6.4). For instance, East Asia's fertility rates have plummeted from 5.5 to 2.3.[6] In the Western world, birth rates have remained at levels that barely maintain the size of its population. Given African economic stagnation, Asian economic growth since World War II, and Western affluence, there seems to be a relationship between income and population growth.

Population Growth vs. Economic Growth

It is often assumed that rapid population growth is a detriment to economic growth. There are a number of potential problems with this assertion. First, there are costs and benefits from a growing population—both for individual families and for a country. Second, it is more likely that the supposed causation goes the other way—that lower incomes lead to larger families and higher population growth. Third, anecdotal and empirical evidence indicate a positive relationship between the economic prosperity and the population *density* of a country.

In general, having additional children involves short-run costs and long-run benefits for a family. Of course there are substantial costs involved in raising children. These include direct expenditures and, especially, the value of the parents' time needed to raise children. However, there are benefits as well—children become productive after a certain age and this ability to produce for the family increases over time. (And obviously I'm ignoring substantial non-monetary costs and benefits.) For a nation, the primary benefit of additional children is that they develop into adults—people who work, generate economic activity, and contribute ideas that advance technology.

The relative size of the costs and benefits differs between poor and rich individuals and thus between poor and rich countries. Families in poorer countries tend to have more children for many reasons: (1) to offset high mortality rates and also, if families are averse to risk, to guard against the possibility that a relatively large number of their children might perish; (2) to take advantage of the fact that there are minimal costs to raising children who will begin to contribute when they are five or six years old; (3) to someday have grown children, who are often the lone support for parents in their old age; (4) to gain the political power that may come from having a large family. And in less civil nations, large families can provide protection from rivals or criminals.

The story is different in wealthier countries. Capitalism and the subsequent economic prosperity have allowed children to be free from the need to work for the family's survival. As a result, children in wealthier countries typically obtain an education while their parents support them. Often, personal savings and the government provide an income for the elderly; children are no longer the sole means of support for their parents later in life. Thus, the gains from having children are fewer. Risk aversion is also not an issue given relatively low mortality rates for children. Moreover, the costs are higher as well given the higher (money) value of both parents' time. In addition to being friendly to children, capitalism has enhanced the freedom of women who previously spent most of their lives bearing and raising children.

In sum, wealthier individuals tend to have fewer children because the costs are higher and the benefits are lower. Likewise, wealthier countries tend to have lower fertility rates. These class differences are also evident within countries; regardless of a country's affluence, poor families tend to have more children than wealthier people.

Finally, a higher population density may not be a detriment to economic growth. Anecdotal evidence illustrates that it is probably not a primary factor; Singapore and Hong Kong both have booming economies with highly concentrated island populations.[7] One could even argue that population density is positively correlated with productivity because of the improvements in communication, transportation of goods and services, specialization, economies of scale, and the exchange of ideas. Using this argument and the fact that Africa is the most sparsely populated continent, Osterfeld reasons that Africa is, in fact, under-populated.[8]

Thus, population is not a primary determinant for the plight of LDCs. In fact, the causal relationship would seem to imply that economic outcomes cause different population growth rates, not vice versa. To the extent population is a concern, the best way to slow population growth may be to encourage economic growth in poor countries. Again, we return to the impact of institutions on the economic prosperity of individuals and nations. What poor countries have in common is not population problems but the burden of "poor policies" that cause low incomes.

Natural Resources

Is the rapidly growing LDC population a problem for the rest of the world? Concerning the negative impact of increasing population on natural resources, there is compelling theory but no compelling historical evidence to support such a notion. If one looks at the record of the catastrophists, it is plagued by universally apocalyptic and incorrect predictions. In this field, the doomsayers have a well-established record of failure.

Are We Running Out of Natural Resources?

The intuition behind the catastrophist position is appealing: If resources are finite, they will eventually be exhausted by human consumption. Further, as population grows, the rate of depletion increases. (Some argue that economic growth also increases the depletion rate. However, economic growth is largely a function of technological improvements, which imply a more efficient use of resources.) Such reasoning is compelling, but it is also incorrect.

The fallacy in the catastrophist position is that all resources are not finite. They forget the most important resource—the capacity of human ingenuity to expand and innovate. (Julian Simon calls this "the ultimate resource" in a 1981 book by the same name.) With this seemingly infinite resource, individuals and markets respond to the higher prices that result from relative scarcity. These prices send signals to entrepreneurs to look elsewhere for resources, to refine them more effectively, to find close (and less expensive) substitutes, and to become more efficient in their use.

These two competing worldviews were aptly demonstrated in a decade-long bet between an economist and an ecologist.[9] In 1980, economist Julian Simon challenged ecologist Paul Ehrlich to choose $1,000 in futures contracts on five resources to be paid in 1990.[10] Each party would pay out of his own pocket—if the prices rose, Ehrlich would win the difference; if they fell, Simon would win. The intuition behind Ehrlich's bet was that if resources became more scarce, they would become more valuable and their prices would rise. With Ehrlich's static worldview, the bet seemed a sure thing. (In addition, world population rose by an unprecedented 800 million in the 1980s.) Simon, however, knew he had economic theory and history on his side; prices for natural resources have been falling for thousands of years.[11]

The outcome? In 1990, Ehrlich mailed Simon a check for $576.07; the price of *each* of the five resources *he* had chosen had decreased in price since 1980. Simon offered to renew the bet with a wager of as much as $20,000, but Ehrlich declined. Ehrlich also said that he had not changed his views. Today, he still professes the same worldview and voices the same apocalyptic predictions.

Someday, Ehrlich may prove to be correct. The key to resource scarcity is how the market responds. If this mechanism is ever disabled, Ehrlich's static worldview might come to pass. Thus, it is crucial that economic incentives remain strong so that it is always in individuals' self-interest to innovate. Ironically, the additional government intervention advocated by doomsayers would impede the market's ability to use the "ultimate resource." With government setting the prices of resources or taxing incomes at a higher rate, the incentives are reduced; in a more socialistic world, we might truly be in trouble. Osterfeld expresses it this way: "The kernel of truth in the catastrophist position is that a completely closed or controlled society would, in fact, face the ominous prospect of resource depletion."[12]

The Resources of LDCs

We know that falling real prices for natural resources are good news for consumers. (Also, price decreases signal a growing availability of those resources.) But the same outcome is bad news for countries that rely on the sale of natural resources for income. Whereas LDCs are certainly capable of making other products, raw materials are a comparatively easy way to generate income.

One should also note that natural resources are neither a necessary nor a sufficient condition for achieving economic prosperity. Russia and Africa are rich in resources but struggle in abject poverty; Hong Kong and Singapore are located on what amount to glorified rocks but have still achieved excellent standards of living.

As we saw with Simon's "ultimate resource," natural resources encompass more than what you can dig out of the ground. However, trade in some of these arenas is condemned and even forbidden by our government. In each case, wealthier countries with ad hoc morality systems are offended by mutually beneficial trade in poorer countries. They respond by trying to eliminate the trading opportunities of poor individuals and countries that would like to make themselves better off.

Vital Organs

Our government has decided there should not be a well-functioning market for vital organs in the United States; organs can only be given away by donors. This keeps the price at zero for potential suppliers, providing little economic incentive for people to donate their organs. The result is a shortage of organs and frequently, death. In India, people are allowed to sell their organs—after death or while still living as in the case of kidneys (when only one is needed).

The United States puts pressure on India to restrict its market for vital organs. But this would prohibit mutually beneficial trade between recipients (who do not have to wait in line) and donors who have their expenses paid and receive $1,800—greater than seven times India's average annual income (equivalent to nearly $150,000 here). Selling an organ allows impoverished people a voluntary opportunity to move to the middle class, start a business, buy a home, or otherwise improve their lives. Some argue that the trade in organs exploits the poor, but both parties enter into the agreement knowing the potential costs and benefits. (Would it seem reasonable if someone here chose to sell one of their kidneys for $150,000?) Further, if other people benefit financially from organ donations (doctors and technicians, for example), shouldn't donors benefit as well? Instead, the United States tries to prevent poor individuals from helping themselves.

Cows and Chickens Versus Elephants and Trees

The markets for certain animals also receive our government's attention. For instance, the United States has led a "developed" nations' ban on ivory and has imposed trade sanctions on Taiwan for selling tiger parts. These policies hurt the countries that have these resources and, ironically, make it more likely that the animals will not survive.

The key is property rights—if someone owns the animals, they will survive; if not, nobody has an economic incentive to protect them. (An example from American history is the fate of cattle versus bison.) For elephants, Zimbabwe has instituted a system that provides property rights to villages. As a result, its elephant population is burgeoning, even to the point where it exports elephants to other countries.[13] In most of the rest of Africa, where officials try to stop poaching without allowing property rights, populations are dwindling. In those countries, the elephants are "owned by everybody"; thus, they are owned by nobody. Without the proper economic incentives, such a policy implicitly encourages wild animals to be hunted to extinction. Further, poor individuals are needlessly prevented from earning income from their animals, just as people in our country earn income from theirs.

The same can be said of rain forests. In each case, wealthy countries try to tell poor countries what they can do with their resources. Restrictions on others' natural resources roll off the tongues of the affluent too easily. But who are we to interfere with poor countries' attempts to improve their incomes by using their natural resources? We should remember that no such restrictions were placed on the United States on its way to becoming a wealthy country. We should encourage these countries to establish property rights as incentives to wise management and preservation of resources. If that approach is not sufficient, the relevant countries should be well compensated for not using their resources to improve incomes.

Food and Starvation

Given famines and mass starvation, there is clearly a problem with either food production or distribution. But is it a problem of population?

Although this is seemingly plausible, given the environmentalists' lack of success in predicting outcomes or understanding markets, I want to look at alternative explanations.

How much food is produced each year? Is it enough to feed the world? At least since 1948, world food production has surpassed population increases by about 1% per year.[14] As a result, the real price of food has been declining over the same period. In 1985, world surplus of grain stocks exceeded 190 million tons, "enough to feed all of the hungry people in sub-Saharan Africa for 50 years."[15] Moreover, arable land is still widely available—hundreds of millions of acres, especially in poorer countries. And primitive agricultural methods are used on hundreds of millions of other acres. In sum, we currently produce more than enough food to feed the world's population, and we are capable of producing much more even without further technological advance.

Increases in food production have outpaced population growth because of persistent and dramatic improvements in farm technology over the past 200 years, as much as 100-fold with some crops.[16] For instance, in 1790, 90% of the U.S. population produced the nation's food; today that number is only 3%. If technology continues to advance, our capacity to grow food will also increase.

So why are LDCs unable to grow enough food? The problem is "poor policy." The governments of LDCs are frequently anti-business and anti-farmer. They typically pursue some combination of the following: nationalization of land or restrictions concerning property rights; minimum wages and tariffs on imported inputs; high tax rates, price controls, or monopolistic purchasing boards. These lower the rate of return for farming and make long-term investments in capital unwise. Further, one would expect to see large-scale foreign investment given the low cost of labor, and other inputs, but restrictions and the uncertainty inherent in dealing with such regimes make investment less attractive.

LDC governments typically blame their problems on wealthier countries and trade conspiracies, but many LDCs restrict trade and foreign capital investments. Restricting trade prevents LDCs from being able to specialize in their comparative advantage. In contrast, the idea that individuals and thus countries should specialize and engage in trade is one of the basic tenets of economics. In that sense, it is ironic that "growing food may not be the best way for hungry people to feed themselves."[17] For individuals and countries, it may be best to specialize in other products and trade for food.

Africa provides an excellent example of these policies in action. Africa's record features abject poverty and famine despite abundant natural resources and tremendous agricultural and economic potential. The World Resources Institute says Africa has much more land that can be cultivated—an area it estimates as more than three times the size of the United States; unfortunately, only one-fourth of Africa's arable land is currently in use.[18] Africa was actually food sufficient in the early 1950s. But between 1960 and 1985, per capita food production declined by 25% as governments inflicted poor policies on their people, especially farmers.

With Africa's low per capita incomes, starvation is not a "food problem" per se but a productivity problem. The crucial issue is low income, not an absence of food. One reason is that people have few skills. But a larger problem is government policies that distort the economic incentives to work hard and be productive, to engage in trade and to make investments in capital and human capital. These combine to ensure that most people on the continent suffer through lives of unmitigated poverty.

Notes

1. Financial aid often targets population goals for LDCs. "It remains an unquestioned article of faith that development is . . . a million condoms away." (W. McGurn, "Philippine Development and the Foreign Assistance Trap," in *Perpetuating Poverty: The World Bank, the IMF, and the Developing World,* ed. D. Bandow and I. Vasquez [Washington, DC: Cato Institute, 1994], p. 239.)

2. Sometimes blame is attributed to "exorbitant" consumption by wealthier countries.

3. P. Gwynne, "The Cooling World," *Newsweek,* April 28, 1975. See P. J. O'Rourke (*All the Trouble in the World: The Lighter Side of Overpopulation, Famine, Ecological Disaster, Ethnic Hatred, and Poverty* [New York: Atlantic Monthly Press, 1994], pp. 167–170) for a damning compilation of quotes from the "experts." Read O'Rourke's chapters 2–6 for a funny and colorful, yet informative, look at the issues of population, food, and resources.

4. D. Osterfeld, *Prosperity Versus Planning: How Government Stifles Economic Growth* (New York: Oxford University Press, 1992), p. 105.

5. B. Wattenberg and K. Zinsmeister, *Are World Population Trends a Problem?* (Washington, DC: American Enterprise Institute, 1986), p. 49.

6. Ibid.

7. Also, densely populated Western European cities emerged from poverty in the 1900s.

8. Osterfeld, *Prosperity Versus Planning,* p. 128.

9. J. Tierney, "Betting the Planet," *Louisville Courier-Journal,* December 16, 1990.

10. Ehrlich is known for his best-selling books and his apocalyptic and wildly inaccurate predictions about resources; Simon is a less popular contributor to the field, perhaps because his writings are not apocalyptic and are thus less exciting.

11. See C. Maurice and C. Smithson's *The Doomsday Myth: 10,000 Years of Economic Crises* (Stanford, CA: Hoover Institution Press, 1984) for an excellent account of how and why resource prices have fallen for 10,000 years.

12. Osterfeld, *Prosperity Versus Planning*, p. 102.

13. E. Larson, "Elephants and Ivory," *Freeman*, July 1991, pp. 261–263.

14. Osterfeld, *Prosperity Versus Planning*, p. 61, citing J. Simon and H. Kahn, "Introduction," in *The Resourceful Earth*, ed. J. Simon and H. Kahn (New York: Basil Blackwell, 1984), pp. 1–49.

15. Ibid., p. 64.

16. S. Lebergott, *The Americans: An Economic Record* (New York: Norton, 1984), p. 301.

17. Osterfeld, *Prosperity Versus Planning*, p. 80.

18. World Resources Institute, *World Resources* (New York: Basic Books, 1986), p. 42, cited by Osterfeld, *Prosperity Versus Planning*, p. 74.

19

Foreign Aid: Stepping Stone or Stumbling Block?

There are two general schools of thought about the primary cause of poverty in LDCs. Some believe LDC legal and economic institutions (which determine the degree of property rights, freedom, taxation, and so on) are primarily responsible. If so, the optimal prescription would be to change or improve those institutions; foreign aid would be mostly irrelevant. Others believe the LDCs' economic markets do not allow most of their people to reach a reasonable standard of living. If so, they conclude that the optimal prescription is government intervention.

In the next chapter, I analyze the impact of government interference by LDCs. In this chapter, we will look at the role of governments in wealthy countries who intervene by providing financial assistance—foreign aid—to LDCs. Again, the importance of foreign aid in the minds of its advocates stems from the belief that LDCs are unlikely to rise from abject poverty (as quickly) on their own; a helping hand from an outside government is important.[1]

Foreign assistance to LDCs is often maligned because "we're giving money to foreigners when we have needs at home." Independent of the merits of that opinion, there are sufficient efficiency and equity concerns regarding whether foreign aid is effective or appropriate. In looking at these, I will revisit many of my contentions about foreign aid's domestic cousin—welfare programs—and conclude that the problems with foreign welfare are generally worse.

Why Aid? The Supposed Need for Government Intervention

The most popular rationale for foreign aid is that LDCs suffer from a "capital shortage," which presumes the need for ample capital stock and a developed infrastructure for economic growth. Without those, advocates of foreign aid reason that LDCs will be stuck in a vicious circle of poverty. Foreign aid is seen as a way to jump-start LDC economies by providing them with the means to make the necessary investments.

The "human capital shortage" is a similar story—there are not enough skilled people to allow an economy to grow. If this is true, it would point to the need for advice from foreign "experts" and the guiding hand of an elite group of domestic leaders who understand how to make an economy function better. Sometimes, this view is voiced in a more paternalistic manner—LDC natives lack the requisite knowledge and motivation.

The problem with these two stories is that if capital or human capital is relatively scarce in a given country, then investments in both should be relatively productive and profitable. In other words, entrepreneurs and educated people should be attracted to the opportunity to use their relatively scarce, therefore valuable, skills. Instead, LDCs are (net) exporters of highly educated people and are unable to attract much foreign capital investment. A compelling explanation for this is that poor policy encourages human capital to leave and prevents capital from entering the country.

However, given the observation that the system is broken and the assumption that individuals cannot fix it, one will conclude that government must be actively involved. Thus, domestic and foreign government intervention are deemed indispensable to effect the requisite changes.

Foreign Aid or Foreign Hindrance?

Foreign aid is assumed to be just that—aid. Its necessity is taken as a given; its effectiveness is taken as axiomatic. However, Thomas Sowell observes that there is "no a priori reason to call it 'foreign aid' or 'foreign hindrance.'"[2] The effectiveness of foreign aid should be a theoretical and empirical question, not merely an assumption.

It is a mistake to view foreign aid as critical to an LDC's economic development. This assumption ignores the fact that poor countries somehow experienced economic growth before the advent of foreign aid; if not, we would all still be in the Stone Age. It also ignores more contemporary evidence that countries have achieved recent economic success with little or no foreign assistance. Moreover, many countries that have received aid remain pathetically poor. Clearly, foreign aid is neither necessary nor sufficient for economic prosperity.

But those who question the efficacy of foreign aid are often branded as hard-hearted. As with welfare policy and education "reform," the pursuit of additional funding is assumed to be compassionate; to suggest true institutional reform instead is often viewed as the height of animosity. However, we know there are serious disincentive and public choice problems with welfare; the same can be said of foreign assistance to LDCs.

Alan Waters draws a comparison between South Korea and Sri Lanka to support his case that economic growth is not related to foreign aid.[3] This comparison is useful because after World War II, the two countries were very similar at the outset—except one received assistance and the other did not—and the outcomes have been very different. South Korea (like other Asian countries) was able to achieve economic prosperity despite not having the factors many development economists say a country needs in order to develop—including foreign aid. Instead, South Korea has what are often ignored as primary factors: property rights and generally free markets. In contrast, Sri Lanka has much of what is supposedly needed, including foreign aid, but remains an economic basket case. Waters argues that foreign aid is, at best, irrelevant and also argues that Sri Lanka's centrally planned economy (socialism) is largely responsible for its poor performance.

Proponents of foreign aid cite assistance efforts they perceive to have been successful. (This closely resembles the penchant of advocates of government training programs to highlight their relatively few successes.) The foremost of these is the Marshall Plan, which provided financial assistance to the Europeans after World War II. Ron Sider reasons too hastily that "one has only to look at the material prosperity of Western Europe today to realize that [the Marshall Plan] was the most successful aid program the world has ever seen."[4] Europe certainly rebounded after the war, but its recovery may have been independent of or even in spite of our assistance.[5]

Advocates of foreign aid can recite only a few examples of seeming effectiveness. In general, aid and growth do not appear to be related. Doug Bandow notes that "the IMF has been subsidizing the world's economic basket cases for years, without apparent effect." He then cites many cases of long-term addiction to IMF assistance.[6] Regardless, "proof by example" is not conclusive for either side in the debate. As with discussions about educational reform, meaningful debate must move from anecdotes to institutions.

Is Aid Effective? The Welfare and Samaritan Dilemmas Revisited

The potential problems with foreign aid parallel those of welfare programs. In the context of the welfare dilemma, the concept of work disincentives for individuals is replaced by disincentives for LDC governments. If a country experiences economic growth, donor countries will be less likely to send assistance. As with the benefit-reduction rate for domestic welfare, the rewards for improving economic performance are diminished by definition, as donor countries decrease their financial support.

The Good Samaritan's dilemma reappears here as well: short-run assistance may promote long-term dependence.[7] Thomas Sowell has observed that Africa (long a net food exporter) lost its ability to feed itself precisely when donor agencies began to "smother Africa with project aid."[8] A coincidence? Maybe, but we know the Good Samaritan's dilemma arises with domestic welfare. It is certainly a plausible, if not compelling, explanation in this context as well.

A related issue is that our foreign "aid" may subsidize harmful government policies. The leaders of LDC's may want to keep per capita incomes low to avoid a reduction in assistance—money that would pass through their hands. Another problem is that LDC leaders have an incentive to underestimate economic growth and income statistics. Also, many LDC leaders reveal that economic prosperity is not their top priority by their policy decisions—for example, excessive military spending, massive government intervention, and restrictions on foreign investment.

Hobart Rowen notes that half the countries that receive loans from the World Bank refuse to report the size of their military budgets. Of those that do, India spends 17% of its budget on its military (versus 4% on health and education); Pakistan spends 27% (versus 3%); and Syria spends 32% (versus 6%).[9] These numbers may be further exaggerated by the breadth of the definition of "capital spending," which may include building government offices and purchasing military equipment.[10] During the Cold War, the United States subsidized grain purchases to the USSR while the Soviets extended their military arsenals. In 1989, 16.5% of International Monetary Fund (IMF) credit was extended to six communist countries (China, Kampuchea, Laos, Romania, Vietnam, and Yugoslavia).[11] Whereas LDCs become addicted to aid, we have a destructive habit as well—providing financial assistance to countries that embrace military power and economic backwardness.

Local Versus Federal and International Aid Revisited

Chapter 15 illustrated that the problems with providing financial assistance become worse as one administers a program from further away (federal versus local). Federal administrators are more likely to lack the categorization and discernment necessary to determine whether a recipient is using assistance as a safety net or a hammock. Further, it is less likely that optimal solutions will be uniform as one deals with a larger and presumably more diverse population. These problems are exacerbated as we move from the federal to the international level; the difficulties with foreign aid are even greater than those of welfare programs.

The problems with "bilateral aid" (country to country) are bad enough. However, for the same reasons, the current trend toward "multilateral aid"—many countries distributing aid through international agencies such as the World Bank and the IMF—is even worse. Strangely, advocates of foreign aid insist that multinational efforts are more effective.[12] This is correct to the extent that the $70 million paid by the United States to the World Bank in 1990 allows our government to have some leverage over $15 billion in new loan approvals.[13] But in terms of helping LDCs, it is difficult to imagine any advantages to this method, and it seems likely that multilateral efforts would aggravate flaws already inherent to foreign aid programs.

From the early 1970s to the early 1990s it was largely accepted that aid should not be conditioned on certain economic reforms. This was an international version of "blaming the system" and a move away from individual (LDC) responsibility. However, to ignore the culpability of LDC governments and their poor policies is wrongheaded and irresponsible.

Aid agencies have required more reforms since the 1990s, although their prescriptions have not been without controversy. Moreover, in organizations that dispense aid, the now-preferred method of representation by country puts donors in a minority. Thus, even if donors wanted to require categorization and discernment, a few votes do not constitute a majority. Some critics have compared this to "borrowers running the bank." Given this ideology, short of leaving the system, donors can do little or nothing to affect LDC policy.

Finally, on occasion, LDC governments are totally unwilling to distribute aid. Sometimes starvation is an explicit policy used to quell rebellions (for example, of Cambodians during the Khmer Rouge rule, Ukranians and Russians under Stalin, and Ethiopians since the mid-1980s) or is the direct result of poor policy (25–30 million Chinese deaths from 1959 to 1962 because of nationalized agriculture).[14]

Public Choice Economics Revisited

Another problem with domestic redistribution (to the poor and nonpoor) is that it creates entrenched special interest groups engaging in mutually beneficial trade with bureaucrats and politicians at the expense of the general public. The public is "rationally ignorant" because the costs for each individual are relatively small and very subtle.[15]

With foreign aid, this problem is worse. The agencies and organizations distributing financial assistance create bureaucracies in both the recipient and donor countries. These are a drain on the resources of both countries, but especially of LDCs. Further, the budget-maximizing behavior for which governments are famous appears here as an incentive to simply distribute funds rather than question aid's effectiveness in a given situation—a "have money, must lend or spend" mind-set. These incentives also bias expenditures toward larger projects to spend money faster. Finally, the inflated costs of bureaucracy often limit the transfer of aid.[16]

In addition, whereas U.S. civil servants are well-paid, "world" bureaucrats (for the United Nations, World Bank, International Monetary Fund, and so on) make them look like paupers—U.N. staffers receive 24% more in compensation than U.S. government workers.[17] It is said that these organizations pay high salaries "to attract the best people." But they also employ 150,000 "foreign experts" per year (80,000 in Africa alone), often paying in excess of $100,000.[18] In 1988, the World Bank spent nearly $1 billion on consultants for advice that "is often overpriced, poorly researched and irrelevant ... simply recycled standard off-the-shelf reports."[19] Besides, if they hire the best, why do they need so many additional experts?

The perquisites are lucrative as well. For conferences on world poverty, staffers typically travel to plush resorts, not to LDCs. In 1989, the World Bank's travel budget was $85 million with per diems in excess of $100 per day. Traveling employees get two rest days before and after each overseas trip in addition to an average of six weeks of paid vacation.[20] Of course, all of this amounts to a familiar story: redistribution from the general public to an elite special interest group—which Gordon Hancock has labeled the "aristocrats of mercy."

There is additional redistribution to those who sell goods through these programs. Virtually all of our food aid goes toward buying our farm surpluses.[21] Overall, about 70% of World Bank loans are used to purchase or provide in-kind transfers of products made in "wealthy industrialized countries."[22] This is akin to giving credit cards to poor countries. To the extent that the debt is not repaid, recipient countries and domestic firms have received income transfers from taxpayers. As one might imagine, there is lobbying by the affected industries, which argue that such foreign aid makes Western countries even more prosperous. However, these programs cannot benefit our country overall, although they can certainly improve the revenues of specific interest groups.

Finally, the mind-boggling corruption of leaders in some recipient countries is well documented: Marcos in the Philippines, Duvalier in Haiti, Mobutu in Zaire, to name a few. These rulers and their families have built up tremendous wealth at the expense of their own people and U.S. taxpayers. Surely there are countless other cases of less dramatic graft— at the local government level if not at the national level. How does this occur? William McGurn argues, "There are only two explanations, neither of them flattering to the development community. Either they knew what was going on . . . and said nothing, or they had no idea that hundreds of millions of dollars were being ripped off right under their noses. The former would make them accessories; the latter criminally negligent."[23]

Redistributing money to poor countries does not mean that assistance will get to poor individuals in poor countries. To the contrary, foreign aid must go through the hands of well-paid bureaucrats and the rulers of the recipient countries.[24] Much of our financial assistance never finds its way to the supposed beneficiaries.

Other Problems

Foreign aid further politicizes life and economic markets. Redistribution of income from donor countries to recipient countries and then from the governments of recipient countries to their people increases the use of political markets. This promotes (1) greater concentration of wealth and power in the hands of the politically active, (2) greater centralization of government activity, (3) the coercive nature of political markets over the voluntary transactions of economic markets, and (4) the inefficiency of subsidized activity over the efficiency of market-driven behavior.[25]

I have pointed to some of the hazards of cash assistance, but in-kind aid can have a devastating impact on LDC producers. American consumers are often warned of the supposed perils of "dumping" by other countries—the practice of exporting inexpensive goods to this country. Of course, if this occurs, it is good news for consumers and bad news for producers. (This is why domestic producers seek protectionist legislation to limit trade from their foreign competition.) In this sense, sending free products (food, etc.) to foreign countries under the auspices of foreign aid is truly "dumping." Such free in-kind assistance can harm domestic suppliers of the product. Sometimes, our food assistance "arrives too late to help the hunger and just in time to drive down prices for producers who have tried to adjust."[26]

Finally, as mentioned earlier, there are significant equity concerns surrounding the practical use of foreign aid. In theory, the purpose is to take money from relatively wealthy Americans to help poor individuals in LDC's.[27] In practice, the money must pass through the hands of domestic and LDC bureaucrats. It may also detour through the hands of LDC rulers, foreign "experts," and domestic firms. A few questions: Is it fair to take money from taxpayers here to send it overseas? Is it fair to reduce the income of poor and moderate-income families to support well-paid bureaucrats, foreign leaders, and domestic firms, even if the supposed intention is to help the poor? Given that LDC leaders frequently invest their personal wealth outside of their own country, why should we force U.S. taxpayers to invest there? In some countries, it is considered wrong for women to work and immoral to kill animals. Is it fair to take money from our working class to subsidize tastes and preferences in another country?

At the least, we need to realize that foreign aid does not go (at least directly) to people in the pitiful portraits that are familiar to us. To some extent, our "assistance" subsidizes the lifestyles of wealthy people. Unfortunately, foreign aid goes directly to governments, not to poor people in LDCs. It is one thing to provide foreign aid; it is often an entirely different matter to provide assistance to needy people in LDCs.

Why Aid? The Role of Guilt

Surprisingly, foreign assistance to LDCs did not begin as a response to pressure from poorer countries. As with welfare, wealthier nations "discovered" poverty, felt they had the resources to devote to the problem, and had faith in the ability of government to improve the situation. They reacted to the problems by implementing income transfers—redistributing money from taxpayers in wealthy countries to LDC governments.[28]

Another feature common to foreign aid and welfare programs is the donors' burden of guilt toward those receiving the transfer. Advocates of foreign aid have succeeded in transferring much of the blame to external (non-LDC) sources. "Western responsibility" for the condition of LDCs is a recurrence of a popular theme—"blaming the system," not poor policy in individual countries. In response, wealthier countries have exhibited a readiness to accept guilt and have failed to assign primary responsibility to the rulers of LDCs. It may be the case that wealthier countries are merely soothing their guilt by giving away relatively small sums of money. In either case, aid largely serves as restitution for perceived wrongs. But what are the crimes for which wealthier countries should have to pay? Why the guilt?

Some argue that contact with wealthier countries allows the exploitation of people in LDCs. On the contrary, access to foreign investment, improved technology, and the general principles of free trade make "contact" the primary avenue for growth in LDCs. The only exception to this would be political market arrangements between companies and LDC governments. Some argue that wealthier countries have benefited at the expense of LDCs by manipulating resource prices. This reflects a failure to understand how markets function. In addition, as noted in Chapter 18, advancing technology continues to make resources more abundant, lowering their relative prices. Although this is bad news for those who own the resources, it is far from a conspiracy.

What about the impact of colonialism? There is no clear correlation—for instance, the United States, Australia, New Zealand, and Canada were all colonies at one time to no apparent detriment (and prosperous Hong Kong *is* a colony). In contrast, Ethiopia, Liberia, Tibet, and Nepal have never been colonies and yet suffer from tremendous poverty.[29] In fact, some countries in post-colonial Africa are now less "free" than when they were colonized. "The political independence of black Africa went hand in hand with the subjection of large members of black Africans."[30] What about the slave trade? Again there is no clear relationship. Africa's most affected areas (West and South Africa) are the continent's most affluent regions.

Some Case Studies

Whether private or public dollars, much of our assistance to Israel goes to support the bureaucracy of a largely socialistic nation. Conventional wisdom holds that Israel is hampered by a huge defense burden. Instead, Barry Chamish argues that it is primarily hamstrung by regulation and taxation.[31] The dilemma is that we want to help Israel, but our assistance largely subsidizes socialism and a bureaucratic class of workers.

The debate over foreign aid to the former USSR and Eastern Europe has been predicated on concerns about the dilemmas related to providing assistance. Another worry has been that the money would not get to the people but would instead end up in the pockets of bureaucrats and players in political markets. Again, the question is how one can help without promoting poor policy.

Since emerging from colonialism, Africa has received tremendous amounts of foreign assistance—in the form of aid, loans, and advice. Despite the assistance, Africa remains the world's poorest continent. More sobering, Africans were poorer at the end of the 1980s than the beginning of the decade. And if its economy (excluding South Africa) grows at the rate projected by the World Bank, it would take 40 years to reach the income levels experienced in the 1970s.[32]

India has been the largest single recipient of aid ($55 billion since 1951) but is still tremendously poor with an annual per capita income of about $300. In sum, it seems likely that the best policy may be to stop "assisting" LDCs.

Policy Recommendations

What can we do, if anything? As with welfare, the answer would seem to be that any prospective solutions are fraught with the capacity for unfortunate, if not dangerous, consequences. And because aid is not a primary determinant of economic growth, one could easily argue that concern over foreign aid is damaging because it deflects dialogue from the true causes of poverty. As with the market for education in the United States, LDCs have "bad institutions"; the best way to reform them is not to spend more money but to dramatically change the system. To even discuss money completely misses the point. "If the mainsprings of development are present, material progress will occur even without foreign aid. If they are absent, it will not occur even with aid."[33]

The importance of LDC institutions is the subject of the next chapter, but is there a way to provide useful foreign aid? There are lessons to be drawn from the analysis and policy recommendations for welfare programs. First, *if* we provide aid, we should insist on categorization and discernment for LDC economic (and political) policies. Many governments fail to "provide the basics" (freedoms, property rights, stable monetary and responsible fiscal policy, infrastructure, and so on) while they are busy pursuing destructive policies. Any aid should be contingent on structural and institutional reform. Without that, we subsidize poor policy and make the poor in LDCs worse off. Second, we can feel fairly comfortable about assisting LDC's after major (unexpected) disasters. In such cases, we can avoid the Good Samaritan's dilemma and limit the problems associated with providing aid. Third, Julian Simon argues that if we give assistance, it should be desired by the recipient; in other words, the recipient country will not hate the donor country afterward.[34]

A much better idea than foreign aid is to eliminate our countless trade barriers (tariffs, quotas, and so on) against imports from LDCs.[35] Trading goods, services, or inputs is mutually beneficial. When we protect our industries, we prevent poor people in LDCs from improving their incomes by selling their goods here. While we lecture the world about free markets, we lock them out of our markets. It should trouble us to further impoverish people by restricting imports of sugar from the Dominican Republic, clothing from Bangladesh, aluminum from Russia, and so on. In sum, we should pursue "trade, not aid."

James Bovard cites repeated examples of the United States providing foreign aid to countries while restricting their trade. He concludes that "the federal government acts as if the United States is obliged both to help foreign nations and to prevent them from helping themselves."[36] Bovard then asks, "Are we rich enough that we can afford to give ... shiploads of handouts—yet so poor and fragile that we cannot allow them a chance to earn a few dollars honestly?" He quips that "apparently it is not enough for the U.S. government to tilt the playing field in American industry's favor; the U.S. government is also obliged to lock all foreign teams out of the stadium."[37] With freer trade, in addition to helping consumers here, we allow people living in abject poverty in LDCs an opportunity to work and make themselves better off. Absent the use of political markets, contact with the West is very helpful for economic growth.

With foreign aid, "many maintain that the more fortunate have a moral obligation to help those who are less fortunate. As we have just seen however . . . transferring wealth from rich to poor countries is not the same as transferring wealth from rich to poor individuals. Many of the taxpayers in the rich nations are themselves either poor or middle-income wage earners; many of the recipients in the poor nations are the economic elite."[38] As Hancock notes, "The real trick, throughout the expropriation, is to maintain the pretense that it is the poor in the poor countries who are being helped."[39]

What is needed in LDCs is not a transfer of wealth but a transfer of the ability to earn income. This will not happen through the redistribution of political markets. It is more likely to be the product of individual activity in well-functioning economic markets.

Notes

1. For the most part, I will ignore foreign aid for political objectives.

2. T. Sowell, *The Economics and Politics of Race: An International Perspective* (New York: Morrow, 1983), p. 239. With the release of the latest world income statistics and the threat of the impending Republican majority to cut foreign assistance, the *New York Times* and *Washington Post* opined on January 2, 1995, that world poverty "should give pause to the new leadership in Congress that seems intent on cutting off the small amount of aid that the U.S. spends in Africa" (quoting the *Times*). Whether aid will truly assist LDCs is often taken for granted.

3. A. Waters, "Economic Growth and the Property Rights Regime," *CATO Journal,* Spring/Summer 1987, pp. 99–115.

4. R. Sider, *Rich Christians in an Age of Hunger* (Dallas: Word, 1990), p. 209.

5. See T. Cowen, "The Marshall Plan: Myths and Realities," in *U.S. Aid to the Developing World,* ed. D. Bandow (Washington, DC: Heritage Foundation, 1985), pp. 61–74.

6. As of 1989, 6 nations (Chile, Egypt, India, Sudan, Turkey, and Yugoslavia) had been relying on IMF aid for more than 30 years; 24 countries for 20–29 years; and 47 countries for 10–19 years. ("The IMF: A Record of Addiction and Failure," in *Perpetuating Poverty: The World Bank, the IMF, and the Developing World,* ed. D. Bandow and I. Vasquez [Washington, DC: Cato Institute, 1994], p. 19.)

7. The welfare and Good Samaritan's dilemmas are developed in Chapter 13.

8. Sowell, *The Economics and Politics of Race,* p. 239.

9. H. Rowen, "No Aid for the Overarmed," *The Washington Post,* April 14, 1994.

10. T. Gillick, *Development Economics in Action: A Study of Economic Policies in Ghana* (New York: St. Martin's Press, 1978), p. 149 (cited in G. Ayittey, "Aid for Black Elephants," in Bandow and Vasquez, *Perpetuating Poverty*, p. 137).

11. J. Williamson, "The Lending Policies of the International Monetary Fund," in *IMF Conditionality* (Cambridge, MA: MIT Press, 1983), p. 653 (cited in Bandow, "The IMF: A Record of Failure and Addiction," p. 22).

12. D. Bandow and I. Vasquez note that U.S. bilateral aid decreased from $10 billion per year during the 1980s to $6.8 billion in 1992 and that payments to multilateral aid distributors rose from $8 billion in 1985 to $16 billion in 1992 ("Introduction," in Bandow and Vasquez, *Perpetuating Poverty*, p. 2).

13. M. Tammen, "Fostering Aid Addiction in Eastern Europe," in Bandow and Vasquez, *Perpetuating Poverty*, p. 101.

14. D. Osterfeld, *Prosperity Versus Planning: How Government Stifles Economic Growth* (New York: Oxford Press, 1992), p. 149. J. Bovard notes that Julius Nyerere's government in Tanzania "received more aid per capita than any other country." At the same time, Nyerere was using his army to "drive the peasants off the land, burn down their huts . . . take them where the government thought they should live." ("The World Bank and the Impoverishment of Nations," in Bandow and Vasquez, *Perpetuating Poverty*, p. 60.)

15. This aspect of public choice economics is explained in Chapter 4. In addition, many of the lending practices of multilateral aid agencies are kept secret. (Bandow and Vasquez, "Introduction," pp. 5–6.)

16. T. Funiciello, *Tyranny of Kindness: Dismantling the Welfare System to End Poverty in America* (New York: Atlantic Monthly Press, 1993), p. 215.

17. G. Hancock, *Lords of Poverty: The Power, Prestige, and Corruption of the International Aid Business* (New York: Atlantic Monthly Press, 1989), pp. 95–96.

18. Osterfeld, *Prosperity Versus Planning*, p. 156.

19. Ayittey, "Aid for Black Elephants," p. 141.

20. Hancock, *Lords of Poverty*, p. 92.

21. "The White Man's Burden," *Economist*, September 25, 1993, pp. 49–50.

22. Hancock, *Lords of Poverty*, p. 159.

23. Ibid., p. 242.

24. In this context, Okun's "leaky bucket" (Chapter 13) has bigger holes.

25. In addition, aid is likely to bias development projects toward improperly chosen external models, that is, leaders and bureaucrats may commit a "fallacy of composition," incorrectly imitating other countries.

26. Osterfeld, *Prosperity Versus Planning*, p. 148.

27. As discussed in Chapter 1, measuring poverty is not a simple matter. For instance, we tend to underestimate LDC standards of living because we measure only income, which ignores subsistence farming. As discussed in Chapter 3, it is important to understand the source of low incomes in a given country, for example, low skills or a young population.

28. Ironically, these gifts have created an enemy of sorts. Donor countries are often subjected to rhetorical attacks from LDCs that now perceive it as their right to receive redistribution.

29. P. T. Bauer, *Reality and Rhetoric: Studies in Economic Development* (Cambridge, MA: Harvard University Press, 1984), p. 58.

30. D. Osterfeld, "The Liberating Potential of Multinational Corporations," in Bandow and Vasquez, *Perpetuating Poverty,* p. 297.

31. Barry Chamish, "Giving 'Til It Hurts," *Reason,* October 1991, pp. 32–35.

32. "A Flicker of Light," *Economist,* p. 21.

33. P. T. Bauer, *Dissent on Development: Studies and Debates in Development Economics* (Cambridge, MA: Harvard University Press, 1972), pp. 97–98.

34. J. Simon, "Population Growth, Economic Growth, and Foreign Aid," *CATO Journal,* Spring/Summer 1987, pp. 159–186.

35. Actually these trade barriers have been "counted." See J. Bovard's *The Fair Trade Fraud* (New York: St. Martin's Press, 1991), *The Farm Fiasco* (San Francisco: ICS Press, 1989), and his essays in *Perpetuating Poverty.*

36. Bovard, *The Fair Trade Fraud,* p. 48.

37. J. Bovard, "The U.S. War on Macedonia," *Wall Street Journal,* June 9, 1993.

38. Osterfeld, *Prosperity Versus Planning,* p. 160.

39. Hancock, *Lords of Poverty,* p. 181.

20

The Road to Recovery:
Get Government (Mostly)
Out of the Way

In this chapter, I continue to analyze the conventional wisdom that leads to the questionable conclusion that governments should intervene to help LDCs emerge from abject poverty. In Chapter 19, I looked at government intervention by donor countries who provide foreign aid with the stated goal of assisting LDCs. In this chapter, I consider the efficacy of government intervention *by* LDCs. I will argue that LDC government interference is the primary cause of international poverty, not the means of escape.[1]

Thus, reversing much of the LDCs' current policies, that is, ending most political control over economic markets, is the optimal perscription. There will still be a role for government—the type of government that has promoted economic growth in currently wealthy countries. This system involves the protection of property rights and freedoms (from criminals in the private sector and politicians in the public sector), a capable judicial system to enforce and punish violations of those property rights, free trade in products and capital investment, limited regulation, and stable monetary policy, among others. Although not exactly paragons of virtue in this regard, countries like the United States—who have at least a tradition of protecting property rights relatively well, have lessons to teach LDCs about limited but effective government.

Problems with LDC Government Intervention

Government control over economic markets is troublesome for many reasons that stem from the fact that it concentrates greater power in the hands of rulers. First, this power is used in political markets to enhance the incomes of rulers and interest groups at the expense of the general public. (This form of government is sometimes referred to as "kleptoc-racy"—a government of thieves.) As a result, the largest degrees of income inequality are in the most centrally controlled economies. George Ayittey claims there are "6 Nigerian billionaires, 6,000 multimillionaires, 55,000 millionaires" but that "22 million Nigerians earn [about $1.50] per day."[2]

Second, "markets produce classes, states produce castes."[3] Political markets are used by incumbents to restrict competition and promote the status quo. This limits individual access to markets and opportunities to achieve a higher standard of living. Third, government control tends to reduce political and religious freedoms as well.[4] People in LDCs often have few liberties along with their limited incomes.[5] Fourth, as government control increases, the acquisition and exercise of political power becomes more important. Government activity politicizes economic decisions, replaces voluntary transactions with directives, and inefficiently diverts energy and resources to the political arena. Fifth, governmental control generally harms consumers—with restricted choices, "demand" is mostly ignored. Remember also that discrimination is more likely in these contexts because it is made costless by market distortions. Finally, government's politically motivated decisions distort the usual workings of a market economy, moving resources to lower-valued uses. This inefficiency lowers national income. In sum, where government is active, the poor receive a smaller part of a smaller pie.

In contrast, well-functioning economic markets minimize the power of individuals and interest groups. In economic markets, income is derived from satisfying other people. The more people you please, the higher your income. Thus, to become wealthy in a pure market economy (outside of an inheritance), one must produce goods or services the masses want to consume. With the use of economic markets, wealth comes from engaging in mutually beneficial trade (benefiting both parties) rather than from the income transfers of political markets (benefiting some at the expense of others). Cooperation in economic trade also promotes social cohesion, since both parties benefit from the trade; political markets promote friction, since government is used by Peter to rob Paul.

The Role of Heavy Taxation

Control over economic markets and freedoms is derived through restrictive laws and confiscatory taxation. The latter is especially heavy on the wealthy—the rich are "soaked." Some rationalize heavy taxation as necessary because people would not save enough on their own to allow ample capital investment. This notion omits the fact that private saving is reduced by "compulsory saving" and is predicated on the specious assumption that government spends ("invests") individuals' money better than they do.

Further, heavy taxation gains more credence in the minds of its advocates with the assumption that high incomes primarily originate from wealth, not work or entrepreneurship. Given this viewpoint, wealth and income could be taxed away with little fear of work disincentives. The only problem is that incentives *do* matter for saving, investing, and working. Capital, especially human capital, will leave a country if the costs become large enough. Training opportunities become less attractive because the higher incomes resulting from the training will be heavily taxed. Why train and work for only a marginally higher after-tax income?

Another form of taxation is the "inflation tax"—when a government prints money to pay for its programs. Unfortunately, this devalues any wealth held in the country's currency, destroying jobs normally created by the private sector. If taken to an extreme, this strategy can lead to hyperinflation and its subsequent problems. Milton Friedman notes that "inflation is always and everywhere a monetary phenomenon." Having an independent central bank is probably essential to avoiding inflation. Unfortunately, this is a rarity among LDCs.

Eliminating Trade

Another critical error in LDC policy is the restriction or elimination of trade. Advocates of this position argue that trade is ineffective, if not harmful. Sometimes, they arrive at this notion by claiming that cheap imported consumer goods are a deterrent to economic growth because they lower private saving. Apparently, allowing people to stretch their incomes further is harmful to an economy.

A more frequent rationale is the perception among LDCs that they need to be self-sufficient in food and other major commodities. The push for national sovereignty leads to massive protectionism, the worst thing for LDCs and their people. As Osterfeld notes, "Withdrawing from the world market means a country must produce what it needs within its own borders. . . . But since the only reason they were not produced domestically in the first place was because they could be purchased more cheaply from abroad, factors are diverted from areas where they were used more productively into areas where they are utilized less productively."[6]

Restricting trade and foreign investment prevents consumers from getting lower prices, props up inefficient monopolies, and eliminates important injections of foreign capital investment. It also harms workers by reducing productivity and thus the growth of real wages. It is impossible to name a wealthy country that severely restricts foreign capital and imports. Trade and external contact have always been the best way to experience economic prosperity.

Trading is crucial to the development of an individual's income and a country's standard of living. One of the basic tenets of economics is that individuals should specialize and then engage in mutually beneficial trade with others who specialize in different goods and services. The same is true of countries. Trade provides greater opportunities for consumers and producers. Trade also provides an economic inducement to improve performance.

The dreaded multinational corporations are the primary LDC vehicles for trade. Despite their reputation, it is only when multinational corporations use political markets that they may cause net harm to a country. They are constantly vilified for any number of supposed crimes. But multinational corporations are just companies—outside of political markets, they are purely voluntary institutions.

Manipulating Prices

Another favorite policy of LDCs is to enact price controls in product markets. They are usually called commodity price stabilizations after their spoken rationale—to eliminate price fluctuations. But the real goal is to artificially raise prices to monopolistic levels in order to engage in political market trades with interest groups that benefit from higher prices. Sometimes these markets are converted to "monopsonies" (monopolies from the demand side), allowing government to pay producers of inputs less than market value, either directly or through heavy taxation.

Others argue that government intervention is necessary because there is a vast "oversupply" (surplus) of labor, that is, unemployment. But again, government intervention is the cause of the malady; its removal is the cure. There are surpluses of labor because it is too expensive for firms to use it efficiently. This is caused by poor policy—LDC rulers enact laws that make unskilled labor prohibitively expensive, especially with minimum wages. Markets do not work well because the government does not allow them to work well.

External contacts, political and economic freedom, and limited taxation should be the prime instruments of material progress in LDCs. Instead, since the 1960s, LDCs have pursued poor policies: state monopolies, restrictions on trade, licensing, ethnic quotas in employment and licensing, capital restrictions, wage and price controls, and limited or rescinded property rights. These laws serve the interests of the rulers and the politically organized at the expense of the general public. These policies restrict individual opportunities, dampen or prevent economic growth, and allow inefficiency to become entrenched.

Why Interventionism?

If government interference is bad for individuals and the country as a whole, why do LDC leaders pursue it? We have returned to the same question that was encountered in the domestic arena: Do politicians harm the general public out of self-interest or because they fail to observe the hard-to-see costs associated with activity in political markets? As with domestic policy, the motivations are unclear and probably vary by situation. But as before, it is largely irrelevant because the results are the same regardless of motives or intentions.

First, rulers have clear incentives to pursue interventionist policies. Public choice economics acknowledges that people try to benefit themselves in both economic and political markets. As I have detailed throughout the book, such self-interest promotes mutually beneficial trade in the former and coerced income redistribution in the latter. As before, "good stories" are useful: "Nationalist myths and protectionist dogma become a veil for the parceling out of favors to protected interests."[7] Second, to some extent, these policy choices may originate in "bad religion"—a misplaced faith in government's ability to achieve objectives for a nation.

Third, Bauer places some of the blame on economists' shift to primarily quantitative methods of analysis. Although empirical work can improve knowledge, it can also be misused. Because of the difficulties inherent in modeling and forecasting macroeconomics, vital mistakes are made that lead to improper policy conclusions. Important variables are often omitted because they are not easily quantifiable—for instance, political variables such as ideology and legal and economic institutions.[8] Then, improbable conclusions are uncritically accepted and put into practice.

Bauer argues that the movement toward statistical work has caused an "atrophy of direct observation" and thus "a disregard of reality."[9] In this context, many developmental economists have ignored the contemporary and historical evidence that many LDCs have not needed central planning to accomplish rapidly growing economies. Such an oversight has caused some of the profession's most celebrated economists to advocate massive government intervention. For example, Nobel Prize–winner Gunnar Myrdal argued that "a sort of super planning *has to be* staged by underdeveloped countries ... and this is, of course, the explanation why grand-scale national planning is at present the goal in underdeveloped countries all over the globe and why this policy line is *unanimously* endorsed by governments and *experts* in advanced countries" (italics added).[10]

Finally, an important aside about the practical difficulties of reducing the role of government in the face of opposition from interest groups. Whether in the United States or elsewhere, reducing the level of government requires hurting groups who are the beneficiaries of existing government activity. They currently receive concentrated benefits; with reform, they will sustain concentrated losses. This will not be popular. In settings where interest groups are particularly powerful, a "benevolent dictator" may be the optimal form of government.

In recent years, Peru and Mexico have accomplished successful variations on one-party rule that have the power to fend off special interest groups and their hold on the redistributive mechanisms of political markets. In 1990, Peru's president, Alberto Fujimori, inherited an expensive civil war with the Shining Path guerrillas, a deep recession, and very high inflation.[11] In April 1992, he dissolved the Congress, suspended the constitution, and seized nearly absolute power. The result has been tremendous progress in the civil war and one of the fastest-growing economies in the Americas. Despite these accomplishments and the approval of the Peruvian people, our government has roundly condemned his approach.[12] Although we have a reflex to advocate democracy, it is not always the best form of government given the power of interest groups.[13]

The Market Economy

Proponents of government interference insist that "market failure" is a frequent occurrence. If so, it would seem reasonable for government to be active in promoting solutions to problems the market cannot fix. But then the key question is whether the subsequent "government failure" is an improvement over the imperfections of economic markets. There are many occasions when government can theoretically improve the efficiency of economic markets, but theory and practice are often widely different. Goals and intentions are noble, but results put food on the table. In general, economic markets win the competition easily. Heilbroner notes that "however inequitably or irresponsibly the marketplace may distribute goods, it does so better than the queues of a planned economy."[14]

Market-based economies dominate centrally planned economies because they provide better incentives to be productive. The optimal role of government then becomes protecting those incentives through the law rather than trying to artificially simulate them through the political allocations of resources. Bauer argues that economic growth comes through individual voluntary responses to emerging opportunities in the market. This points to the importance of "external contacts" (trade and foreign investment) and firm but limited government.

Bauer provides an illustration of this by describing economic development of the rubber industry in Southeast Asia: "There was not a single rubber tree in Asia *until,* in the late 19th century, rubber seeds were brought from Brazil. . . . At that time there were only meager local labor forces in Southeast Asia, and plantation rubber is a very labor-intensive activity. *But* it was possible to attract many hundreds of thousands of workers from India and China. There was little local capital, *but* enterprising trading companies found capital in the West to finance the opening-up and equipping of estates. . . . Most of these activities and responses took place in regions far away from the ports and were made possible by the establishment and extension of public security" (italics added).[15]

Hong Kong also provides a fine example of the merits of limited government and strong external contacts. With few natural resources, Hong Kong focused on allowing multinational corporations to function unimpeded, keeping taxes low, and providing a limited government to provide essentials such as law and order. The result of such openness to investment is a quite prosperous economy.[16]

Still a Valid Role for Government

The foregoing remarks should not be construed as an argument for anarchy but rather as support for government activity that protects individual liberties. This encourages productive activity that directly benefits the individual and thus inadvertently helps other individuals and the country as a whole. What can government do to promote these incentives?

In sum, government needs to protect individual property rights—from foreign powers through the provision of national defense; from domestic criminals through the provision of a police force and a credible judicial system; from the public sector through only limited redistribution and thus low taxation. Ironically, in pursuit of political market interventions and self-interested economic gain, rulers of LDCs have often eschewed these vital functions. The resulting presence of "bad laws" and absence of "good laws" is responsible for the abject poverty LDCs face today. Why are property rights crucial to economic growth and personal prosperity?

The Importance of Property Rights

The existence and strength of property rights facilitate trade between individuals. For example, if government can appropriate all of my wealth at a moment's notice, I have little incentive to accumulate wealth or even to work hard, pursue additional training, or save money. To the extent I am unsure about my property rights, I am likely to limit my efforts. Further, contract law and a good judicial system are important to the exchange of property rights. I often use the illustration that if contracts were difficult to enforce, I would not work for the university because it would be unclear whether I would be compensated for my efforts. Likewise, students would not enroll in school without the assurance they would receive the service for which they had paid. The same can be said of uncertainty's effect on behavior in war-torn countries. Trading opportunities disintegrate in the absence of secure and transferable property rights.

Without trade, individuals cannot specialize in producing a few things. Instead, they must be self-sufficient because they cannot rely on trade to obtain the goods and services they need to survive. Instead of specializing in economics and then trading the subsequent income for the things I need, I would have to grow my own food, make my own clothes, and so on. Such diversity is admirable in some sense, but it is not efficient. Without specialization, economic growth and individual prosperity suffer tremendously. Thus, to the extent property rights are restricted, economic activity, investment, and risk-taking are severely limited.

Another important feature of property rights is that they instill personal responsibility. In such a world, people fully bear the costs and rewards of their actions. In contrast, the distributional characteristics of socialism penalize effort and diffuse the costs of shirking. If we are all in this together, our incomes will be drawn from a common pool. Thus, my lack of effort will slightly reduce all of our incomes. But the key is that my shirking will cost me only a little bit; I will not bear the full costs of being a sluggard. Thus, the incentives behind socialism's limited or absent property rights are not conducive to encouraging productivity. "The tragedy (of socialism) is that in all such cases, individuals find themselves in positions where their utility is maximized by not producing. Individuals continue to respond rationally to the incentives confronting them."[17]

In contrast, an economic system with secure property rights provides strong incentives. It is not only that it benefits those with property rights; it gives owners sufficient incentive to add value to their resources by investing and innovating, thus increasing national wealth. Douglass North, Nobel Prize–winner in 1993, attributes the Industrial Revolution to the advent of patents and greater enforcement of contracts (possible because of an effective judiciary and notaries, for example). With innovators able to recoup rewards from their efforts into the future, rapid technological advances naturally followed.

Taxation is one of the public sector's methods of reducing personal property rights. High taxation lowers the rate of return for effort and lowers the cost of shirking. "Good tax policy" can then be easily defined. Taxes should be just high enough to allow the government to provide its essential services (as defined earlier in the chapter). There should be few if any loopholes, since these are caused by political market pressures and amount to subsidies to interest groups. (A flat tax would remove these.) Finally, taxes should be as low as possible for the poorest individuals in a society. Of course, one could make the standard equity argument on this point. But further, lower taxes would encourage effort, since government would not be lowering the poor's rate of return from working through taxation.

DeSoto's Peru: *The Other Path*

Peru has undergone significant economic reform in recent years. Hernando DeSoto's 1989 descriptive tale of Peru's horrific bureaucracy has stunning lessons for us about poorly defined property rights and massive government intervention.[18] His narration begins with the migration of Peruvian peasants to the city. Because their presence was not welcome, legal barriers were established in education, housing, and business. The "challengers" were forced to compete against the incumbents *and* the system or to go outside the system altogether. The result was a vast array of "informals" (black markets), formed in response to the various restrictions and prohibitions and constituting 48% of the people and 39% of Peru's GDP.[19]

Interestingly, the development of property rights in informals is exactly the opposite of their evolution in "formals." Challengers occupy, build, and *then* acquire limited degrees of implicit property rights. For example, in housing, a group of peasants occupies a piece of land through "invasion"—typically, an organized, unexpected, and forceful appropriation of idle state land. From there, property rights grow slowly as the state fails to take action, as the settlers build, and so on. Although inefficient and risky, it is the only reasonable strategy given that permanent (but still imperfect) rights would require seven years and more than 200 bureaucratic steps.[20]

It is admirable for people to find creative ways of circumventing the system to provide for their families, but such an approach is far from optimal. Their property rights are limited—"owners" are not allowed to sell (since there is no legitimate title to the land), renting is difficult, resources are wasted trying to protect implicit property rights and obtain explicit property rights, and there is a level of uncertainty that makes investments of any type less attractive.[21]

DeSoto estimated the cost of accessing the legal markets in trade by establishing fictitious entities and "jumping through the bureaucratic

hoops." The massive red tape, the compliance with bureaucratic procedures, and the mandated taxes and fees usually amounted to an insur-
mountable barrier for the average Peruvian. To open a small store
required 43 days and $600; to open a market legally took 17 years.[22]
Setting up a small industry required 11 permits, 9 months, 2 bribes, and
a total economic cost of $1,231 (equivalent to 32 months of earnings at
the minimum wage).[23] In transport, there was no legal access at all; only
the state could award rights (and rarely did).

DeSoto describes "the costs of informality" that stem from Peru's system of incomplete property rights. In trade, the key is that merchants try
to avoid detection and punishment by the authorities, making their
activities inefficient for many reasons. The informal market promotes (1)
an inefficiently low level of production because operations are on a
smaller scale; (2) an inefficiently low capital-labor ratio, since capital
(machinery and plant) is easier to detect and more difficult to transport
and the chosen quantity of goods and services is not efficiently produced; (3) an inefficiently low level of inventories; (4) subsequently, a
greater burden from "inflation taxes" because people hold more money
than is optimal; (5) limited growth in reputation and recognition (advertising through a variety of media is impossible); (6) additional costs for
bribes and other expenditures to protect and extend property rights; (7)
contracts that are more difficult to enforce outside the law and the judicial system; and (8) higher interest rates if one is able to borrow at all,
because using property as collateral is difficult or impossible.

The failure of the state to provide basic services prevents individuals
from maximizing their opportunities and income. As in the case of labor
market interventions in the United States, poor people are especially
harmed because they face higher prices and fewer labor market opportunities. In addition, these interventions lower national wealth. The inefficiencies associated with limited property rights needlessly diminish
productivity, reduce investment, and retard technological progress.
Finally, with the vast activity in informals, gauging the economy's performance is difficult; this makes macroeconomic policy more difficult.

So why did "bad laws" dominate Peru? DeSoto calls this "Peru's redistributive tradition"—a penchant for transferring rather than creating
wealth. Government views the law as "a mechanism for sharing a fixed
stock of wealth among different interest groups that demand it."[24] The
result is "good law" from the vantage point of the politically successful
groups and "bad law" for society as a whole, especially the poor. The
upshot is that competition is alive and well in political markets and thus
is greatly hampered in economic markets.

DeSoto's discussion of the public choice aspects of political market
activity are fascinating as well; Peru took the concept of the rationally

ignorant general public to new heights. All legislation emanated from the executive branch and passed without recorded debate in Parliament. Legislation was constructed in a complex manner that blurred its true costs. Finally, most legislation was never published. These features of the Peruvian political system perpetuated the need for bureaucracy, encouraged bribes, increased lobbying efforts by interest groups, and made uncertainty a way of life, since the rules of the game could change at any moment.

Did Peru have a free market? DeSoto emphatically answers no. It was instead immersed in mercantilism—government granted privileges to producers and consumers through subsidies, taxes, regulations, licenses, and other measures, usually under the guise of helping the general public. DeSoto also describes Peru's bout with "left wing and right-wing mercantilism." Both groups were more concerned with redistributing rather than creating wealth; one group redistributed to the poor, the other to business interests. Either way, interest groups benefited at the expense of the general public and to the detriment of the nation's economy.

A Wall of Separation

With respect to the role of laws and political markets, Osterfeld advocates a "wall of separation" between the economy and the government.[25] He argues for privatization and—to the extent government is involved—decentralization.[26] His prescription summarizes the ideals of a limited but effective government—one that protects property rights and freedoms, allowing the incentives of economic markets to prevail.

DeSoto argues that "modern market economies generate growth because widespread, formal property rights permit massive, low-cost exchange, thus fostering specialization and greater productivity. Without formal property, a modern market economy cannot exist. . . . The differences between the developed and the developing countries is in no small measure the difference between countries where property has been formalized and those where it has not."[27] By far, the most important reform LDCs can undertake is to provide secure and complete property rights for all individuals.

Notes

1. In this context, P. J. O'Rourke concludes: "Poor polluted, exploited, resource-depleted, population-pressured, deforested, and desertified countries. And none of their problems are of their own making. None of their problems proceed from fatuous oligarchies, wild corruption, or whimsical economic rights

... fondness for violence ... religious zealotry, fanatical nationalism, tribalism, xenophobia, or peculiar ideas about the nature of the world." (*All the Trouble in the World: The Lighter Side of Overpopulation, Famine, Ecological Disaster, Ethnic Hatred, Plague, and Poverty* [New York: Atlantic Monthly Press, 1994], p. 222.)

2. In his book review of G. Ayittey's *Africa Betrayed* (New York: St. Martin's Press, 1992), T. Hazlett comments that "the massive skimming operation would make a mobster blush." See chapter 18 of M. Kimenyi's *Economics of Poverty, Discrimination and Public Policy* (Cincinnati: South-Western, 1995). Kimenyi notes the difficulty of comparing such data across countries. Such considerations also make the use of LDC data rather questionable.

3. D. Osterfeld, *Prosperity Versus Planning: How Government Stifles Economic Growth* (New York: Oxford University Press, 1992), p. 39.

4. If we hold tax revenue constant, rulers have a preference for higher tax rates because this allows them to exert greater control over resources and freedoms. For example, if tax rates of 30% and 70% raise equal amounts of income, a political leader would prefer the higher tax rates. Thus, independent of the fear of a revolution, the "optimal" tax policy for rulers diminishes freedom and income.

5. The causation from freedom to economic incentives and performance is certain; it is also often the case that economic growth promotes additional political freedom.

6. Osterfeld, *Prosperity Versus Planning*, p. 288.

7. P. Roberts, "Developing Planning in Latin America," in *Perpetuating Poverty: The World Bank, the IMF, and the Developing World*, ed. D. Bandow and I. Vasquez (Washington, DC: Cato Institute, 1994), p. 152.

8. Another difficulty with these models is that people are implicitly assumed to be homogeneous. If this were so, government action would be more effective. But in reality, there are vast individual and cultural differences among groups, which are almost taboo in discussions on the issues. These subjects deviate from the realm of economics, but they are nonetheless important. Concerning the role of cultural factors, see Chapter 2 in Osterfeld's *Prosperity Versus Planning*, P. T. Bauer's *Reality and Rhetoric: Studies in Economic Development* (Cambridge, MA: Harvard University Press, 1984), and T. Sowell's *The Economics and Politics of Race: An International Perspective* (New York: Morrow, 1983).

9. P. T. Bauer, "The Disregard of Reality," *CATO Journal*, Spring/Summer 1987, p. 29.

10. Bauer, *Reality and Rhetoric*, p. 20.

11. The Shining Path is largely funded by the illegal drug trade's artificially high prices and profits. The costs of prohibition in LDCs is high; see Chapter 10 for the impact on poor individuals in our country.

12. The same method was used by President Yeltsin in Russia with U.S. government approval. There appears to be no relevant distinctions between the two situations, except our government's reaction.

13. Clearly, this is a risky strategy. If the dictator is not benevolent, life will be rather unpleasant. But perhaps people in LDCs would be willing to take this risk. Another example of democracy entailing large costs is where ethnic or tribal conflicts are tremendous. Africa and Yugoslavia provide contemporary examples.

14. R. Heilbroner, "The Triumph of Capitalism," *New Yorker*, January 23, 1989, p. 98.

15. Bauer, *Reality and Rhetoric*, p. 24.

16. Chile was a success story in the 1980s for similar reasons, featuring privatization and vouchers programs. (See T. Castaneda, *Combatting Poverty: Innovative Social Reforms in Chile During the 1980s* [San Francisco: ICS Press, 1992].)

17. Osterfeld, *Prosperity Versus Planning*, p. 53.

18. H. DeSoto, *The Other Path: The Invisible Revolution in the Third World* (New York: Harper and Row, 1989).

19. Ibid., p. 12. In addition to the gross inefficiencies and the removal of opportunities for poor individuals, DeSoto found that people had a general disrespect for the law—in many cases, mere survival entailed violating the law. This resembles Murray's finding that previously "virtuous" behavior had become "dumb" because of the financial inducements of welfare programs.

20. Ibid., pp. 134–143. In the likely event one cannot purchase the land legitimately, this waiting time includes 43 months for the adjudication of state wasteland (involving 207 requirements with 48 government agencies); 28 months to meet zoning requirements for minimum safety and maximum density; and 12 months for acquiring building permits. Note that this still allows one to receive only partial property rights with restricted rights to resell the property.

21. The same method of obtaining and extending property rights is used in trade. Street vending is mostly outside the law because of taxation and the legal requirements for permits. Again, "invasion" of a location on a street is the means by which merchants begin to acquire property rights for a "store." In this context, property rights are even weaker, since streets are public. This makes it even less likely that long-term investments will take place. In both cases, the failure of government to understand the importance of property rights and stability is regrettable.

22. DeSoto, *The Other Path*, pp. 143–144.

23. Ibid., p. 134.

24. Ibid., p. 189.

25. Ibid., p. vii.

26. As discussed in Chapter 15, local government has a number of advantages over federal efforts, including responsiveness and efficiency. Further, Osterfeld notes that privatization is not equivalent to "contracting out" while allowing the private sector firm to maintain monopoly power. Such decisions are bound to be political and are subject to the same type of economic inefficiencies.

27. H. DeSoto, "The Missing Ingredient," *Economist: 150 Economist Years*, September 11, 1993, pp. 8, 11.

21

Conclusion

Walter Williams jokingly tells how to get a roomful of fiscal conservatives to agree: Start bashing AFDC (Aid to Families with Dependent Children). He then notes that the tenor of the gathering shifts when one changes the subject to aid to dependent farmers or aid to dependent textile workers—or any other subsidies to national or local industries. We typically focus on redistribution to the poor while we ignore the redistribution that goes to the non-poor. Further, if a group receives subsidies from government, it argues, "That's different." Former representative Fred Grandy describes this ambivalence: People are "torn between their addiction to bacon and their aversion to pork."[1]

Herbert Stein expresses it this way: "The problem in America today is that we have two welfare states. One is aimed, however imperfectly, at 'the extinction of mass misery.' . . . The other mainly sloshes money around among people who are not poor. . . . This welfare state for the non-poor is about five times as big as the welfare state for the poor."[2] James Donahue estimated that taxpayers would pay $51 billion in direct subsidies to business and $53 billion in tax breaks for companies in 1994.[3] Yet the public complains vociferously about spending a combined $50 billion on food stamps and AFDC.

In government's efforts to transfer income to the non-poor—interest groups engaging in trade in political markets—it inadvertently drains the general public and hammers the poor. There's a joke about a man who needed a heart transplant and was amazed when he was offered three possible replacements by his doctor—one from a 20-year-old college student who died in a car accident, one from a 45-year-old jogger, and one from a 95-year-old free-market economist. When asked which one he preferred, he didn't hesitate: "I want the free-market economist's heart because it's never been used." And so it goes—the perception that allowing (economic) markets to work is a raw deal for the poor.

Government Compassion?

But what about the compassion of government activism? How much compassion is involved in forcing poor people to attend pathetic schools for the sake of the status quo—bureaucrats and teachers' unions? How much compassion is there in the prescription to spend more money on our monopolistic and socialistic educational system instead of changing a fundamentally flawed approach? How much compassion is there in a drug war that exposes inner-city kids to spectacular violence, seduces them with profitable but illegal careers, and promotes negative role models? How much compassion does it take to vote to increase the prices of food and clothing? How much compassion does it take to lock the relatively unskilled out of labor market opportunities? It would seem the free-market economist's heart has been used after all.

OK, so we shouldn't redistribute to the non-poor. What about the compassion of our welfare programs? A few more questions: How compassionate is it to have a welfare system that indiscriminately gives money with little regard for short-run or long-run incentives? How compassionate is it to penalize hard work, saving, and marriage while subsidizing single-parent households? How compassionate is a bureaucrat who indiscriminately allocates money from the state capital as opposed to a volunteer who works one-on-one with someone who needs individualized assistance?

The questions answer themselves. We have established a political system that is mostly unconcerned with the plight of the poor. Instead, those who govern are primarily concerned with promoting the economic well-being of interest groups, bureaucrats, and politicians. They use "good stories"—consumer and worker protection, nationalism, and even helping the poor—to reach their goals. The use of political markets is not about compassion, it is primarily about force—the power of government to take from one group to enhance the incomes of others.

Besides, by definition, government cannot be compassionate: "Compassion that is not costly to its giver is ultimately no compassion at all. . . . A 'loving government' is not just an oxymoron. It's something that can't be, just by its very nature. It can't be because government really has nothing of its own to give. Everything it has it gets from others, and so there is no way that it . . . can sacrifice."[4] Only individuals can be compassionate, both because individual solutions are more effective and because only individuals can voluntarily sacrifice their own resources to help others.

The Morality of Redistribution

The outcomes alone should cause one to doubt the morality of redistribution. Is it moral to give people welfare payments without requiring responsibility—something we would never do with our own children? Is it moral to increase the price of food and clothing for the poor so that wealthy farmers can have greater incomes? Is it moral for the state to mandate an inadequate level of education to protect the educational establishment? Is it moral to prop up corrupt and despotic foreign rulers with the money of lower-middle-class taxpayers?

Remember that governmental redistribution requires force; it is not voluntary. What is the difference between using a gun to take $10 from 20 individuals to buy medicine for someone's sick child and government coercing taxes from the general public to pay for Medicaid? Is it moral for anyone to take something from one individual by force even if the purpose is to give it to another? Or as Robert Heinlein asks, "Under what circumstances is it moral for a group (government) to do that which is not moral for a member of that group to do alone?"[5]

The purpose of the law is supposedly to protect property rights and freedoms. We expect the law to capture and punish those who steal our possessions, violate our person, and limit our freedoms. Yet we give government the right to do the same to us. The law has been perverted in such a way that it legitimizes the taking of others' property—not by criminals but by public officials.

The Disproportionate Impact of Poor Policy on the Poor

As we have seen throughout the book, there are tremendous efficiency concerns with government activism. But this book is not primarily about government waste or how to cut inefficiency out of current programs. The key issue is that many of these policies work to the detriment of the poor more than anybody else. If the cost of goods and the tax rates increase, the non-poor will still lead comfortable lives. If the public schools deteriorate further, the non-poor will respond by paying for private schools or home-schooling their children. If the minimum wage is increased to $10 per hour or $12,000 per year is available in welfare benefits, the non-poor won't lose their jobs or be tempted to rely on welfare. The rules of the game are changed only for the unskilled and the poor.

For the poor and lower-middle class, it is a different story. Impose the same set of policies on a middle-class working family and you cause someone to pick up an additional part-time job or require both parents to work instead of just one. Try the same experiment on the poor and you get lives of abject and permanent poverty.

The problem is that our forays into government activism and interference are no mere experiment. The consequences are borne in the lives of real people, and unfortunately the test group often takes a beating. As Thomas Hazlitt quips, "When it comes to government experiments, sign me up for the control group." This is not like a farmer who experiments with the optimal amounts of seed and fertilizer. The stakes are higher and the variables are much more difficult to measure or even determine. The suggestion that there are some who know how to manage the lives of others (and should be given that power) is ripe with paternalism and elitism.

On the way to helping interest groups, we have hammered the least able in our society. On the way to trying to help the poor, we have locked them out of labor markets with minimum wages and tempted them to use a guaranteed income from government as a hammock. The bottom line is that the policies described in this book combine to make life a needlessly difficult struggle for many of the poor in our country.

This book is a plea to civil rights leaders as well as advocates of the poor. Some of these leaders benefit from the focus remaining on political markets, where they derive their power and income. But others are truly concerned for members of their respective communities. I would encourage the latter group to question the efficacy of government interference in general, especially for the poor. The government route may have appeared to be the best, but it is certainly more difficult to maintain that argument after looking at the facts. Do not try to make government programs function better; work to get government out of the way of poor people and individuals who want to help.

Theory Versus Practice

Government intervention looks like an attractive option as long as we (1) assume the current system is primarily market driven, (2) focus on the "market failures" of that system, and (3) interpret the resulting distribution of economic rewards as inequitable. Independent of the last concern, it would be a mistake to think our system (or those of LDCs) consists of economic markets with only "a little politics on the side." Not only is government heavily involved in virtually every aspect of economic life, more often than not, its interference contributes to the misery of the poor. Further, it would be a mistake to depart from economic markets merely because their outcomes do not measure up to our standards

(however defined). Instead the question must be, Are government interventions and the subsequent failures an improvement over allowing
economic markets to work?

To omit this question and blindingly grasp for government solutions is
negligence. To believe government intervention will help is usually a
matter of misplaced faith in its effectiveness and beneficence. Many
times, advocates for government activism argue that "it will be different
this time"—with more money, better people running the program, and
so on. David Friedman notes that "the ideal socialist state will not attract
power freaks. People who make decisions will show no slightest bias
toward their own interests. There will be no way for a clever man to bend
the institutions to serve his own ends. And rivers will run uphill."[6] It is
not a matter of more money or more efficient programs. Government in
a democracy is fundamentally flawed in its ability to help the general
public; it is best at helping specific groups. The solution for the poor is
not more government; more often than not, the problem *is* government.
As Dwight Lee and Richard McKenzie note, "There is no reason to
believe that those who do not do well in the marketplace will do any better on the field of political battle."[7]

Of course, government is well able to deliver the goods to some groups
of people. To that end, Albert Jay Nock, commenting on Lincoln's phrase
"of the people, by the people, for the people," said it was "probably the
most effective single stroke of propaganda ever made on behalf of State
prestige."[8] Which people did Lincoln mean? If we substitute the agents in
political markets—"of the politicians, by the bureaucrats, for the interest
groups"—we would be very close to the truth.

Given government's record, it is sad, amusing, and paradoxical that we
rely so heavily on government. "State power has an unbroken record of
inability to do anything efficiently, economically, disinterestedly or honestly; yet when the slightest dissatisfaction arises over any exercise of
social power, the aid of the agent least qualified to give aid is immediately called for."[9] Thomas Paine thus concluded that "government, even
in its best state, is but a necessary evil; in its worst state, an intolerable
one." Why do we continue to run to a god that has failed us so often?

Why Free Markets Are Difficult to Defend

P. T. Bauer notes that "the market provides no mechanism for its own
survival."[10] First, it is not necessary to understand how economic markets work to benefit from them. Just as a tennis player may not understand physics and a business owner may not be able to derive a marginal cost curve, intricate knowledge of the workings of economic markets
is not essential or even important to benefit from them.

In contrast, the use of political markets requires knowledge about how to use them—how to play the game. Agents in political markets tend to be more articulate because they need that skill to be more effective in their "marketplace." Because players in political markets know more about their markets, they are often able to eloquently defend their use. Given this disparity, Bauer concludes that "in spite of its productivity, the market order may well go under unless its participants and supporters have the clarity of thought and the will and courage to work for its survival."[11]

Second, people confuse activity and good intentions with results. The irony here is that economic markets deliver the goods, but it is difficult to explain how it does so. However, to the extent government activism is effective, one can easily explain the results. Economic markets have a reputation of being based on greed. If one defines greed as self-interested behavior, this is certainly true. Even charity is offered because it makes the donor feel better. But political markets operate with the same self-interested, greedy parties. The key is their ability to persuade the public that their actions are for the benefit of the community. Ironically, political trades that take from one to give to another are assumed to be based on compassion, whereas economic trades that benefit both parties are often vilified as being motivated by greed.

Finally, as I have noted throughout the book, political solutions often appear more attractive than they really are because people fail to see the subtle and relatively small costs per person. We usually see the advertised and otherwise easy-to-see benefits of government activity. Without a similar knowledge of the costs, government interference appears to be the only reasonable solution.

Amazingly, free markets receive the blame for many of society's ills. Yet "in spite of popular myths about capitalism oppressing the poor, the poor are worst off in those things provided by the government, such as schooling, police protection and justice."[12] In contrast, under capitalism, the poor usually have possessions of reasonable quality (from the private sector).

And of all economic systems, capitalism is the kindest to children, women, and the poor. It is only in our prosperity over the past 100 years that we have achieved a standard of living sufficient to free children from the need to work for the family's survival. It is only with the high incomes spawned by capitalism that women have been freed from lives that amounted largely to bearing and raising children. Under capitalism, at least the poor have an opportunity to progress. Economic markets reward hard work and allow advancement, but political markets protect the status quo, eliminate individual opportunity, and produce a caste system.

There is nothing new about poverty—it is as old as time. What's new is the high standards of living achieved by a large proportion of the population in several countries. Those are directly attributable to the economic markets of capitalism.

The Prospects for Political Reform

Outside of a "revival"—a public with renewed interest and educated about the costs of redistribution—a strong leader with a passion for economic markets and freedom is probably a requirement for substantive political reform—someone along the lines of the "benevolent dictator" discussed in the context of fighting interest groups and bringing reform to LDCs. Under this scenario, if a president embraced a line-item veto and used it with great vigor, one could avoid many of the complications of reforming political markets.[13] Another option would be to end the withholding tax and require people to send the government a personal check every month for the amount of their taxes. It would be fun to watch the diminution of government that would certainly follow as people more fully realized where much of their earnings go.

But what about a revival? First, we need to blame ourselves, not "them." We are responsible for those we elect to represent us.[14] Because of our faith in government's ability and our belief that redistribution is moral and just, we indirectly support the compendium of poor policies detailed in this book. On the prospects for reform, Herbert Schlossberg notes that "it requires unusual decadence for an entire population to acquiesce in mutual pick-pocketing, to allow itself, that is, to be bribed with its own money. The growing list of government dependents makes it less likely that we can reverse the trend."[15] Without a change of heart, reforming the government will be impossible.

It has been said that "democracy does not rest on truths, but on the opinions of men." We need to stand primarily on principles, not pragmatism. We need to make it safer for politicians to "do the right thing." J. Vernon McGee, a biblical scholar and noted preacher, remarks that "sometimes majority opinion means a lot of people going the wrong direction." With current public policy, unfortunately the "sometimes" is closer to "always." Until our system of government or those opinions change, we will travel down this road until we reach bankruptcy or revolution.

Second, most of us need to realize that we are part of the redistributive game. Most in the middle class overlook their share of political market activity or believe they are too poor to be part of the problem. But much of the middle class benefits from subsidized college tuition at public universities, subsidized health insurance, and a plethora of other policies detailed in this book. To accomplish substantive reform, members of the middle class must be willing to part with the political market transactions that benefit them. As Ronald Reagan once said, "There are simple answers, but not easy answers."

Third, a political leader or an effective spokesperson for the efficacy of economic markets could make a difference. "I can think of few important movements for reform in which success was won by any method other than that of an energetic minority presenting the indifferent majority with a fait accompli, which was then accepted."[16] The majority are indifferent ("rationally ignorant") because they fail to see the costs of the activism—to themselves or the poor. If the costs ever become visible (in a specific market or in general), the redistributive game will end.

David Friedman notes that the Socialist party's presidential candidate never received a million votes, but he argues that "it may have been the most successful political party in American history. It never gained control over anything larger than Milwaukee but it succeeded in enacting into law virtually every economic proposal in its 1928 platform—a list of radical proposals ranging from minimum wages to social security."[17]

Thus, the important thing is not gaining power per se, but spreading ideas. Truly, ideas have consequences. If reform is to come, if government is to quit making some better off at the expense of the many, if the poor are to be allowed an opportunity to achieve economic prosperity, then the ideas and ideals of political freedom and free economic markets must triumph over political markets.

Notes

1. *U.S. News and World Report,* November 14, 1994, p. 39.

2. H. Stein, "Who's Subsidizing Whom?" *Wall Street Journal,* September 15, 1993.

3. J. Donahue, "The Corporate Welfare Kings," *Washington Post National Weekly Edition,* March 21–March 27, 1994.

4. J. Belz, "Real Compassion Is Costly," *World,* February 26, 1994, p. 3.

5. R. Heinlein, *The Moon Is a Harsh Mistress* (New York: Ace Books, 1965), p. 63. Toward the end of the last century, President Grover Cleveland said, "I will not be a party to stealing money from one group of citizens to give to another group of citizens, no matter what the need or apparent justification." (Quoted in L. Burkett, *The Coming Economic Earthquake* [Chicago: Moody Press, 1991], p. 33.)

6. D. Friedman, *The Machinery of Freedom: Guide to a Radical Capitalism* (LaSalle, IL: Open Court, 1989), p. 108. D. Lee and R. McKenzie explain it this way: "No matter how committed and informed political leaders are, their ability to achieve particular objectives is severely limited by a host of competing interests to which they have to respond if they are to remain political leaders."

(*Failure and Progress: The Bright Side of the Dismal Science* [Washington, DC: Cato Institute, 1993, p. 105.)

7. Lee and McKenzie, *Failure and Progress*, p. 131.

8. A. Nock, *Our Enemy, the State* (San Francisco: Fox and Wilkes, 1992), p. 25.

9. Ibid., p. 83.

10. P. T. Bauer, *Reality and Rhetoric: Studies in Economic Development* (Cambridge, MA: Harvard University Press, 1984), p. 36.

11. Ibid., p. 37.

12. Friedman, *The Machinery of Freedom*, p. 130.

13. See M. Friedman, *The Tyranny of the Status Quo* (San Diego: Harcourt Brace Jovanovich, 1984), and G. Kolko, *The Triumph of Conservatism* (New York: Free Press, 1963). The former describes the difficulties surrounding attempts at reform in the 1980s; the latter was written by a socialist describing the use of regulation by those who were being regulated—to restrict competition.

14. Another explanation is that we fail to elect fiscally conservative representatives because it eliminates our pork but leaves our tax burdens little changed. Although this "prisoner's dilemma" story is somewhat compelling, it seems unlikely that it is the primary reason for redistribution.

15. H. Schlossberg, *Idols for Destruction: The Conflict of Christian Faith and American Culture* (Wheaton, IL: Crossway Books, 1990), p. 281.

16. V. Brittain, quoted in *Prism*, December/January 1994, p. 6.

17. Friedman, *The Machinery of Freedom*, p. 228.

Selected Bibliography

Aaron, H., B. Bosworth, and G. Burtless. *Can America Afford to Grow Old?* Washington, DC: Brookings Institution, 1989.

Auletta, K. *The Underclass.* New York: Random House, 1982.

Ayittey, G. *Africa Betrayed.* New York: St. Martin's Press, 1992.

Bandow, D. *The Politics of Envy: Statism as Theology.* New Brunswick, NJ: Transaction Press, 1994.

Bandow, D., ed. *U.S. Aid to the Developing Countries.* Washington, DC: Heritage Foundation, 1985.

Bandow, D., and I. Vasquez, eds. *Perpetuating Poverty: The World Bank, the IMF, and the Developing World.* Washington, DC: Cato Institute, 1994.

Bauer, P. *Dissent on Development: Studies and Debates in Development Economics.* Cambridge, MA: Harvard University Press, 1972.

_____. *Reality and Rhetoric: Studies in Economic Development.* Cambridge, MA: Harvard University Press, 1984.

Bennett, W. *The Book of Virtues: A Treasury of Great Moral Stories.* New York: Simon and Schuster, 1994.

Bernick, M. *Urban Illusions: New Approaches to Inner-City Unemployment.* New York: Praeger, 1987.

Boaz, David, ed. *The Crisis in Drug Prohibition.* Washington, DC: Cato Institute, 1990.

Bovard, J. *The Farm Fiasco.* San Francisco: ICS Press, 1989.

_____. *The Fair Trade Fraud.* New York: St. Martin's Press, 1991.

Brace, C. *The Dangerous Classes of New York and Twenty Years' Work Among Them,* 3rd ed. New York: Wynkoop and Hallenbeck, 1880.

Browning, E., and J. Browning. *Public Finance and the Price System,* 3rd ed., New York: Harper-Collins, 1987. (4th ed., New York: Macmillan, 1994.)

Buchanan, J., and G. Tullock. *The Calculus of Consent: Logical Foundations of Constitutional Democracy.* Ann Arbor: University of Michigan Press, 1962.

Burkett, L. *The Coming Economic Earthquake.* Chicago: Moody Press, 1991.

Castaneda, T. *Combating Poverty: Innovative Social Reforms in Chile During the 1980s.* San Francisco: ICS Press, 1992.

DeSoto, H. *The Other Path: The Invisible Revolution in the Third World.* New York: Harper and Row, 1989.

Ellwood, D. *Poor Support: Poverty in the American Family.* New York: Basic Books, 1988.

Felten, E. *The Ruling Class: Inside the Imperial Congress.* Washington, DC: Heritage Foundation, 1993.

Ferrara, P. *Social Security: Averting the Crisis.* Washington, DC: Cato Institute, 1982.

Friedman, D. *The Machinery of Freedom: Guide to a Radical Capitalism.* LaSalle, IL: Open Court, 1989.

Friedman, M. *Capitalism and Freedom.* Chicago: University of Chicago Press, 1962.

_____. *The Tyranny of the Status Quo.* San Diego: Harcourt, Brace and Jovanovich, 1984.

Frum, D. *Dead Right.* New York: Basic Books, 1994.

Funiciello, T. *Tyranny of Kindness: Dismantling the Welfare System to End Poverty in America.* New York: Atlantic Monthly Press, 1993.

Gillick, T. *Development Economics in Action: A Study of Economic Policies in Ghana.* New York: St. Martin's Press, 1978.

Goodman, J., and G. Musgrave. *Patient Power: Solving America's Health Care Crisis.* Washington, DC: Cato Institute, 1992.

_____. *Patient Power: The Free Enterprise Alternative to the Clinton Health Plan.* Washington, DC: Cato Institute, 1994.

Gwartney J., and R. Wagner, eds. *Public Choice and Constitutional Economics.* Greenwich, CT: JAI Press, 1988.

Hall, R., and A. Rabushka. *The Flat Tax,* 2nd ed. Stanford, CA: Hoover Institution, 1995.

Hancock, G. *Lords of Poverty: The Power, Prestige, and Corruption of the International Aid Business.* New York: Atlantic Monthly Press, 1989.

Harrington, M. *The Other America: Poverty in the United States.* New York: Macmillan, 1962.

Harrison, B., and B. Bluestone. *The Great U-Turn: Corporate Restructuring and the Polarizing of America.* New York: Basic Books, 1988.

Hazlitt, H. *Economics in One Lesson.* New York: Crown, 1946.

Heinlein, R. *The Moon Is a Harsh Mistress.* New York: Ace Books, 1965.

Herrnstein, R., and C. Murray. *The Bell Curve: Intelligence and Class Structure in American Life.* New York: Free Press, 1994.

Higgs, R. *Crisis and Leviathan: Critical Episodes in the Growth of American Government.* New York: Oxford Press, 1987.

Irving, J. *The Cider House Rules.* New York: Bantam Books, 1985.

Jencks, C. *The Homeless.* Cambridge, MA: Harvard University Press, 1994.

Jencks C., and P. Peterson, eds. *The Urban Underclass.* Washington, DC: Brookings Institution, 1991.

Kaus, M. *The End of Equality.* New York: Basic Books, 1992.

Kimenyi, M. *The Economics of Poverty, Discrimination and Public Policy.* Cincinnati: South-Western, 1995.

Kingson, E., and E. Berkowitz. *Social Security and Medicare: A Policy Primer.* Westport, CT: Auburn House, 1993.

Kolko, G. *The Triumph of Conservatism: A Reinterpretation of American History 1900–1916.* New York: Free Press, 1963.

Lebergott, S. *The Americans: An Economic Record.* New York: Norton, 1984.

Lee, D., and R. McKenzie. *Failure and Progress: The Bright Side of the Dismal Science.* Washington, DC: Cato Institute, 1993.

Lindbeck, A. *The Political Economy of the New Left: An Outsider's View.* 2nd ed. New York: Harper and Row, 1977.

Maurice, C., and C. Smithson. *The Doomsday Myth: 10,000 Years of Economic Crises.* Stanford, CA: Hoover Institution Press, 1984.

Murray, C. *Losing Ground: American Social Policy 1950–1980.* New York: Basic Books, 1984.

_____. *In Pursuit of Happiness and Good Government.* New York: Simon and Schuster, 1988.

National Conference of Catholic Bishops. *Economic Justice for All: Pastoral Letter on Catholic Social Teaching and the U.S. Economy.* Washington, DC: U.S. Catholic Conference, 1986.

Nee, W. *The Normal Christian Life.* Wheaton, IL: Tyndale House, 1957.

Nelson, R. *Reaching for Heaven on Earth: The Theological Meaning of Economics* (Lanham, MD: Rowman and Littlefield, 1991).

Nock, A. *Our Enemy, the State.* San Francisco: Fox and Wilkes, 1935 (reprinted 1992).

Okun, A. *Equality and Efficiency: The Big Tradeoff.* Washington, DC: Brookings Institution, 1975.

Olasky, M. *The Tragedy of American Compassion.* Washington, DC: Regnery Gateway, 1992.

_____. *Abortion Rites: A Social History of Abortion in America.* Wheaton, IL: Crossway Books, 1992.

O'Rourke, P. J. *All the Trouble in the World: The Lighter Side of Overpopulation, Famine, Ecological Disaster, Ethnic Hatred, Plague, and Poverty.* New York: Atlantic Monthly Press, 1994.

Osterfeld, D. *Prosperity Versus Planning: How Government Stifles Economic Growth.* New York: Oxford Press, 1992.

Page, B. *Who Gets What from Government?* Berkeley: University of California Press, 1983.

Perkins, J. *With Justice for All.* Ventura, CA: Regal Books, 1982.

Rand, A. *Anthem.* New York: Bantam Books, 1946.

_____. *Atlas Shrugged.* New York: Bantam Books, 1957.

Reynolds, M. *Economics of Labor.* Cincinnati: South-Western, 1995.

Ryan, W. *Blaming the Victim.* New York: Random House, 1971.

Schlossberg, H. *Idols for Destruction: The Conflict of Christian Faith and American Culture.* Wheaton, IL: Crossway Books, 1990.

Sheffrin, S. *Markets and Majorities: The Political Economy of Public Policy.* New York: Free Press, 1993.

Sider, R. *Rich Christians in an Age of Hunger.* Dallas: Word, 1990.

Simon, J. *The Ultimate Resource.* Princeton, NJ: Princeton University Press, 1981.

Smith, A. *The Theory of Moral Sentiments.* Oxford, England: Clarendon Press, 1976.

Sowell, T. *The Economics and Politics of Race: An International Perspective.* New York: Morrow, 1983.

_____. *Compassion Versus Guilt and Other Essays.* New York: Morrow, 1987.

_____. *A Conflict of Visions: Ideological Origins of Political Struggle.* New York: Morrow, 1987.

_____. *Race and Culture: A Worldview.* New York: Basic Books, 1994.

Thurow, L. *Generating Inequality: Mechanisms of Distribution in the U.S. Economy.* New York: Basic Books, 1975.

_____. *The Zero-Sum Society: Distribution and the Possibilities for Economic Change.* New York: Basic Books, 1980.

Tullock, G. *Welfare for the Well-to-do.* Dallas: Fisher Institute, 1983.

U.S. Bureau of the Census. *Statistical Abstract of the United States.* Washington, DC: U.S. Department of the Treasury, various years.

Vedder, R., and L. Galloway. *Out of Work: Unemployment and Government in Twentieth-Century America.* New York: Holmes and Meier, 1993.

Vonnegut, K. *Welcome to the Monkey House.* New York: Dell, 1961.

_____. *Hocus Pocus.* New York: Berkeley Books, 1990.

Wagner, R. *To Promote the General Welfare: Market Processes vs. Political Transfers.* San Francisco: Pacific Research Institute, 1989.

Wasley, T. *What Has Government Done to Our Health Care?* Washington, DC: Cato Institute, 1992.

Wattenberg, B., and K. Zinsmeister. *Are World Population Trends a Problem?* Washington, DC: American Enterprise Institute, 1986.

Williams, W. *The State Against Blacks.* New York: McGraw-Hill, 1982.

_____. *All It Takes Is Guts: A Minority View.* Washington, DC: Regnery Gateway, 1987.

Williamson, J., ed. *IMF Conditionality.* Cambridge, MA: MIT Press, 1983.

Wilson, W. *The Truly Disadvantaged: The Inner City, the Underclass, and Public Policy.* Chicago: University of Chicago Press, 1987.

World Resources Institute. *World Resources.* New York: Basic Books, 1986.

About the Book and Author

Challenging the conventional approach most "poverty" books take—a focus on how government attempts to assist the poor with welfare programs—D. Eric Schansberg instead presents in this volume a dynamic and timely alternative to the idea. Using public choice economics, he illustrates how special interest groups advocate policies that benefit themselves but inadvertently hurt the poor. The author demonstrates how this inequity occurs in both product and labor markets—from farm subsidies to protectionist trade policies, from drug prohibition to the government's provision of public education.

In addition, Schansberg provides the reader with a thorough analysis of welfare policies, focusing on the intractable problems built into the current system. He then argues for radical welfare reform advocating case-by-case solutions centered on "tough love" and to the extent possible, private charities. The author also provides statistical information on income distribution and redistribution, a discussion of discrimination, and a section devoted to international policy issues.

Poor Policy is highly engaging, readable, and accessible for anyone interested in public policy. It provides concise and intuitive explanations for a vast array of those policies whose impact on the poor is usually ignored.

D. Eric Schansberg is assistant professor of economics at Indiana University–Southeast.

Index